"There are few women who will not settle for killing relationships, with destructive men or pills or liquor, rather than walk through loneliness. If you read this book, you will have met someone to guide you through that walk—there are no epiphanies, no miracles, only the promise of growth, and Miss Gordon makes us trust that promise."
—Jill Robinson,
The New York Times Book Review

"SPELLBINDING SEEMS TOO MILD
A WORD."
—*Detroit Free Press*

"I can hardly remember the last time I stayed up half the night because I couldn't stop reading. But that's what happened with *I'm Dancing as Fast as I Can*."
—*Chicago Tribune*

I'M DANCING AS FAST AS I CAN
Barbara Gordon

I'm Dancing as Fast as I Can

BARBARA GORDON

BANTAM BOOKS

TORONTO • NEW YORK • LONDON • SYDNEY • AUCKLAND

*This low-priced Bantam Book
has been completely reset in a type face
designed for easy reading, and was printed
from new plates. It contains the complete
text of the original hard-cover edition.*
NOT ONE WORD HAS BEEN OMITTED.

I'M DANCING AS FAST AS I CAN

*A Bantam Book / published by arrangement with
Harper & Row, Publishers, Inc.*

PRINTING HISTORY

*Harper & Row edition published May 1979
6 printings through September 1979
Literary Guild edition July 1979
Doubleday Book Club edition November 1979
Cook Book Guild—Doubleday edition Fall 1979
Serialized in* LADIES' HOME JOURNAL *November 1979
Bantam edition / May 1980
11 printings through April 1982*

ISBN 0-553-20861-6

Published simultaneously in the United States and Canada

*Bantam Books are published by Bantam Books, Inc. Its trade-
mark, consisting of the words "Bantam Books" and the por-
trayal of a rooster, is Registered in U.S. Patent and Trademark
Office and in other countries. Marca Registrada. Bantam
Books, Inc., 666 Fifth Avenue, New York, New York 10103.*

PRINTED IN THE UNITED STATES OF AMERICA

20 19 18

*For my mother and father,
and for Edie*

I have told my story as honestly as I can.
Obviously, it has been important to me to
protect the identity of the other people involved
in the story, so names and details have
been changed for this purpose.

I have a favorite joke. A man and a woman meet at a singles resort in the Catskills. They are dancing together on a Saturday night. He says, "I'm only here for the weekend." She replies, "I'm dancing as fast as I can."

1

My Favorite
Time of Life

I was making a film about a dying woman. Compared to what I had been doing, it seemed as if this one would be easy because there were no facts to verify, no painstaking research, no bad guys, just directing the cameras and interviewing Jean. She had cancer. The only villain was time. After an exhausting year of producing tough investigative films about Nazi war criminals and slumlords, following Mayor Jean Barris through her daily round as she fought for her life would be a piece of cake. Now, locked in the editing room with Steve Isaacs, my film editor, we sat side by side in high editing room chairs, peering at the Moviola, listening to Jean, staring at her face. She never looked as if she was suffering. The phone rang. I motioned to Steve to keep screening: I had developed my own way of handling people who interrupted my work in the editing room.

"Well, is she gonna die or isn't she, Barbara?" It was the voice of CBS's crackerjack salesman, Martin Ryan.

"I don't know, Marty. She's still in the hospital."

"Well, what do you think? Will she be dead by air time?"

I sighed as I watched Jean on the Moviola. She was standing in line at the laetrile clinic in Mexico. "I'm a film-maker, not a doctor," I said after a few seconds.

"Then you'll have to make two versions," he said

flatly, "one 28:13, the other 23:13. If she dies we'll kill the commercials."

If she dies we'll kill the commercials. I hung up muttering to myself, then went back to the private world I loved so much: my film, the editor and me. But Martin had ruined it. I reminded myself that he sells documentary advertising time, and that isn't easy when *Charlie's Angels* is the barometer of America's taste buds. Let him gaffe. It pays my rent.

Now Jean was on the beach in Tijuana, walking with her husband, Ben, talking of life, her family, suburban politics and what it was like to become mayor of her hometown at forty-five, Nixon, blacks. She had so much to say. She looked great. A tall, blond woman, she was attractive in a healthy, sturdy, American kind of way. Sturdy but vulnerable. Her crooked smile betrayed a little-girl fragility, and that, in combination with her tall, almost imposing body, made her charming. I remembered how curious she had been about me, my career, why I lived with the man I loved instead of marrying him, of the trouble I'd had when I aimed my cameras at the CIA and the FBI. I didn't blame her. If I were dying and sharing my most intimate thoughts and fears with a stranger, I'd damn well want a closeness, too.

So we had to become close. At first our relationship was cursory and casual, a business relationship, and that's all. But as we spent time talking, walking, filming, eating in restaurants together, we began to like each other a lot. I shared with Jean's oldest friends a sense of outrage that this forty-seven-year-old woman who was just beginning to emerge from housewivery and PTA meetings, this woman who was making a place for herself in the rough-and-tumble world of politics, had to be stricken with this hateful illness. Just when she was blooming, enjoying her life—cancer of the pancreas! I also shared with her oldest friends the conviction that she would be cured. She was going to live.

I watched the screen as Jean and Ben strolled back to the clinic for Jean's daily dose of laetrile. They had taken a mortgage on their house to pay for the trip for this "alternative cure." She had made me promise to call it an "alternative cure" and then swear never to mention that it was laetrile. I wondered why and one day she finally told me. Always the consummate politician, Jean said that if people found out she had taken laetrile, it could hurt her politically. When I looked confused, she went on to explain that the John Birch Society believed that American Communists were battling to make laetrile illegal in America so that the Soviet Union could claim that they had discovered it as the cure for cancer. Jean didn't want to be associated with any right-wing craziness. She just wanted it to work. She wanted to live. So we had called it an "alternative cure."

I winced as I remembered our days together in Tijuana—the cash-and-carry Lourdes of North America. There was fear mixed with hope on the faces of the stricken patients and their families and loved ones as they stood in line for hours at the laetrile clinic, waiting for their daily injection. I had filmed the signs plastered on the walls—NO CHECKS ACCEPTED, CASH ONLY—and I remembered the cold, hard looks on the faces of the Mexican nurses as they herded the people like sheep into the tiny rooms where the injections were given. Stories of miracle cures spread through the line like wildfire. Everyone had heard of a daughter, a husband, a wife, a grandmother, from Texas, Arkansas, California, Canada, someone who had been called terminal and was now cured. Why wouldn't America make it legal? It had cost so much to travel to Tijuana. They all talked together softly as the line edged toward the gray counter where the sullen nurses filled out forms, and the clanging of cash registers provided a grim accompaniment to their voices. The merchandising of hope. Jean had let me follow her and film it, but she never once complained about the whole tawdry business. She had only exacted that one promise: call it an "alternative cure."

But she wasn't cured at all. Now she was isolated in a hospital room in a small Connecticut town and no one knew if she would make it. She had planned to move on to national politics; she fantasized about a job in Washington, maybe even a cabinet post. She wanted so to be a star, to be famous outside her own hometown. For weeks Steve had shown me the ravages of illness on her face, showed me that even he could see she was getting worse. I never saw it. Everyone else saw it in her face. Not me. Hold on, Jeanie, I thought to myself. You'll love yourself on television. Hang on, but don't suffer. If she dies we'll kill the commercials. But what if she lingers?

Steve and I shook our heads over Martin's televisionese. We made jokes about how working in this business could turn anyone into a robot. And then I left the editing room to take care of the day's business. Walking through the sprawling CBS production complex, I remembered that I had to read the promotional copy for Jean's film. I knew it would be cloyingly sentimental and Edgar Guesty. I would have to refashion it, and that meant a battle with the head witch of the publicity department. But Jean was a classy lady, and I wasn't going to let this film turn into a maudlin, nauseating television number. Jean was going first class. Then I had to try to rope John O'Connor, the TV critic of *The New York Times,* into a screening before air time. Next a corporate lawyer was coming from Black Rock, the CBS executive building across town, for my deposition. I was being sued for six million dollars because of a film I had done on an "alleged" Nazi war criminal. Someone was contending that my film had depicted him as neither former nor alleged and was out for blood and dollars—my blood and CBS's dollars. From cancer to Nazis. Perfect.

When I got to my office, the clock told me it was lunchtime. I ignored it. I never went out for lunch. Just thinking about crowded streets and noisy restaurants and a gnawing panic would begin, a panic that had become all too familiar, filling my mind, my body, almost immobilizing me. I gasped quickly for air. Dummy. You're a producer, you just came back from directing a film in Tijuana. Why should you feel terror-stricken about going out to lunch? It didn't make any sense. I reached into my purse. I didn't want anything in particular; I was just checking to make sure everything was there, intact, whole—the wallet, the keys, the plastic vial of pills. All was right with the world.

I lit a cigarette and sat down at my desk which always looked as if a kindergarten class had just spent an hour of free play there. How did I ever find anything in that mess? The shelves behind me were filled with books on drug addiction, New York's housing laws, the *Congressional Record,* the full text of O'Neill's *Moon for the Misbegotten,* the latest statistics on unemployment among Vietnam veterans. What craziness, I thought. I must get rid of some of those books. I must clean up this desk. No, I've got too much to do. Tomorrow.

Fran Ladd poked her head in the doorway. She was my assistant, confidante and friend. A twenty-four-year-old former radical from Chicago, she was the best researcher in the business. From slumlords to Vietnam vets, from Nazis to cancer, the two of us had made dynamite films for three years. We were an unlikely twosome: she blond, Irish, Catholic, from the Midwest; me Jewish, dark, forty, from Miami Beach. I was aggressive and outgoing. Frannie was all internal, shy, almost bashful, yet that didn't keep her from crashing into people's lives, people we would put on film. My main criticism of her was that she chain-smoked three packs of cigarettes a day. I wanted her to stop. I smoked, but not like that. We both loved our jobs, and the differences between us only served as a constant source of laughter and delight. Like Woodward and Bernstein, like Batman and Robin, we were a team.

"Your Emmy arrived, finally," she said, smiling, as she walked into the office. "And I've got you a hero and a beer from Rocko's." She held out a giant hero sandwich in one hand and a shiny statue in the other.

I burst out laughing. Heroes and statues—who would believe it?

"The lawyer is late, and Eric called," Fran said. "He'll meet you at Sucho's at eight and he has a court for Saturday night, so you *can't* work late. And Jean still isn't talking, but Ben says she's resting comfortably. Now I've got to run and do some shopping. Sure you don't want to get out of here? Leave the sandwich and come with me, Barb."

I waved her off with one of my "You know I don't go out to lunch" looks. She made a face and headed for the elevator. I unwrapped the hero and took a bite, looking at my new Emmy, belatedly arrived from the engraver's. It was my reward for last year's documentary and the engraver's block letters loomed into my line of sight: BARBARA GORDON, BEST WRITER, CBS, SUPERLANDLORD. I thought with a laugh of the producer who had won so many Emmies that he put one on his Volkswagen to make it look like a Mercedes. This was my third, but it was still nice to be a winner.

With everyone out to lunch, the office was filled with a sweet silence. I loved it. The rest of the time the noise was deafening, but I loved that, too. The hum of Moviolas, streams of messengers coming and going, sound tracks being mixed, phones jangling, the sounds of life in the television business—a business I adored and had wanted to be part of, even when I was very young. I stared at the statue, forgetting the sandwich, remembering my arrival at NBC at the age of twenty-one properly dressed in a conservative suit, stockings, heels, pearls—the old number. A Barnard graduate with a head full of philosophy, economics, history, psychology, English literature, I had run, just like all the other bright young girls, to Speedwriting school to get that job in television I had always wanted. There was no woman's movement around to tell me that becoming a secretary wasn't the only way. In those days, it *was* the only way. I had poured coffee, taken dictation, written messy letters on an electric typewriter for three years, hating every moment of it. A rare glimpse of Chet Huntley in the elevator was about as close to the "glamour" of television as I could get.

And then it had slowly started to happen. Someone gave me a chance to be a researcher, and from there I became an associate producer, then a writer on a morning show, then a writer-producer of documentaries. It was a struggle, but I was smart, I was a quick study, and finally I had made it. I thought of the films

I had never won Emmies for—films I liked better than *Superlandlord:* the portrait of Dalton Trumbo who, at the height of the Nixon era, had told me about his own experience with the man and how he had been destroyed by the blacklisting of the fifties; Sterling Hayden, who talked about booze, about writing, about being an actor. Somehow I had been able to identify with these men. They had been hurt badly in their lives, but they had survived.

From NBC I had moved to the Public Broadcasting System, where I worked on a film about the FBI and its use of *agents provocateurs* to infiltrate the New Left. In 1969, to say anything negative about or even to question the venerable FBI was considered subversive. The film was censored and I found myself in the middle of a demoralizing battle to get it on the air. My brush with the CIA came a year later, when I filmed the story of Victor Marchetti, the former CIA agent, a hawk turned dove, who was trying to speak out against the agency. I took a film crew to McLean, Virginia, to get pictures of the agency—just exterior shots, from a public road, of the CIA sign on the building. We were approached by a team of agents, and despite my press credentials, they said they thought the crew and I were foreign spies. We left, but they tailed us up the Pennsylvania and New Jersey turnpikes, all the way back to New York. I laughed all through the ride, loving the drama. But that night I had nightmares and the shakes when I thought about what had happened—then anger when I realized that my tax dollars were paying spooks to play hide-and-seek with a film-maker from public television.

It was a long way from pearls and pouring coffee to being chased by the CIA, and after that I went to CBS where I was able to pick the subjects of my own films, write and produce them. I was a lucky lady, lucky to be able to merge my politics, my passion for the First Amendment, my private self, with my career. I was happy with a job where you didn't have to whore. But if I was so happy, why did that creeping terror come over me every time I tried to go out for lunch? Screw it, it's manageable, I told myself. The pills help, Eric understands, Dr. Allen says it's just anxiety. I've got a super job, a super man, a wonderful life—and anxiety. Who doesn't? I just didn't want to make a career of it.

I called home. The service responded. "Nothing for you, Miss Gordon." Damn, I thought, there must be a better way of putting that. I must talk to Telanserphone about new copy. I made that call home every day at lunchtime. Everyone in the world knew I was never home at lunchtime. What did I want, anyway?

My boss, Alan Newman, seldom escaped a date for lunch. So I was surprised to see his pink, boyish face appear in my doorway. He was ecstatic that CBS had decided to cancel the commercials if Jeanie died before air time. I didn't want to hear it again, but I couldn't bring myself to interrupt him. "Wonderful" was all I could summon up for a response. It *was* a mark of good taste to respect Jeanie or death or life in the only way they could And in this instance, respect meant losing money. But Jeanie wasn't going to die.

I finished my sandwich and spent the rest of the afternoon in the editing room with Steve. We had made fifteen films together. Our relationship was like marriage. I knew his wife, Ellen; he had lunch with Eric. I knew how much his mortgage payments were, his parking problems, his cholesterol count, his brand of cigars. He knew my bedtime, how I drank my coffee, when I had my period. A good relationship between film-maker and editor is special and quite marvelous. Even our disagreements—and we had many full-blown differences of opinion that turned into arguments—were healthy and unneurotic. We always knew what we were fighting about. And we amused each other with stories and jokes that diverted us from the sometimes tedious mechanical work of making a film: the endless hours of noncreative splitting of reels, breaking tracks, backsplicing, cueing.

What I loved most about Steve was not his enormous talent and sensitivity, but his wonderfully acerbic irony, a sense of humor as dry as the Sahara. We gossiped about our colleagues, our own crazy lives, our parents, and Steve would make me laugh by reminding me of the time his mother said, "Please get me tickets to see *Boys in the Band*. I love musicals." He had protested, saying it wasn't for her, but she had insisted. And sure enough, the day after she saw it, she called and said indignantly, "How could you send me to such a dirty show?" Then the warm smile, a puff on the cigar, and back to the Moviola and the film.

It was after seven when we finally decided to call it a day. "You got plans?" Steve asked. "How about sharing indigestion with me in the cafeteria?"

"I'm meeting Eric at Sucho's."

"Ah, so," he said. "Everything O.K.?"

"Everything is fine," I said, a little annoyed by the question. "Give my love to Ellen."

And everything *was* fine. I was on my way to meet my love.

Sucho's, our favorite Japanese restaurant, was small, quiet, almost serene. Because of our crazy hours, Eric and I treated ourselves to the raw fish, the gusty Japanese beer and sukiyaki several times a week. As I walked to the restaurant, I realized there was no anxiety, no angst. Why? I wondered. What makes dinner different from lunch? Eric, of course. I smiled, feeling wonderful. I looked forward to our filling ourselves with the food and with each other, sharing the details of our respective jobs, coming together, blending our separate worlds into a oneness that happened at the end of each day. How I loved him!

Maybe Eric Bauer wasn't perfect, I thought, but to me he was a reasonable facsimile of perfection. Nearly six feet tall, with a head of thick black hair, graying slightly at the temples, a gentle smile, he was at fifty a marvelous mixture of man and boy. He always dressed in chinos and tweed sports jackets, and I told myself his appearance was honest, straightforward, nonaffected. We had lived together for five years, years which had been happy, busy, full. We shared everything and I thought that was how it should be. He was my tennis partner, best friend and lover. But my anxiety attacks had increased after we met. Why, at the peak of my career, living with a man I loved, a man who adored me, should I be anxious?

I had to admit that Eric was often a puzzlement to me. He had been married twice and had one child, a girl who was almost ten. I saw his marriages as attempts to create a familiar world he had never experienced himself. But his ex-wives were very strange, as he described them, almost sick. The first had simply left him for no reason, he said. And the second, the mother of the ten-year-old girl, refused to let him visit his own child. Clearly, both marriages had been disastrous.

There were other puzzlements. He was friendless. In all the years we had lived together, he had never received a call from anyone, not a "How are you?" not a "Let's meet for coffee." It was as if he was alone on this planet, as if he had never worked, never been married, as if he had just been born. One night a few months after he had moved into my apartment, I found him sobbing in the bedroom. "What is it?" I asked, wondering what in the world had happened.

"If it weren't for you," he told me through his tears, "if it weren't for you, my whole world would fall apart. No one cares about me, no one but you."

I had reassured him, told him how much I loved him, how much everyone loved him. I had taken enormous pleasure in introducing Eric to my friends—my business, tennis, summer, winter, and especially my year-in-year-out friends. He seemed to love and appreciate having ready-made relationships accessible to him and I knew my friends adored him. So he had two crazy ex-wives, so he cried one night. So who's perfect?

I wasn't. My past was nothing to brag about either. I had been married once, years ago. Stan, my husband. How and why had *that* happened? Then I had fallen in love with a married man. I knew there was something peculiar in me that was attracted to that unavailable species. Oh, he was available up to a point—available for occasional evenings, lunches, trips, even a week in a faraway place. But all the important times, like Christmas and birthdays and Sundays, I ended up alone. There was also something peculiar about me and the way I responded to the loss of love, the end of an affair. It was always more crushing to me than to anyone else I knew. It took me longer to recover, to find myself again.

Everything was so intense with me. I used to tell myself, when I was in the throes of that mad, passionate, dewy-eyed romance with my married man, that the extraordinary pleasure, the ecstasy, the joy when we were together made up for the loss of the living time, the sharing time, the being time. But something inside me always knew that furtive loving with a touch of angst wasn't as good as the all-the-time kind. Still, I had spent six years of my life deeply involved with that man. He had promised we would get married. It never happened.

With Eric it was different. Our love *was* the all-the-time kind. There was nothing furtive about our relationship. He wanted to marry me. But having been married to Stan for four terrible years, I wasn't really interested in marriage. What Eric and I had was superior to marriage, I thought. It had all the commitment, all the sharing, all the love, and none of the terrible obligation and duty and obedience part.

As I walked into Sucho's, I laughed remembering my mother's reaction when I had taken her there a few months before. "How can people who serve such elegant food, who decorate in such good taste, be the barbarians they were in World War II?"

She had not been impressed with my retort: "Remember My Lai."

Eric looked up at me with a broad smile. "Did you read the *Village Voice* today?"

I shook my head. No, I hadn't found time, I told him as I took off my coat.

"In Nat Hentoff's continuing love affair with the First Amendment, you are still his number one courtesan, his favorite muckraker."

I sat down and just looked at him. We were so lucky. Love, happiness, careers—we shared everything.

And it was through sharing similar interests that we had met. I had been doing a film about life in New York's vast crime-ridden housing projects, and Eric was the lawyer for one of the subjects of the film. I went to his office to ask him to agree to my interviewing his client. We had a three-hour talk that first day and soon we found ourselves meeting for coffee, taking walks, no longer talking about the film, but about each other.

He told me that after law school he had gone to work for a Wall Street firm, but in 1952 he had been drawn into Adlai Stevenson's campaign for the presidency. He had been so deeply affected by Stevenson that he gave up corporate law, and ever since, he had gone from cause to cause. At the time we met, he had just opened his own office, a cramped, dusty little space in East Harlem. I loved that he wasn't a fancy corporate lawyer, that he had chosen to use his wonderful head for helping the poor. We had so much in common. Many of my films had been about the problems facing the poor, the voiceless, the most wretched people in our society. Now I had met a man who cared about them, too.

He was married, but he had been separated from his second wife for months and they were getting a divorce. Here was a relationship with a future. It didn't matter that he was making very little money. After I convinced him to appear in a brief segment of my film, his business began to pick up. And when my friends got to know him, they steered even more clients his way. He lived in a terrible Village apartment, and that didn't matter either. For a while we maintained the fiction of separate apartments, separate lives. But we spent most of our time together in my apartment. He brought his clothes, his records, his books, and then he moved in. Now, five years later, he filled my life. He accepted me, my mind, my job—even my anxiety attacks—just as I respected his brain, his straightforwardness, his sense of humor. No sexist, my Eric. He even loved my independence. We had it all.

"No one should be so happy, Eric," I blurted out. "It's indecent."

He gave me a funny smile. "So?"

I knew what he meant. After he got a divorce from his second wife, he had started to pressure me about marriage. It was a gentle pressure, a loving pressure, but that is the hardest kind to resist. And so I had finally promised to marry him. But I didn't really mean it.

"Oh, Eric. Marriage," I said, feeling the old heaviness that came over me whenever we discussed it. "It's so good like this. I'm too old for children. We couldn't be more committed. Why ruin it?"

I remember his answer. "You obey other social conventions," he said. "And it matters to me."

Why? I wondered. He had tried it twice already. Why did he need it so? And if it was so important to him, why couldn't I give in?

During dinner, we talked about the house at the beach. I had bought it three years before as our weekend hideout, our summertime retreat. It was a wreck, but Eric had done marvelous things helping to repair and rebuild it. He knew how to talk to plumbers and electricians, and he had built the staircase from the deck to the beach himself. He was good at everything—carpentry, car-fixing, tennis, love-making. We were planning to rent the house in August, and Eric was telling me about the things he wanted to do first. I didn't know where we would find the time, but he said he would do much of the work himself. I was grateful that he had changed the subject.

Dinner over, we strolled arm in arm, world in world, back to the apartment. We walked across our favorite street, Central Park South, bundled close together to fight a harsh, end-of-winter wind. We saw the horse-drawn carriages outside the Plaza and brushed past the rollicking conventioneers who stayed in the once stately hotels that faced the park. My apartment was on Central Park West, but we always walked home this way. It was a tradition, a ritual that had developed between us without anything being said. Much of our relationship was like that, unspoken, tacit, a silent understanding of the things we shared.

No anxiety now. Eric, the sake, the Emmy. No

terror. I savored the sweetness of the moment. The marriage thing—still unresolved—was pushed aside.

Once home, we fell into bed, holding each other, touching, talking. I loved lying next to him, smelling his clean, strong smell. No Aramis, no Gucci, just soap. Fresh, sturdy, no artifice, no guile. Our conversation was full of plans. We were thinking about going to Europe with the money we would get from renting the beach house. "How about Spain, babe?" He was the only man who had ever called me babe. I loved it.

I had so many other things on my mind: Jean, the lawyer, Steve. And right now I just wanted to sleep. I'll think about Europe tomorrow.

The next morning, half out the door heading toward the elevator, I stopped short. Damn! The National Council of Churches of Christians and Jews or Moslems and Hindus or whatever awards luncheon was today. At "21." And here I was dressed in jeans and an old sweater, a scarf covering my dirty hair and a blotch of color on my lips for make-up. I rushed back to the apartment to wash my hair, put on a respectable pants suit and do what I could to my face. I would have to make a speech. How could I have forgotten?

I tore into the office and a Greek chorus of secretaries shrieked in approval—or amazement—at my appearance. They weren't used to seeing me so put together. Neither was I. I called the hospital for my morning check-in with Jean's husband. He tried to be patient with me and give me the news. I wasn't sure if he hated me for intruding on his family at such a time, or if he understood that I really cared about Jean apart from the film. She wasn't in intense pain, he told me, but she had decided she didn't want me to bring any of the film to the hospital, which she had made me promise to do if she had to be hospitalized before it was broadcast. I knew that meant she was too sick to watch it, in too much pain to care. But before I could say anything Ben had hung up. Into the phone I whispered, "Ben, don't let her suffer, please."

I suddenly felt depressed. I had counted on being

able to cheer Jean up when she was in the hospital. I had hoped I would be able to lift her spirits. I knew if she saw herself in the red pants suit on the beach in Mexico, walking past the balloon man, she would feel better. In spite of the depressing laetrile episode, the trip had been like a second honeymoon for her and Ben. But this morning she wanted nothing, wanted to see no one. She had to be suffering.

The phone rang. It was Steve, calling from the editing room to tell me our boss had heard from John O'Connor. Eleven Monday morning. He also had a film clip for me to show at the awards luncheon.

Fran came through the door with her perennial morning Coca-Cola, the last vestige of her college persona. "Greg wants you to drop by whenever you get a chance. Something about a speech to the affiliates, and the Nazi is superquiet today."

"Watch it, Frannie." I laughed. *"Alleged."*

"Alleged is quiet but our lawyer wants your deposition."

"What does Greg want me to talk about?"

"Don't know. Documentaries. What else?" She left the office.

What else indeed? There's more to me than documentaries. I was strangely stung by Fran's comment. Still, Greg Donnolly was the general manager of the station and I was pleased that he thought enough of my work to ask me to make a speech to the affiliates. Maybe it would take my mind off Jean.

Fran must have seen the worry on my face. The next time she popped her head into my office, she said brightly, "Time to go—award time." But she was looking at me nervously. "Is something the matter? Is it Jean?"

"No—yes," I stammered as I reached for my coat. "It's Jean—it's nothing." She looked unconvinced. "Really, Frannie, it's nothing. I've got to run. Where's Steve with that clip? I'll dash over and pick it up."

You don't dash, I said to myself, you flee, as if moving quickly will somehow help you beat the terror. There it was, the old fear, back again, whenever I had to go someplace. And I was, at this point, afraid of the fear. My anxiety attacks had become so intense that I was often immobilized, paralyzed. So I hadn't dashed very far when the terror, greater than yesterday's, less than tomorrow's, swallowed me up like a vacuum cleaner. I walked along holding on to the walls of the corridor, praying I wouldn't bump into anyone I knew.

What *are* you frightened of? What was it? I was going to a shrink once a week and still the anxiety increased. Why didn't Dr. Allen help me? Dammit, I'd been seeing him religiously for ten years, ever since about the time I left my husband. It was a routine, like brushing my teeth, a normal part of my life, as it was for most of the people I knew. He gave me Valium and I was taking it by the handful. So why was the terror growing? I must talk to him, must get more pills, must do something.

Somehow the anxiety decreased when I reached Steve's editing room and saw him smiling at me. I was safe. He handed me the clip I would show at the luncheon.

"I hate this awards thing. It takes time away from us," I said. "But when I get back, we'll make magic for Mr. O'Connor."

"Don't pout, Barb. We're in good shape. You're just in a bitchy mood because you have to go out for lunch." It had become a joke between us. Only a few people knew the reason I preferred Rocko's sandwiches to "21."

"I know you," he said as he hugged me goodbye. "Now get out of here and be wonderful."

I decided to walk to "21," but I had taken only a few steps east on Fifty-seventh Street when the terror began again. My hands became drenched in perspiration. I held on to the sides of the buildings for support and struggled to catch my breath. My God, if anyone saw me, he would think I was drunk. I made it to Tenth Avenue and went into a grimy diner filled with the truckdrivers who claimed Fifty-seventh Street as their territory.

"Please," I said to the harried waitress, "I only want

a glass of water." I fumbled for the pills in my purse. "I'll pay you. I won't take up your table at lunchtime. I'll pay you." I closed my eyes and tried to catch my breath. How long have I been living like this?

The waitress set a glass of water on the table and I gulped it down with two Valium. I inhaled deeply as I waited for the anxiety to subside. In about ten minutes I felt better, or at least able to walk out of the diner. I hailed a cab and urged the driver to hurry. I was late. Be gracious, be cool. You're winning an award.

The private dining room at "21" was crammed with other winners, all beaming, all drinking white wine and chatting with animation. I tore into the room and began the social thing. And when it was time for my speech, I forgot my terror of just a few moments before. The pills, the wine, or maybe it was just being involved and not thinking about it.

My film was about the former mental patients of Long Beach, and when I saw their faces on the screen, I remembered the anguish I felt for them. They had returned to life in the town after years in institutions, dumped on a community that was not prepared to receive them. The town, faced with an influx of mental patients, many of them poor, many of them elderly, had passed a law stating that no one who needed daily medication to function could live in the rooming houses along the boardwalk on the ocean. What a law! I had thought. Next it will be people with blue eyes or dark hair. I had dug into that town and Steve and I had made a moving film in which a mental patient named Gladys had spoken eloquently about what it was like to be unwanted by a community, to be denied a home, a right to live like other people—what it was like to be stigmatized. I had spent days poking around the rooming houses, talking to the people on the boardwalk, trying to be fair to both sides. Were property values really going down? Were the mental patients a threat, were they violent, did they disturb the children? Despite all the fears and accusations of the townspeople, I couldn't find one incident in which they had bothered anyone. The show had been an essay on the anatomy of prejudice. It was one of my favorite films, one that had pained me deeply, one that disturbed me for months after it was completed.

I talked about the film and then gave my standard rap about the First Amendment and the people's right to know. I reminded the audience that we documentary film-makers were aware that our work would never change the world. But certainly we could affect the way people looked at their government. We could alter their perceptions about those who controlled their lives. And if my films did that much, I was happy. But to myself I thought, Twenty years after Edward R. Murrow's documentary report on the lives of migrant workers, nothing has changed. Our films create horror and outrage at the outset, but society has a wonderful repressive mechanism. The cries of social and political indignation that my films evoked were generally lost in a whirlwind of more pressing and immediate problems. The lives of the former mental patients of Long Beach remain wretched.

Still, I was proud of the way I made my living, and I said that perhaps together, my film, CBS's genuine concern for social issues, and this award would at least provide a beginning for change. I thanked the National Council of Churches—it was them after all—and sat down to a burst of applause. The luncheon over, I made a graceful exit and left "21." I was still feeling the glow of the wine. Heady with attention, filled with pride, I felt brave. I would walk back to CBS, and this time I would make it.

It was a cold, clear, brilliant March afternoon, and the brisk, almost brutal wind blowing off the Hudson stole my breath and burned my eyes. I'm alone. All alone. No Eric, no Frannie, no Steve. I felt fine, and I realized I hadn't had time to buy clothes in months. How long had it been since I'd spent a day alone with me, shopping, walking, thinking? Ages. I turned around and headed toward Bergdorf's.

I strolled past the windows. The elegant mannequins with their stylish clothes beckoned me inside. But their plastic smiles seemed to mock me. They knew better. They knew their clothes were safe. For months I had been unable to enter a department store without fleeing back to the street gasping for air, darting into a cab for safety, then running into the protected environment of my apartment. There the terror always subsided. When I was really desperate for clothes, I would take two Valium and tear into a small boutique, preferably one located on the ground floor. No crowds, no elevators, a small selection to choose from, no hassles. I would quickly inspect the limited number of things available, make my choice, and get out. I turned away from Bergdorf's windows. I could live without department stores. Besides, Steve will need me, I rationalized. Too much to do. Who needs clothes?

Eric and I had a date with Edie and Jonathan Samson that evening in the Village. I never had dinner below Fifty-seventh Street if I could help it. It wasn't snobbery; it was the same old terror that seemed to increase in proportion to the distance I was from home. But with Edie and Jonathan it was different. Edie was my dear friend.

We had met at a party given by a mutual friend and it had happened instantly. Click. Laughter, sensitivity, smarts—it was as if we had known each other all our lives. It began with a simple conversation. When Edie heard I was doing a film on the aged, she told me she had worked with some people who were doing innovative things with the aged in nursing homes. She gave me their names and numbers. Then it turned out she had also worked in communications, teaching and publishing. When she was through, I wasn't quite sure what she actually did. Her interests seemed to encompass everything. I loved that she was eclectic, superinvolved in so many disciplines. I loved the intensity with which she spoke about art, politics, an off-Broadway play, the women's movement.

We met again a few months later in the Hamptons and spent a day walking on the beach, talking about ex-husbands, lovers, sex, careers. We laughed until we hurt about the foibles of the men in our lives, about our own foibles. Neither of us had a sister, but soon it seemed as if that's what we were to each other. And I loved her.

Her husband, Jonathan, was a tender rock. They had two children who were in their teens and they lived just off Gramercy Park in an apartment that went on forever. Jonathan was one of the best plastic surgeons in the business, and in addition to everything else, Edie was deeply involved in her husband's career. How did she cram it all in, how did she know so much, digest so much, where did she find the time? Friends, lovers, parents. They had a marriage I envied.

We met at a new Italian restaurant near their apartment: black cane chairs, black-and-white tile floor, everything black and white except for the hundreds of plants that hung from the ceiling. We ordered the northern Italian food that was the house specialty, and a superb white wine. Edie and Jonathan were going to Israel that summer, and Edie was on a crash course to learn everything about the place: the history, the culture, the food, the artists, the politicians. As she talked, I remembered the first time I introduced Eric to both of them. Rosy with new love, filled with romance, I wanted to share my happiness. I told Edie all about him: how we met, the kind of work he did. I had no secrets from Edie. She knew that Eric had just moved into my apartment, she knew that I was trying to get him more work and that I was paying the bills. She knew about the two ex-wives. But if she and Jonathan had reservations, they hadn't expressed them. Jonathan suspended judgment, and Edie's curiosity overcame her skepticism. I loved them for giving Eric a chance, for wanting me to be happy. I knew they would like him. I knew it. Now, five years later, we were all friends. And I was still happy.

But that evening, even with Eric, even with my dear friends Edie and Jonathan, my thoughts were sad. "It's Jean, isn't it?" Edie said, sensing my mood. "Is she going to die?"

"No." I said, shaking my head vehemently. "I can tell just by looking at her face on the film. She's going to make it. There's so much she wants to do in her life. But I feel so helpless."

"The film will help her," Eric said, taking my hand. "It will help a lot of people."

"How do you make a film, not knowing the ending?" Edie asked.

"How do you live your life?" Jonathan said. He smiled and suddenly I felt better. When we left the restaurant the four of us walked back to their apartment, where Jonathan brewed some mainland Chinese tea he had bought in Chinatown. Eric and I didn't stay long. Jonathan had surgery at eight the next morning. Edie had a zillion appointments. Good night, good night, see you soon.

We took a cab back to the apartment and that night, filled with a sense of sharing, having delighted in being with our friends, we were not too tired to make love. Eric made love like no man I had ever known. He was strong, tender and totally uninhibited. He touched, he felt, he laughed, he talked. As I fell asleep in his arms, the small of my back embraced by his body, I silently thanked my guardian angel for all my happiness, for the richness of my life.

2
Sundays, Sundays

The phone rang sharply, almost insistently, startling
Eric and me out of our sleep. It was Sunday morning.
Damn! I pulled the covers over my head to try to fall
back asleep as he reached for the phone. I heard nothing for several minutes, then I heard him saying in his
gravelly morning voice, "You're dissembling. Catherine, you're dissembling."

Catherine was ex-wife number two, who now lived
in Chicago. She had never called the apartment before,
at least not when I was there. Dissembling, I thought
in my twilight sleep, what does *that* mean? Why is she
calling now?

"I'll send it when I have it," Eric said. "I told you I
don't have any now. When I have it." His voice was
more than firm; he was angry. I put the pillow on top
of my head. I didn't want to hear one word, not a
fraction of this conversation.

Then Eric began talking in a voice I had never
heard before. It was a strange and frightening voice.
She must have said something awful, something terrible. "You are overwrought, Ca-the-rine. You are not
think-ing clearly. You know how you get when you
don't think clearly."

It was no use. I couldn't sleep through this. I was
up. Sunday morning had begun. I started for the bathroom and turned to look at Eric, sitting on the edge of
the bed. He was listening now, and there was an angry
scowl on his face.

He had hung up when I returned. I went to the

kitchen to make some coffee, and a few minutes later we were back in bed together. I was afraid to ask him about the call; I could see he was still shaking with rage.

The Sunday *Times* was scattered on the floor around the large white platform bed Eric had built for the bedroom; we had devoured it the night before. Eric was the only man I knew who read every section: book review, real estate, business, the arts. He seemed to care about all of it intensely.

We lay there, sipping the coffee. The bright morning sun poured in through the bedroom shutters. Finally I mustered the courage to say softly, "What was that? What's the matter?"

"The bitch."

I had never heard him talk like that, never seen him so furious.

"She wants me to pay her bill at Mercy Hospital. You remember I told you she hurt her back when she had that accident."

"What accident?"

"When she fell down."

I nodded. He had said something about it to me. But she must have medical insurance, I thought. "Why does she want you to pay it?" I asked a little nervously.

"She says I promised to—I don't remember. And, Barbara, I'd rather not discuss this now. It's morning. I'm barely awake."

I didn't want to discuss it either, but I was disturbed by his tone. Catherine was the mother of his only child. And she had had an accident. How could he talk to her like that? "If Catherine needs money," I said, "we can send it to her."

"Damn it, Barbara, I said I didn't want to talk about it!" He got out of bed and went to the kitchen. I lit a cigarette, thinking, We do have secrets, Eric and I. We don't share everything after all.

His mood had changed when he returned. "I'm sorry, babe," he said, handing me another cup of coffee. "It's just that she's always after me for money. Not all women are like you, living on your own, paying your own bills. As a matter of fact, you're really supporting me."

I didn't want to hear that either. I was paying for the rent and the food. I had to pay those bills before him; why shouldn't I pay them now? He took care of his office expenses, a part-time secretary, alimony, child support, although I sometimes had to lend him money to meet those payments. "Eric, stop talking like that," I said. "We love each other. We share everything. I don't mind. When you start making more money, you'll pay for things, too."

I sat up and he took me in his arms. "What do you want to do today?" he said.

It's Sunday, I thought. I've always hated Sundays, always had to fight the gray gloom that comes over me on Sunday afternoons. I remembered being home in Florida on Sunday, homework unfinished, Monday coming, the weekend over. Or being in New York on a Sunday afternoon after a concert or a visit to a museum and having to get on the dirty, rickety train back to Vassar. I remembered the hundreds of Sundays I was alone, while the married man I loved romped with his children on a suburban lawn. I had thought then that when I die it will be on Sunday afternoon around four o'clock. But since Eric had come into my life, he made Sundays light. I had someone who loved me, someone I loved, to share the day with me. It was our most treasured time together —away from our jobs, just us.

"I know," Eric said. "Let's go out to the house and see what the winter did to it."

I wasn't sure. Part of me wanted to hang out in the apartment doing nothing. The water out there was still turned off, the electricity hadn't been turned on yet, and it was a two-hour drive each way.

Eric loved the house at the beach. In a way, I was sure that he felt it was more his than mine, even though I paid the mortgage and the other bills. We had spent our first summer together in a rented house in the Hamptons and then we decided to look for one to buy. It was a commitment—a home on the ocean with no memories of anyone else, a home of our own. It took almost another year to renovate the old beach cottage we found. We raised the roof, extended the living room; Eric had done most of the work himself, happy to contribute to our relationship by saving me money. There were still a lot of things he wanted to do, and watching him every summer weekend busy with some new do-it-yourself project, I wondered if he had ever lived in a house before.

"How about it, babe? Let's go to the beach," he said again. "It's a gorgeous day. We'll take wine and cheese and have a feast on the deck."

I smiled and nodded yes. He was always so happy at the beach. Maybe he would forget the call from Catherine. Maybe I could forget the tone of his voice when he spoke to her.

We hurried out of the apartment. I thought about calling the hospital to ask about Jean but stopped myself. No, this is our day, just the two of us. No gloom, no doom. Just me and my man and the sunshine.

"There's a leak under that window," he said as we stood in the middle of the living room. "And I'd better check the roof to see if the shingles are still tight."

"Is that hard?" I asked. I was worried. I never understood structural things: beams, shingles, two-by-fours, copper wiring. I was so grateful he knew about all that.

"It's nothing, babe. I can caulk the window myself, and we've still got a guarantee on the roof." I heard him walking around overhead and then he was off to look behind the house for some snow fencing. He wanted to string it along the dunes in front of the house to trap the sand that would be blown our way by the winds of the last weeks of March. I unpacked our lunch and we sat on the deck awhile, sipping wine and looking at the sea. Then Eric went back to work and I took a walk along the beach. It was untouched by footprints this time of year. It was sparkling, the sand so clean, the water a shocking blue. The waves were breaking close to the shore and although the water was cold, I took off my sneakers and walked barefoot along the water's edge. I looked at my neighbors' dunes. This year we were lucky. The wind and the water had added a great deal of sand. It hadn't been a bad winter. Everything was intact. We had survived.

When I returned to the house, I found Eric deeply engrossed making notes and taking measurements for some new project. There really wasn't much for me to do. I couldn't clean; the water wasn't turned on yet because the pipes could still burst in a spring freeze. So I just puttered around, checking to see that everything was in place. I always felt a little guilty, a little left out and useless, when Eric got involved with the house. It was like a romance, and I was the stranger, the intruder. So I went out to the deck and sat in the sun, staring at the sea.

After a few minutes I felt his arms around me. He was standing behind me and leaned over to kiss me softly on the lips. I looked up at him. The beach was deserted. And there in the bright sunlight, with the waves crashing on the shore, we made love. It was a bit risky since the house sat high on the dunes facing the sea. But if anyone walked by we wouldn't have noticed. And we knew the dunes wouldn't tell. We lay there in each other's arms looking at the ocean, me trying to regulate my heartbeat to his rhythm, something I often did after we made love.

We didn't speak for a long time. Anything we said would have been trite. And then the late afternoon sun began to turn cold and hard, and we were getting chilled.

"I love you, babe."

"I know, Eric. And me you."

"But it's time to get old Sammy on the road."

Sammy was the name of our car. It was a present from a marvelous friend, Sam Gold, who had given it to me when I bought the house. Years before, I had been able to help him get his mother into a nursing home in New York. I had produced a number of films on the aged, and Sam had called, asking my advice. The car was his way of saying thanks. And though it was no beauty, it got us back and forth to the house. Eric had spent hours working on it, replacing the carburetor, tinkering and tuning it up. That, too, was like a romance, the car and Eric, and I knew enough not to intrude on that relationship either. I was no mechanic. In fact, I didn't even like to drive. When I first moved to New York and saw the frenetic, congested roads, the cars cutting in and darting out, I simply let my Florida license expire. Eric decided to give me some brush-up lessons one summer, but it just didn't work. I was too nervous, he was too impatient, and after a couple of close calls on back roads we gave up. Our love had survived some bad moments on the tennis court. Why tempt fate with driving lessons? I had teased. Besides, Eric was a beautiful driver. In old Sammy, with Eric behind the wheel, I alway felt safe.

"Take care, house," I called as we pulled out of the driveway. "Stay dry. We'll be back soon." Then suddenly I thought of Jean, and the weekend she wanted to spend with Eric and me at the beach. We had talked about it as we walked along the beach in Tijuana. She, too, adored the sea. You'll make that weekend here, Jeanie, you will. But just thinking about her reminded me of the week ahead: my appointment with Dr. Allen in the morning, the screening for O'Connor. And slowly that old Sunday heaviness came over me, enshrouding me in a terrible gray pall.

Eric, sensing my mood, said tenderly, "Got the Sunday demons, babe? Right on the button." He smiled and showed me his watch. It was four o'clock.

"Just a little, Eric, just a little."

As I walked into the apartment the phone was ringing. Not thinking, not really knowing that I knew who the call was from, I dropped my beach basket on the hall floor and hurried to the bedroom. Eric was parking the car in the garage. He would be back in about ten minutes.

"Barbara? Is that you?" It was my mother in Miami. She always called on Sunday—always. "Where have you been?" she said. "We've been trying to get you for hours. I've been worried to death."

"Eric and I went out to the beach," I said.

"Isn't it a little early to go out there? Isn't it cold? I hope you dressed warm. Wait a minute while I get your father. Lou! Lou! Barbara's on the phone. Pick up the extension. Don't you want to talk to your daughter?"

I tightened inside. As many times as this scene had been played out, I was never prepared. Rarely had I ever picked up the phone to hear my father's voice, there, ready, eager to talk to me. Why? Today was no exception. I lay back on the bed as she called to him again, hoping Eric would come soon, wanting him there with me.

Finally my father, as always, picked up the phone and said, "How are you, baby? Are you O.K.? Your mother's been worried sick. You know she always calls on Sunday. You should have let us know where you were."

"Now, Lou, I wasn't worried. Barbara's a big girl. She doesn't have to tell us every single move she makes."

"O.K., O.K. You weren't worried."

"So, Barbara dear, what's new? How's Jean?" my mother began. As usual, she *was* genuinely interested in my life; too interested, I sometimes thought. But she was always there, always ready to listen, always ready to help. So I began to fill her in about Jean. Then she asked if I thought the laetrile was helping. No, I thought it was useless.

"Oh. I'm sorry," she said. There was a pause and then she said, "Anything new with you and Eric?" I could hear the reluctance in her voice as she asked the question.

My father, sensing that her indirect approach would never work, decided to assert himself. "Let me handle this, Sally," he said firmly. "Just what are your plans about marriage, Barbara?"

It was the inevitable question, every Sunday, and I still hadn't learned how to handle it. "I have none," I said. "If I did, you'd be the first to know." I hated my wise-ass sarcastic tone, but I couldn't help it. I looked up and saw Eric standing in the hallway. He knew about the Sunday phone calls, he knew what was going on. He smiled and shook his head as he went to the kitchen to make drinks.

"Well, your brother has children," my mother persisted. "And we love Melinda. She's a wonderful daughter-in-law. But we won't be a real family until you make me a grandmother, too."

"Oh, Mother, stop it, please," I said. "You *are* a grandmother. I make films, not children."

Now it was my father's turn. "It's only because we love you, Barbara. You never think about the future. You and Eric can't go on like this."

I was getting angry. I always got angry. "Why not?" I said. "Why the hell not? What's wrong with two people who love each other living together? What the hell's the matter with that?"

"Nothing is wrong," my mother added softly. "It's just that you would make us so happy . . . and if you really love him . . . and our friends—"

I cut her off. "I don't give a damn about your friends and I do love him. Please, Mother, why can't you let me live my own life?"

I took a long sip of the Scotch Eric had handed me, and tried to calm down. He walked back to the living room, leaving me to conclude this phone call on my own.

My mother changed the subject and began to talk about her grandchildren, the trip to Europe they were planning this summer, anything to end the conversation on a happy note. I listened, made a few comments and finally said, "I've got to get off now. I'll talk to you both soon. Next Sunday. Do you want to say hello to Eric?"

"No dear. You just give him our love," my mother said and the phone clicked off.

I walked into the living room and sat next to Eric on the couch. "I can't stand it," I said. "I can't bloody stand it another second. Every Sunday, every phone call. They even phone me at the office about it, when they know you aren't around. Why does it matter to them so?"

"Because they love you and you're important to them," he said. "They need to care about you. They need you to fill in their own lives. I feel the same way, babe. You know that."

I looked away. I didn't want him to go on. And in a few seconds he saw how unhappy I was and put his arms around me. But I couldn't shake my mood. The day had been totally ruined. I hated Sundays for good reason, I thought, and I always will.

In the kitchen making supper, I still couldn't get the call out of my mind. Why did my parents always make me feel so guilty? Guilty because I wouldn't make them happy. What about *my* happiness? Didn't that matter? It was a curious conspiracy, my parents and Eric. But he didn't really understand. He didn't realize that it wasn't *him* they wanted me to marry. It was just the idea of marriage that was so important to them.

I remembered how nervous I had been when I introduced Eric to my parents. I had told them by phone that there was a man in my life, a man I adored. I wanted desperately for them to like him. So I lied. I told them that he was getting a divorce, but I didn't mention that he had been married twice. On their way to Europe that summer my parents had stopped in New York to see me, to meet him. They were a little shocked to find that we were living together in my apartment—I had somehow failed to mention that, too. But then the prospective-son-in-law questions began: What did Eric do for a living? What were our "plans for the future"?

In their minds that meant only one thing: marriage. So I finally gathered my courage and told them the truth. Even when Eric's divorce was final, I said, we did not plan to get married. I assured them that it was possible to live together, to love together, without benefit of matrimony. I was a grown woman, and they would just have to accept it.

I remembered the forlorn look on their faces when I said that. Living together without marriage? I had challenged all their values by telling them that, upset many of their dreams. And they had never really accepted it. Once they learned that the divorce was final, the questions began all over again, and now they were waiting, waiting to hear me say the magic word. I had assaulted their values, but they would win, anyway. Eventually Barbara would come to her senses.

Eric came to the kitchen at least twice to refill his wineglass while I was making supper. Maybe because my nerves were so raw, I snapped at him. "Why do you need that? It's rotten to drink so much."

"It's my Valium," he said sharply. "It makes me feel good. You've got your pills, I've got my wine. Now drop it, Barbara."

Oh God, I thought, now I've ruined the day for him, too. I knew he hated my taking the pills. He hated Dr. Allen for giving them to me. In fact, he thought Dr. Allen was less than terrific on every count. He couldn't understand what we had talked about all these years. And even with the pills, my anxiety attacks were growing worse. Eric had the solution. How many times had he said to me, "If you'd only marry me, babe, I'd make sure they went away"?

Pressure. And his remark about wine being his Valium—was that some kind of subtle blackmail? I decided not to think about it.

We talked about inconsequential things during supper: who we might get to rent the beach house, new tires for Sammy. I did the dishes, and when I went back to the living room, Eric was fussing with the plants. He was marvelous with them. If I looked at them they died. So I left him to his plants and got ready for bed.

Tomorrow, I thought, I've got to talk to Dr. Allen about these attacks. O'Connor. Maybe Jeanie will be better and can talk to me. And I've got to start thinking about a new film when this one is over.

I was tired but I couldn't fall asleep. I remembered the way Eric had spoken to Catherine. I remembered the way I had spoken to my parents. I hated phone calls. I heard music from the living room. Eric was listening to Mozart. Why didn't he come to bed? I hated Sundays.

Finally he came in the bedroom and began to undress. I pretended to be asleep when he lay down next to me, taking me in his arms to hold me through the night.

3

Each Day
from Now On

I turned the corner on Riverside Drive, surprised again by the fresh, sweet air that came off the polluted Hudson. I was on my way to see Dr. Allen. Most of my friends went to doctors with German accents on upper Park Avenue. They rode up in elevators with baby carriages and laundry bags. I had a shrink on Riverside Drive, with no accent and a view of the river. I'd been helping him pay the rent for ten years.

I felt a deep fatigue as I waited for him to buzz open the door. I sat in the empty, dimly lit waiting room, drinking coffee from the container I had brought with me, leafing through the morning *Times*. It was eight-thirty. I was all alone. I always had the first appointment on Monday mornings. Somehow, the furniture looked tacky today. The magazine rack was filled with *House Beautiful, Better Homes and Gardens* and ancient copies of *Newsweek*. So many visits, I thought to myself, for so many years. What *am* I doing here? Then I reminded myself: Even though we don't seem to talk about anything that matters, I get the Valium from Dr. Allen. And I knew how much I needed that.

He walked halfway down the corridor to greet me as he always did, nodded and then headed back as I started to gather my things. In his office we sat in our traditional seats facing each other, my back to the analytic couch.

"Well, Miss Gordon, how are you today?" he asked, giving me what seemed to be a significant stare. I felt a familiar heaviness inside when he spoke those words. The man knew everything about me—my loves and my hates, my joys and hurts, my fantasies and fears. And still he called me Miss Gordon.

I looked at the carefully pressed suit, the white shirt, the characterless tie, the angular face, the sterile room. How old was he? I realized I had no idea. He could have been forty-three or fifty-one. He had revealed so little of himself in the past ten years that I knew nothing about him—not so much his private life, but what kind of person he was. That's the way it is supposed to be, I thought; cool, detached. He must remain so distant in order to help me, I told myself. But he seemed so detached that it was hard for me to believe that he was trying to stay distant. God, I thought, maybe he *is* that detached. I knew he didn't sense the urgency I felt. Years before when he was on vacation, I had visited a doctor he had recommended in case I needed to talk to someone. I had remarked to that doctor, You are so engaged, so immediate, I really like talking to you better than Dr. Allen. You hear me. But then I had felt terrible, guilty. Dr. Allen knew me better. I didn't want to start the whole thing all over again.

I was shocked to hear myself burst into a monologue of almost feverish intensity. "What's new, Dr. Allen, is that I can't walk the streets of the city I love alone. Unless I'm stoned on pills or with someone, I can't do it. I can't function without Valium. I'm growing too dependent on something other than myself to function. I'm growing too dependent on pills. Why? Tell me why!"

He interrupted, "But I've told you many times, Miss Gordon, they are not addictive. They can't hurt you." And he crossed his legs and sat back in his chair to hear my response.

The words started pouring out of me. I hadn't planned to say all these things, but now they were coming out and I didn't seem able to stop. "I'm in love with a wonderful man, I have a super job, a terrific life. Why do I have these terrible anxiety attacks? Why can't you help me? They are restricting my movements, closing in on my life. Please, Dr. Allen, please help me!"

He didn't respond. He was still staring at me, the expression on his face unchanged from when I had entered his office. "Look, you're a doctor," I said. "The pills aren't working anymore. I'll face whatever it is that's causing this. I'm not a coward. I need your help."

"Perhaps," he began softly, "you need more medication to make you less hysterical. Now tell me what is making you so upset. Did you and Eric have a fight?"

I assured him that Eric and I hadn't fought, that the weekend had been fine except for my parents' pressuring phone call. And soon I felt quiet again and began to talk about Jean. "I'm worried about her. She won't talk to me, she's stuck there in the hospital and I hope she's not suffering." Then I got caught up in telling him about the laetrile, how much Jean had counted on it working, that she couldn't die, she was too young.

"I'm thinking of switching you to a stronger medication," he said.

He wasn't hearing me. He wasn't listening. I had spoken of my concern about Jean calmly, quietly. But now I felt like a raving lunatic. I crushed my cigarette in the ashtray and I heard myself screaming, "Pills, pills—there has to be another answer! I hate taking them, Eric hates my taking them!"

He got up from his chair and walked to his desk. I sat there staring at him, wondering what he was going to say. He picked up a large book on his desk and then came back to his chair. He began leafing through the book, not saying anything. "I think," he said finally, "you should go on Thorazine. It will help you get through these attacks."

"Thorazine!" I shouted at him. "That numbs the mind, kills the soul. They use it in hospitals. I don't want it."

"It will help you," he said with a smile.

"I don't care," I said angrily. "I'm not that sick. I don't want to be a zombie."

"Just a little, or perhaps you'd like some lithium?" His voice was confident. He was secure talking about all these pills.

I got out of my chair and began pacing the office, back and forth. I was trying to think clearly. Valium. Lithium. Were pills the only answer?

"The session is almost over, Miss Gordon," he said. "What is your decision?"

What is your decision? Would you like chocolate, vanilla or strawberry? Oh, I'll take Thorazine, on a sugar cone, please Daddy. My mind was racing. I was confused. I didn't know what to do. Finally I looked at him and said, "Just give me a prescription for the Valium."

He reached for his pad and pen. "What strength is that you take, Miss Gordon?"

I couldn't believe my ears. He didn't even know what strength medication he had been giving me. "Five milligrams," I said quietly.

"Would you like to have an additional session this week?" he asked, handing me the prescription. "Would that make you feel better? You know I really think the Thorazine would help you. I wish you'd consider it."

"No to the session. I don't have time. And no, no, no to the Thorazine. I wish I didn't need this," I said, shaking the prescription in my hand.

"Very good; then I'll see you next Monday." He started to get up to let me out, but this morning I wanted to leave without the ritual. I walked to the door and left it open as I fled down the corridor.

Outside, clutching the prescription in my hand, I ran for a cab. I had to get crosstown in a hurry. Steve and Fran would be waiting. Again I had the prescription and no answers. The same anxiety. It had all happened before. In my head I heard Dr. Allen's voice saying, "You're just hysterical." Why? Why am I hysterical? I had asked him so many times. And his answer was always pills. I wasn't that weak, goddammit. I wasn't. Someday I'll learn what's behind all this shit, I promised myself. But right now I'll get more Valium. I'll work on the film. Everything is all right when I work.

As usual, the man from the *Times* was impassive. I talked through the rough spots in the film, using the old film-maker's trick of coughing at a still unsolved bad edit, dropping my pad during an overexposed scene, hoping to divert his attention from the problem areas. Without opticals, the music and dissolves were only indicated by Steve's inscrutable marks, so O'Connor had to have a good imagination. He made cryptic notes and I thought, Oh, Mr. O'Connor, this is my eightieth film, so please be kind. Then to myself, He can't pan cancer, not even O'Connor. But if he perceives sentimentality and self-pity rather than admiration for Jean's courage, her humaneness, her honesty —who knows? How lucky the producers of feature films and plays or writers of books are! They don't have to sit here, almost like partners in their own possible execution, and endure the suspense of showing their work to someone who can make mincemeat of you or make you a hero. Executioner or Santa Claus? Which will it be?

Steve and I watched as O'Connor returned his note pad to his jacket, reached for his coat and breezed out the door waving goodbyes. Steve and I smiled at each other. We had performed well, stifling a "Hope you like it," repressing a "Jeanie would love a good review." No, we had remained cool, as professionals should. We wouldn't know what he thought for a week.

Strung out from the tension and excitement, Steve and I fled to a nearby retreat and watering hole, the Slate, for Bloody Marys and second-guessing. Our nonprofessional selves tried to psyche O'Connor out: "He smiled there." "He was too quiet." "He was intrigued." "He looked sad." Inevitably we saw rough spots in the film that we had not noticed before. It was as if the presence of two new eyes triggered a fresh set of brain cells in each of us. It was fun and intoxicating. It would have been more exhilarating if the subject of our film were other than what it was, or if Jean were not in the hospital.

Still, we both knew that our work on this film was

almost over and Steve asked me if our boss had mentioned the wonderful idea he had for my next one. I was feeling so tired, so exhausted that I didn't want to talk about it. I realized that was unusual. Whenever Steve and I were finishing a film, I always worried about my next project. What would it be? What would I do if I didn't get an idea? Would it be good? I never really rested between films. When other producers finished a film, they took time off to see friends, be with their families. Not me. Even when the film was in the lab and there was nothing to do, I was at my desk reading the *Times,* talking on the phone, looking for ideas. But this time I heard myself telling Steve that I didn't mean to be rude but I couldn't think about that right now.

"Why do another show right away?" Steve said. "Play a little tennis. Take a break."

I looked at him and we both laughed at the impossibility of that suggestion. Me, rest? I'd never not worked. What would I do? Who would I be?

"Are you and Eric still talking about Europe?" he asked. "A honeymoon?"

"You sound like my mother," I said uneasily. "Look, this place is too noisy. Why don't we go back and do some more work on the film?"

"There's nothing to edit until the new footage comes out of the lab," he said. "Go shop."

Me, shop? How funny, I thought, and smiled to myself remembering a phone conversation I once had with Ellen, Steve's wife. "I just don't know what to do with myself," she said. "I'm shopped out." Steve knew I couldn't go into department stores. He knew how I felt about marriage. Why is everybody nudging me? No, I thought, he's a friend.

"Come on, let's go," I said brightly. "Let's go look at Jeanie. I have an idea." On the way back we stopped to buy sesame seeds because they were good for Steve's cholesterol.

That afternoon, Frannie told me something I didn't want to hear. "I've done some research, Barbara," she said. "Jean can't have a remission. It's impossible.

Pancreatic cancer is worse than leukemia." She was begging me to be realistic.

I wasn't having any of it. I told her I had been with Jean in Mexico. She had never complained about the pain. I knew she was just suffering from that Mexican food. I myself had had a mild bout of Montezuma's revenge while I was there, so it had to be worse for her.

Fran looked at me incredulously. "You're some objective journalist," she said.

I had trained her to be a good researcher. She had done her job and now I was shutting her up. "I *am* being realistic," I told her. "Jean's only forty-seven, just getting her life together. It's too unfair. Besides she's not dying and that's that. I have to go see Greg."

I wandered from the production area to the adjacent building, the management side. The thicker rugs, the greener plants, the subdued lighting, were always a jolt to me. It was such a lush habitat compared to the more mundane trappings of my world. Whenever I went to see Greg I felt like a guy from the assembly line called into the boss's office.

Greg Donnolly—Andover, Yale, Darien, Episcopalian—was a born executive. He must have conducted sales meetings in the sandbox. Smooth, unflappable and very smart, he had made his name at CBS as a young salesman. Now, at forty, he was the general manager of CBS's flagship New York station. It made more money for CBS than the network itself, and the pressure was always on Greg to keep ratings up and sales even higher. It was also his responsibility to keep his producers out of trouble. But while others viewed documentary film-makers with suspicion or boredom, Greg treated me and my colleagues with respect. This quintessential salesman often found himself backing a band of muckraking journalists he had inherited from some other regime, and I always believed that he would have been happier if the whole lot of us simply disappeared. Our shows inevitably caused some kind of nastiness. But Greg seemed genuinely proud of our critical success and he was always supportive when the inflamed tempers provoked by our films resulted in law suits and threats at his door. It came with the territory, and as part of that territory he would nourish and defend me when I was attacked.

He stepped in front of his desk to greet me with his traditional "Hiya, Barb, how's it going?" Then he asked, "How's Jean?" I was amazed at how quickly she had become known all over the station. Everyone talked about her as if she were an old family friend. Jeanie, I thought, you *are* a star.

Greg began, "I guess you know, if she dies . . ."

I nodded quickly and thanked him. Enough, I thought. I don't want to hear it again.

Then he switched to the business at hand. It seemed the affiliate meeting was being planned for early May and CBS wanted to urge the other local stations to get into the documentary business. Greg wanted me to do the hype, to remind the stations that it was good for their image, good for the community. They could make money as well as score Brownie points. He urged me to tell it straight, to let them know of the legal hassles, to be sure to include the trouble I'd had on the Marchetti film and my run-in with the FBI. And of course, he reminded me of the Nazi.

I was surprised and flattered. But I've never understood you, I thought. We've never talked. *Candid Camera* reruns sell better and with less grief than my shows. Of course I'd make the speech. As I started to leave, he asked me to have Steve put together a nice montagey thing of my films, congratulated me on the National Council of Churches award and closed with another good word about Jean.

I left his office heady with attentiveness, not feeling the incipient terror, feeling secure. I walked through the bowels of CBS, the rows of editing rooms lining the long, dark corridors that seemed to stretch out endlessly in front of me. Room after room, each one emitting its own sound: gunfire, Budweiser commercials, the late movie being screened for that night's airing, "This is Walter Cronkite. Good night." Then I was standing outside Steve's room and I heard Jean's voice creep through the closed door: "I don't want to die, but if I have to, then each day from now on will be a gift."

I walked into the room and sat silently on the chair next to Steve's. He was peering at Jean's face on the Moviola and turned to me, about to speak. But I pointed to the screen with a gesture that meant let's watch Jean. Then the phone rang. I was furious. The damn phone always rang when I sat down to screen with Steve.

I picked it up with an impatient hello and I heard a man's voice whisper something about "ten minutes ago." It was peaceful. She died ten minutes ago. I recognized Ben's voice, choking on his words. I stared at Jean's face on the screen, looked at Steve, who was looking at me. Then I was choking into the phone myself, feeling anything I said would be wrong. Words stuck in my throat. Breathing deeply, I managed to say awkwardly, "I'm sorry. At least she didn't suffer." Ben didn't seem to hear me. He was saying something about a promise, my promise to Jean. She had wanted the film to be about life, not death.

I was already numb with the loss of Jean as a friend, but Ben was talking about work, taking me away from Jean, taking me back to my professional self. My voice was barely audible as I assured him I'd keep my promise. I would come to the funeral alone, just me, no cameras. But there was no one on the phone anymore.

Steve looked at me. He knew. I stared at him with disbelief. I was so tired. He put his arms around me. I started to cry and then pushed him away. I felt lost, abandoned, sad, used up. I couldn't look at Jean's face, now frozen on the Moviola screen. Her mouth looked as if she was getting ready to speak, her body was moving forward. I cried out, "Steve, I don't care who sees this film. I won't work on it another minute. If she can't see it, who cares? It was only for her. What's the point? It was only for her."

I grabbed my purse, left the editing room and stumbled through the hall toward my office, tears streaming down my face. Jean, I thought, we never said goodbye. It was wonderful knowing you. You enriched my life and I hope I was able to ease some of the anguish of these past weeks for you. We were intimate strangers, Jeanie. What a brave, warm, soft woman you are. It's just that damn cancer. I thought you'd beat it, too. I almost believed in that Mexican voodoo doctor. The film was for you, not for anyone else. What an obscene business I'm in. Yes, Jean, the red pants suit looks great. It *does* make you look thinner, but still dignified and proper, like the mayor you are. As I walked, thoughts tumbling around my brain, feeling a profound sense of loss, the nameless terror returned—dizziness, heart beating wildly, gagging, chills, shaking. I grasped at the walls for support until I reached my office, then collapsed at my desk.

Fran stood in the doorway, her eyes filled with tears. Steve must have phoned her. Quietly, talking in a strange, hushed way, she told me Eric would be waiting for me at Sucho's. She had phoned him with the news about Jean. "I'm so sorry, Barbara," she said. "She was a nice lady."

I kissed Fran good night and walked, stumbled, through the depressing streets that unite CBS and the rest of the world. No, I said to myself, I won't work on this film another minute. Not a second. I don't care about it anymore. It was only for Jean. But then I saw her face, and I remembered how much she wanted the film to be on the air, to be about life, not death. I was falling into the very trap she had warned me about. Her *life* was what was important, *not* her death. Jeanie, you are a star, I thought. And we'll make it a hell of a show.

Soaking wet with perspiration, trembling with anxiety, I walked into the restaurant. My love smiled up at me over the menu. It was warm and safe. The terror began to subside. Looking at Eric in his tweed jacket, his glasses burnished by the soft lights of the restaurant, I felt at peace. I was with him; everything would be all right.

"Sorry about Jean," he said. He kissed me on the cheek and handed me a Scotch.

"Don't bury her yet," I quipped briskly. His words destroyed the moment of peace I had begun to experience. Too soon, Eric. She isn't dead to me yet. Too soon.

He started to talk about the film: was I going to take a camera crew to the funeral, would I have to re-edit to include Jean's death? The more he said, the more anxious I became. He was talking business, just as Ben had begun talking business. I heard nothing more. I went to the john, fished in my purse and took out the vial of Valium.

I swallowed the pills and looked in the mirror, my thoughts zigging back and forth. You have success, happiness, love, friends. My friend is gone. My reflection shrugged back to me sadly, as if to reply, I don't know what to say to you, Barbara. It was too much. I felt chilled, wasted. Oh, God, please end it. Some atheist, praying in bathrooms again. Why doesn't the doctor help me? Why am I a slave to these pills? I can't blame this on Jean's death, I can't. Anxiety. It's been increasing for months, but tonight it's terrible.

The Valium began to work and I was feeling a little better. The Scotch, the soft lights and Eric were waiting. Everything was beginning to be good again. But I can't make another film. I'm so tired. Dead tired. Tomorrow I will tell Alan no more shows. I'll tell Greg I'll go to San Francisco to make the speech but that was it.

I knew how much Eric wanted me to keep working. Every time I even thought of stopping for a while, he reminded me how much Alan needed me, how good work made me feel, how good I was at my job. He was, for some reason, vehemently opposed to my stopping. But this time I'd have to. Things are going to be different. I'm going to take care of everything, including myself.

I'm going to find some peace.

4
Falling Apart

Saint Patrick's Day. Fifth Avenue bisected with a freshly painted green line and filled with crowds of green-and-white people. Traffic a horror all over the city. The radio station droned on, now reminding us all, Irish or no, to wear green. I turned over, burying my head in the pillow, thinking, I should get up, I should get up, it's eleven. Eric left for work hours ago. "Move, Barbara, move."

Jeanie had died two days before the film aired and I had gone to her funeral. I managed it somehow. It had been very important to me to go to the small Connecticut town all alone; no sound men, no cameras, just me. Not just because I wanted to keep my promise to Jean; no, I wanted to be there as a person, a friend. I took a cab to Grand Central and was swallowed up in a sea of anonymous faces. Nervously clutching my purse and the *Times,* I boarded the train and sat by the window, looking out at the dreary Connecticut landscape, still dismal from the winter despite the bright afternoon sunshine. With all my phobias, with all the shrinking of my world, I had done it.

It was a bright, cold March afternoon. The funeral was held outdoors, on the lawn of the modern municipal building where Jean had had her office. It was like a town meeting. Hundreds of people were there; families with children crowded into five hundred seats. The new mayor had closed the schools for the day and flags were lowered to half mast. Senators and congressmen Jean had met in her brief political career arrived by helicopters, which landed behind the building. I smiled as I remembered how she had won them over instantly, this woman who had poured coffee for the PTA, held Girl Scout meetings in her home, and then plunged into politics, rejoicing in the discovery she had made, that at forty-five she had a new life.

The sounds of Helen Reddy singing "I Am Woman" —music Jean had chosen for her possible funeral— blared out of loudspeakers on the makeshift dais. Ben and their three sons sat together in the first row, looking drawn and tired but not numb and shocked like the survivors of people who die suddenly. They had been prepared. Friends of Jean whom I had met before talked with me. Did I know she had picked the music herself, did I know she wanted an open coffin? Yes, yes, I knew. She had said it all in the film. I watched reporters and film crews from my station and others as they did their work, reporting the death of Jean Barris. I would not report that death or film that funeral. I was just there to say goodbye to my friend, but I still couldn't believe she was dead.

There were tributes, prayers, and then it was over and the cameramen packed their gear, running to their crew cars to hurry back to their stations. The film had to be processed, edited, a script written so the footage could be seen on that night's news. I watched the cars leave, watched the long line of people filing past Jean lying in her open coffin. I couldn't look. I didn't go to the cemetery either. I wanted to remember her on the beach in Tijuana, laughing about the John Birch Society.

I walked back to the train station. Helen Reddy's music—the only sound—could be heard for blocks. As I passed the rows of brick houses and manicured lawns, I was suddenly overwhelmed with a bone weariness, a feeling of meaninglessness. I knew now that Jean was dead.

A sunny Saint Patrick's Day, so the crowds should be enormous, the announcer's voice continued. I pulled the blankets over my head. I have to get up, I thought.

Although John O'Connor had written nice things

about the film in the *Times,* I didn't care anymore. She hadn't lived to see it, so it didn't matter. But I couldn't live with that feeling of meaningless—not for long. I had already embarked on a new film. So what had happened to all that resolve, all those promises I made myself, to stop, to rest, to be? I couldn't stop. Who was I kidding? Who would I be without work? I loved it.

I got out of bed, making my morning noises, and stumbled into the kitchen. I made a pot of strong coffee, poured it into a mug and went back to the bedroom. I looked at the phone, looked at the bed. Come on, Barbara, I said to myself, and then went to the bathroom to get ready for the day. But when I peered into the mirror to put on my make-up, I thought of Jean. I saw her face, laughing with merriment on the beach in Tijuana, buying balloons from the vendor, watching the Mexican children build sand castles by the water's edge. I had wanted to walk closer to her, talk more with her, but I had been charged with directing the cameraman, so I followed her like a shadow that day, pushing out of my mind seeing only the joy on her face as she walked along the the thought that she was living under an indictment, ocean, letting the warm water wash over her feet. I had tried to quiet the voice in my head that said, She may never see the ocean again, never buy a balloon again, never laugh again.

The lipstick was shaky in my hand and no matter how I struggled, my face looked smudgy. So I took some cleansing cream, wiped all the make-up off, and told myself, I'll start over, I'll make it right.

I poured another mug of coffee and sat on the edge of the bed. I began to think of the new show I was doing. It was about some agencies that handle children for adoption. The State of New York gave millions of dollars to these agencies, and civil liberties organizations were claiming that some of them, in order to keep getting state money, did *not* place their children for adoption. It was a nightmare of bureaucratic mismanagement. And who suffered? The children, of course, and the childless parents who eagerly awaited a child to fill out their lives.

I was intrigued by the project, but somehow the energy and enthusiasm I usually had for a new film just weren't there. I lay back on the bed and stared at the mirrored ceiling. It had been a present from Eric on my last birthday. "A canopy bed has so much class and so's a ceiling made of glass," Rodgers and Hart had written. I smiled into the mirror. Thank God for Eric, thank God. I felt revived just thinking about him and started again for the bathroom. Move, Barbara, move. The day has begun and you're still hanging around the house like some lady of leisure.

This time the make-up went on effortlessly, as if the mere thought of the work I loved and the man I loved had steadied me. It's just thinking about Jean that makes me shaky, I told myself. I can't think about her so much, I can't. It's over.

I slipped into a silk shirt and a pair of jeans and was about to tie a scarf around my head, when I looked at my purse on the bed. I opeend it and took out the vial of Valium. Pills. They were as much a part of my morning ritual as putting on lipstick. I got a glass of water, sat down on the bed and emptied two yellow pills into my hand. I had almost put them in my mouth when suddenly my body froze. I looked at the pills in my hand. How many times, how many, many times have I taken these pills, popped them like aspirin, like vitamins, thinking only that the anxiety would go away, thinking only that they would help me? Whatever the menace is, the danger, the peril, I should be able to fight it without pills. Why just treat the symptoms? I want to get rid of the symptoms. I want to face the demon so Eric and I can enjoy our lives, so I can shop in department stores, ride buses, walk the streets, without feeling my life is in peril. Impulsively I threw the vial on the floor and watched the yellow pills make a circle on the rug.

At that moment, I felt like someone on the stage, an actress playing out someone else's lines, a writer's thoughts. I had never considered giving up Valium before, never talked to Eric about it, or Dr. Allen. But suddenly I was Barbara again, and I wanted to *be* Barbara, not some zombie. This was *my* idea, and in my conscious mind I was dead certain of what I was doing, convinced of its rightness.

But then I began to feel apprehensive, like a smoker who grinds out a cigarette, swearing that it is going to be his last. Maybe I'd better stay home this morning. Still staring at the pills on the rug, I picked up the phone. My secretary answered. "Susan," I said, "I'll be in the library most of the day doing some research. Tell Fran and Alan for me. I won't be in until later this afternoon. But I'll call in." I felt a little nervous about telling a lie.

"I've got some messages for you," Susan said. She sounded like Susan, efficient, on top of things. I knew she believed me. "Steve has some footage of children's shelters he wants you to see, Jean's husband called, and Eric called. He has a case in court this afternoon and may be home around eight."

"Thanks, Susan," I said, trying to sound light and ordinary. "See you later." But something deep inside me knew I wouldn't see her later. I wasn't sure, but a voice said, You won't go to the office at all today, and you know it.

I held the receiver in my hand. There was one more call I had to make. I dialed the familiar numbers, trying to remain confident, struggling to remain certain of what I was doing.

The voice was quiet and self-assured. "Yes, Miss Gordon, what can I do for you?"

"I won't be able to make my session next Monday, Dr. Allen. I'll be tied up at work." I hate lying, but I had to. Soon there would be no need for lies; soon I'd be sure of everything.

"Will you need a prescription for more Valium before our next appointment?" he asked in that same soothing voice, the voice that had assuaged all the pain, all the conflicts, all the demons. I trusted that voice, but Dr. Allen was talking to a Barbara that I wasn't anymore. The morning had already changed me and I felt adult, filled with joy that I was at last taking charge of my own life.

"I have enough pills for a while, Dr. Allen," I said. "Besides, I've come to a decision this morning. I'm not going to take Valium again—ever."

"Would you like me to send over something else? Where are you calling from?" he asked, a little nervously, I thought.

"I'm home and I'm buried under a pile of work. And no, thank you. I don't want anything else. I don't want to take pills anymore. So many pills for so many years have to be bad for me." And I waited for his response to this new-found independence of mine.

"I've told you many times, Miss Gordon," he said with a hint of impatience, "they are nonaddictive and do a great deal to help you. Perhaps you'd like to try a little Stelazine?"

A little orange juice, a little tea, perhaps you'd like something in green, the chef salad madame? A sea of faces suggesting, offering, titillating, ran through my mind. He still wasn't hearing me.

"No, no more pills, Dr. Allen, no more pills. I'm going off Valium. What do you think of that?" And again I waited for his response, for him to tell me how strong I was, that I was doing the right thing.

"All right, Miss Gordon, then don't take one, not one. Do it absolutely cold. As a matter of fact, don't even have a sip of wine and I'm sure you'll do fine. Call me if you need anything or if you change your mind. But remember, don't take even one."

Later I must have been asked a hundred times why I stopped cold. There is no easy answer, but as usual, once I made up my mind to do something, I did it, and it didn't occur to me to do it any other way. And besides, my doctor had said to stop cold—not an ordinary doctor, but a friend, a man, a psychiatrist, who had known me for ten years. He wouldn't tell me to do the wrong thing.

I knew it wouldn't be easy, of course. I had seen films about heroin withdrawal; scenes from *A Hatful of Rain* and *The Man with the Golden Arm* were etched in my mind. But I wasn't a junkie; I was going off medicine, not drugs, I thought. And it is always done cold turkey. Valium wasn't heroin; it couldn't be such a rough withdrawal.

Valium is an interesting drug. It isn't an upper or a downer. It's a leveler. It evens things out silently, quietly. No rush, no thrill, no charge. It's called the safe and sane drug; millions of prescriptions are written for Valium every year, not counting hospital use. So obviously I was in good company. It had certainly helped my anxiety attacks in the past, but it didn't always work anymore, no matter how many I took. I had started taking Valium for a back problem, beginning with four milligrams a day. Now I was up to thirty and couldn't get out of the house without taking them. I was taking them *before* an anxiety attack, trying to ward it off, or to minimize the terror. And that didn't always work either. Why bother?

I didn't know why Valium worked when it did, or why it didn't. Nor did I know that withdrawal from Valium can cause more serious complications than withdrawing from heroin. Months later, I would see other addicts—and, believe me, tranquilizer takers can become addicts—being withdrawn from Valium five milligrams a week over a long course of treatment. I was taking thirty milligrams a day and I went off it cold. I didn't know I wasn't supposed to do it that way. I only knew I had to change things, I knew I wanted to stop. If I didn't have the courage to say no to more films, at least I could say no to the pills. It was all the same. In a few days I'd be fine, rested, refreshed, ready to face a new day, a new film, Eric, life.

Instead I blew my head open.

Alone in the apartment that sunny Saint Patrick's Day, I ground coffee beans, read the *Times*, listened to music. I was changing my life, I was intoxicated by a feeling of liberation: no pills, no work, just me, *being*. It was probably going to be tough, I knew, but I was ready to face it. I'd see it through. Then slowly strange things began to happen. By early afternoon I began to feel a creeping sense of anxiety. But it was different from my usual bouts of terror. It felt like little jolts of electricity, as if charged pins and needles were shooting through my body. My breathing became rapid and I began to perspire.

Damn. I'd expected something to happen, but not here. I had never had an attack in the apartment before. Outside, yes. In restaurants, elevators, stores, streets. Restaurants were too noisy, streets too wide, stores too crowded, buildings too tall, elevators too fast. But home, home had to be safe. It couldn't happen here. I wouldn't let it. It was safe here, it was always safe at home. I told myself to be still, to breathe slowly. Just breathe.

My scalp started to burn as if I had hot coals under my hair. Then I began to experience funny little twitches, spasms, a jerk of a leg, a flying arm, tiny tremors that soon turned into convulsions. I held on to the bed, trying to relax. It was impossible. I told myself it was just a twenty-four hour withdrawal, that it was nothing. I could take it. If those symptoms meant my body wanted more pills, I would just ignore them. I was strong, I could do it. I wasn't going to call my doctor. He had already told me what to do.

Sometime that afternoon I phoned the office. "Susan, this is Barbara." The hand that held the receiver was shaking, my voice sounded hollow, unreal. "I'm not going to make it in today."

"Have you got a cold?" Susan said. "You sound terrible."

"I've got something," I said with a nervous laugh. "Have Frannie call me at home if anything comes up."

"Take care of yourself," Susan said.

Take care of myself? How could I take care of myself when I didn't even know what was wrong? I lay back on the bed, my head spinning. I had picked up the pills and put the little vial on the table by the bed. Maybe just one, to stop the burning and the twitches. I reached for the vial. No, dammit, no! Dr. Allen said not to take one. I struggled to my feet, took the vial to the bathroom and dumped the pills in the toilet.

Then it was almost seven o'clock. Eric would be home soon. I must make dinner. I thought that working, doing something, would calm me. I went to the kitchen and was so occupied trying to force myself to concentrate on cooking that I was startled to hear his key in the lock. "Hi, babe," he said, and his voice jolted me out of my concentration into his world, the real world.

He put down his briefcase, headed for the refrigerator and started to pour himself a drink. "What can I make you, babe? Would you like some Scotch or white wine?"

I had promised myself I wouldn't blurt out my decision about the pills. Why make a big thing of it? It was just something I was doing, something I had to do. But despite my promises, it all started pouring out. "Eric, I have something to tell you. I've stopped the bloody pills. No more Valium." I was speaking rapidly, excited by my own words, eager to hear his reaction. "I told Dr. Allen and he said do it cold. So I'm not even supposed to have wine. Isn't that wonderful? I'm doing it, darling. I've had it with little yellows."

Eric was sipping his drink. He set it down and put his arms around me. "Wonderful! That's my woman," he said. "But what happened? Why did you decide so suddenly?"

We were walking to the sofa in the living room and I tried to gather my thoughts. I wanted to be clear, very clear, about what I told him. "I don't know, darling. I just found myself throwing the damn things on the floor." I looked into his eyes intently. I wanted him to tell me how strong I was, how independent. I knew he hated the pills as much as I did. He had to be thrilled.

"Are you sure this is what you want to do?" he said in a low voice. "Do you think it's the right thing?" There was a puzzled frown on his face. I was disappointed. I wanted him to be happy, to be proud of me.

He must have seen my disappointment for the troubled frown turned into a reassuring smile. "O.K. It doesn't matter why. So how do you feel?"

"Strange, really strange. I spent the whole day in the apartment and I felt a burning in my head, and then a jumpiness, and then a constant anxiety, the kind I get on the street. It was a little scary because that's the first time I've ever felt that way here. But I'm sure it's only a reaction to the drugs. It'll disappear in a day or so."

He was looking at me apprehensively. But then he was smiling again. "*I'm* going to make you healthy," he said, and now he was suddenly expansive. "Green vegetables, fresh juice, brown rice—this apartment is going to become a shrine to good living and health. We're going to make Adelle Davis look like a degenerate. Good living here from now on. Just call me Prince Valium."

We both laughed. He *was* Prince Valium, I thought. Now I knew I could make it.

He helped me with dinner and I noticed that he refilled his glass several times. I was about to make a comment but then repressed it. I was in no position to criticize. Eric ordinarily didn't drink that much.

"What about the job, babe? You know how Alan counts on you," he said over dinner. Somehow I had been expecting the question, but I couldn't give him a coherent answer. Even with him there, sitting right across the table from me, I felt anxious, insecure. My thoughts were jumbled and I said something about Fran and Steve, and that there really wasn't much for me to do yet. "I just need some rest," I said finally. "I'm sure I'll be fine in a couple of days."

We went to bed, Eric and I, lying in our spoon position—my back cradled against his chest, so we could feel all of each other's bodies. But that night I couldn't lie still and savor the feeling of his skin next to mine. I began to toss and turn.

"Lie still, Barbara. What's the matter?"

"I can't, Eric. I feel so jumpy. It's awful. I don't want to disturb you, really. I'll go into the living room."

He sat up and turned on the light. "Why do you want to get away from me?" he said.

"It's not you. It's me. I feel so damn restless. I don't want to bother you." And I started to get up and put on my robe.

"Lie down, Barbara. I mean it. Stop that crap about sleeping alone." He had never barked at me like that. I couldn't understand why he was so upset.

I didn't sleep at all that night, even though I felt tired. I just lay there in bed, eyes wide open, staring at the ceiling. I was having coffee, reading the *Times,* when Eric got up. We had breakfast together, he left for work, and I spent the morning reading, talking on the phone, chatting with Frannie, making plans with friends. The burning sensation in my scalp, the bursts of excitability, eased that morning. I was exhausted from not sleeping, but really I felt fine. There was just nothing I wanted to do. I only wanted to luxuriate in bed, resting, feeling overjoyed at having no responsibilities, proud to be off pills. It had been years since I had time to be lazy.

But by noon the excitement, the panic, the growing terror, began to return, stronger than before. God, I thought, it's happening again. And again I couldn't believe I was experiencing the terror in my own apartment. I couldn't let it happen here. Where would I go? Where would I be safe? There was nowhere to run. I was home. I couldn't keep my body still. I lay down on the bed, telling myself, Be quiet, be quiet, there's nothing to fear. You're home, it's all right, you're safe. You will be safe. My face turned beet red, my hair felt as if it were sizzling over hot coals. I was frantic. I tried to reach Eric at his office, but he was out to lunch. I had never been so frightened. Then the phone rang.

It was Edie. Immediately I shifted gears. I didn't want to frighten her. We had a theater date that night, she reminded me, and she had heard about the most marvelous restaurant for supper afterward. How could I go to the theater or a restaurant? "Oh, Edie," I said. "I don't think I can make it. I'm really feeling rotten."

"Is it the flu?" she said. "What are your symptoms?"

How could I lie to Edie? She was my friend, my dearest friend. "I have a confession to make, Edie," I said, and then paused to gather my courage. "I have been taking Valium for years and today is my second day off them and I feel very peculiar." Close as we were, I had never told her about the pills. I'm not sure if it was because I was ashamed and hadn't wanted to face her and Jonathan's possible disapproval, or because I just hadn't considered it important enough to share with them. But now I was telling her everything. And I was curious about her reaction.

"Terrific," she said, covering any surprise or apprehension she might have felt. "Why did you start taking the damn things in the first place?"

"Oh, Edie, it's a long and terribly boring story. But sometimes when you called and wanted me to meet you at an art gallery in SoHo or a restaurant in Chinatown, don't you know why I could never come, why we always met at the Russian Tea Room? I couldn't get there, Edie. I was terrified to go anyplace alone below Fifty-seventh Street, and I didn't know how to tell you."

"Well, that's all over now," she said confidently. "There's nothing to be frightened of. We'll meet at the theater and we'll all have a good time together. Eric isn't working late, I hope."

She was right. Everything would work out. We both agreed that my symptoms were just an overreaction, that I was doing the right thing, and we'd see each other later. I felt so relieved when I hung up the phone. Talking with Edie had helped. She always made me feel good about myself. She had diverted me from the terror.

I tried to take advantage of that moment of relief by soaking in a hot tub. Whenever I wanted to feel peaceful, I settled into a long, languid bath. I tried to let go, to surrender to the luxurious hot water lapping at my body, to sink softly into peace, into quiet. But I couldn't sit still. The terror began to mount again and, wrapped in a towel, I rushed to the bed, then to the living room, walking, pacing around the apartment. I had not slept for thirty-six hours, but I wasn't sleepy. Exhausted but not sleepy. In the film business you got accustomed to going for days without sleep, but this was a different kind of exhaustion.

I finally managed to dress for the theater. I felt very fragile. But the thought of being with Edie and Jonathan had calmed me. I was functioning after all. But my hand was so shaky I could hardly control it when I put on my lipstick. I stared at my face in the mirror. That wasn't me. It's lack of sleep, I thought. I'll look better tomorrow.

Suddenly Eric was standing behind me. I looked up at his face behind mine in the mirror. I hadn't heard him come in. "Oh, Eric," I said, turning into his arms. "I feel so strange, like a piece of glass. I don't know if I can make it to the theater tonight. I don't know."

"You can do anything you want to do, babe. It'll be good for you. You've been in the house for two days now. You love Jonathan and Edie, and the play will make you laugh." He gave me a kiss on the cheek and a long hug. "Come on now, don't ruin my evening."

I wanted to stand there, holding on to him. I wanted to lie with him in our big bed. I didn't want to go *anywhere*. But I found myself saying, "You're right. Let's go."

We met at the theater. I thought I detected concern on Edie's face, but we didn't have time to talk as we took our seats. I had trouble concentrating on the play. I felt overly excited, agitated, flushed, with a constant buzz at the back of my head. Even though I could hear what the actors were saying, I didn't have the faintest idea what the play was about. I leaned closer to Eric and said softly, "I can't take much more of this. I've got to get out of here." "Sit still!" he whispered impatiently. Edie heard him and took my hand comfortingly.

After the play we went to Edie's new discovery, a small, quiet Spanish restaurant. As soon as we sat down, Jonathan, who played the classical guitar, became deeply engrossed in listening to the guitarist. But during dinner he started talking about the pills. Edie had told him everything. "It's bad for anyone to take that much medication, Barbara," he said. "I'm glad you've quit, but I want you to take lots of vitamins, and eat properly for a change."

I smiled. In his own incisive way, Jonathan was concerned, too. "I promised Dr. Allen I wouldn't drink," I said, "but do you think it would be all right for me to have a glass of wine?"

"Sure, as long as you don't overdo it," he said with authority. Then he added tenderly, "I'm proud of you, Barbara. It'll be worth it, you'll see. But I think in a day or so you ought to go to your internist for a checkup. Let's make sure your body is handling this withdrawal the way it should. Promise me you'll make an appointment."

"She's doing just fine, Jonathan," Eric said a little defensively. "I'll get the vitamins and see that she eats. She doesn't need any doctors. Look what doctors have done to her already."

"A physical couldn't hurt," Edie said. "Call me when you've made the appointment, Barbara, and we'll go together."

Eric glared at her. I had never seen him look like that. He was acting very strangely. Why did he resent Jonathan's and Edie's advice? They only wanted to help me. But then I realized he felt that we were strong enough to handle this by ourselves.

Edie turned to me. "Are you getting any sleep at all?"

I was about to answer, when Eric interrupted. "None. She hasn't slept the past two nights, but I'm sure she will tonight. Don't worry, Edie. I can handle it."

"I'm not worried," Edie said sharply. "I'm concerned." Then she turned to Jonathan and made a signal that said, Let's talk about something else.

I barely touched my food. I tried to join the conversation, but every time I spoke, the words seemed wrong somehow. No, it can't be happening again, I said to myself. Not here, not with Eric and my friends.

I smoked one cigarette after another to mask the terror that began to fill me. If I can just get some sleep, I thought, I know I'll feel better tomorrow.

But I didn't sleep that night. I spent the hours putting cold towels on my head, walking around the living room, trying to be quiet so I wouldn't disturb Eric. A fire seemed to be raging through my head and the cold towels didn't help. But I had to do something. Then the fire was consuming my whole body. I was incredibly thirsty and downed glass after glass of juice. I tried to read, I wrote notes to myself which I couldn't decipher.

As the night wore on, I became filled with a sense of urgency. I felt so lucid. Bits and pieces of my life flashed before my eyes as if I were watching a Moviola, and I began to think about my parents, old friends, business relationships, aunts, uncles, ex-lovers, everything. By the time Eric woke up, I was eager to tell him about all the new connections I had made. Each fragment of a thought seemed significant, profound. I couldn't wait, I was so excited. I had so much to say. I pounced on him with a rush of chatter while he was still in bed.

"Eric, darling. Eric, I think I understand, I think I know why I took the pills. I've never really been happy until I met you, and now I'm frightened I'll lose you." I went on and on. I couldn't stop talking.

"For Christ's sake, Barbara,'" he said. "I'm not even out of bed yet. Give me a minute, will you?"

I felt chastised like a small child and retreated, pouting, into the living room. I must be quiet, I told myself. But I felt chilled, chilled to the marrow of my bones, and frightened.

I sat on the couch in the living room as Eric made the coffee. It was strange sitting there watching him in the kitchen. I usually got breakfast on weekday mornings, but today was different. I was supercharged with energy, yet I felt completely helpless.

"I'm staying home today," he said, giving me a cup of coffee. "Libby can handle things in the office. You're going to rest, and I'm going to take care of you. Now drink your coffee. I'm just going to run down and get food and some vitamins. Where's your purse? I'll need some money. Do you want anything to read?"

"No. No, I can't read," I said. And I watched as he began efficiently to get our day in order.

When he came back I was still sitting on the couch. It didn't enter my mind to help him put the groceries away. He brought me a glass of tomato juice and a handful of pills. "Let's get some vitamins and good things into you to fight the Valium," he said. "Come on—down you go with them." And obediently, not questioning anything, filled with love for him, I did as he said.

We spent the day together and I began to tell him stories about my past. It was an analytic marathon. I was the patient and Eric was the doctor. At first he just sat and listened, but by the end of the day he was a participant, asking questions, offering advice. He was caught up in the story of my life, in the drama, and he was helping to write the script.

If Eric had been angry at me that morning, now he was all love and tenderness. "Keep talking, babe," he said when it was time for supper. "I'm just going to put the potatoes in the oven. Tonight we're having fresh broiled sea bass and broccoli and salad. A lot of B vitamins. That's what you need, a lot of B's."

So I kept talking about my mother, my father, my brother, my girl friends, my grandparents, everything. I remember thinking how wonderful Eric was, taking it all in, going through it all with me. I felt good, lucky, excited, despite the withdrawal symptoms, despite the terror. I don't need Dr. Allen, I don't need pills to function, I thought to myself. I've got Eric. He *is* Prince Valium.

I phoned my boss the next day to tell him I had to stop working for a while. Alan was tender and kind and told me to get a good rest. "This adoption racket thing isn't going to disappear overnight," he said. I assured him I would be out for only a few weeks and we could talk about the new film then. Eric approved of my decision. But he was worried about money, so we decided to deposit my last pay check in his account, just for groceries and other household expenses.

As the days went by, he began to take on more and more responsibility—talking to people on the phone, buying food, doing the laundry—while I began to function less and less. I spent hours talking to him, pacing, reading, trying to bathe, trying to sleep. I meandered through my past, vomiting up old wounds, unhealed hurts, unresolved relationships. I had an irrepressible urge to tell him everything. The past was beginning to impinge on the present but I wasn't worried. Obviously the Valium had repressed so much.

We had shared so many years, built a house together, lived together like people in love; it seemed natural to be sharing all these thoughts, stories and emotions with him. He was so willing to live through this crisis with me, help me get over the pills. I was safe with him, no matter how terrible I felt. Together we would get me through whatever the hell was going on.

My insomnia persisted. I felt as if I had lost some vital natural sleep mechanism. I was emotionally and physically drained, but still I couldn't sleep. Finally I called my gynecologist and told him I needed sleeping pills. He had my druggist send me eight. They didn't work for very long.

During the day, I saw myself behaving in ways I had never behaved before. I had always dressed and raced out of the apartment, but now I found myself not caring how I looked. At first I put on jeans and a sweater, but now I stayed in a nightgown all day, a soiled, messy nightgown. I couldn't think of putting on make-up, or washing or combing my hair. I was beginning to look like some kind of wild animal, but I seemed unable to change. I was on the verge of exploding, screaming with rage, trying to hold on to every minute. Clothes and make-up, looking pretty, feeling sexy—all that was becoming alien to me. I was engaged in solving a puzzle and I had to devote all my energy to that.

I was only dimly aware of the passage of time, but after about ten days I seemed to enter a new phase. I felt a heaviness in my heart and I began crying about everything. Childhood hurts now seemed as if they had happened yesterday, and I couldn't stop weeping. Eric talked to me, telling me to get it out, feel the guilt, feel the pain. My sadness grew in intensity and I walked around the apartment crying and crying.

I didn't dare leave the apartment now; I didn't think I could control my body on the street. So Eric continued to do all the shopping and the other chores. He was beginning to look tired. I had to be a drag, I knew, but there was nothing I could do. I couldn't stop talking, sobbing, talking. Sometimes he seemed to be bored and other times he would snap at me, saying strange things like "You're like all women. You remind me of my mother." I thought he was angry with me for not going outside, for making him do all the shopping and cooking. I would make anyone feel exhausted. But then he'd laugh and get over it.

At night in bed, he had always taken me in his arms, but now I would turn away from him, incapable of feeling that kind of love. When I first went off the pills, after the initial shock we made love a few times. And although I had been restless and uncomfortable, I found that I experienced more, a deeper feeling of joy, of freedom, of exaltation than I ever had. Maybe Valium had repressed part of my sexuality. But now I just couldn't respond, and that made him angry, too. "Dammit, Barbara," he said one night. "How long do you think I can stand this? And look at you. You're a mess!"

"Oh, God, I'm sorry," I cried. I ran into the living room and threw myself on the couch, sobbing.

A moment later he was on his knees by my side, stroking my hair, comforting me. "It's O.K., babe. I'm here. I love you. Everything is going to be all right."

When did everything turn from two loving people going through a storm together into something else?

One evening I sat in the living room, sipping a glass of wine, while Eric did the dishes. I always hoped the wine would make me sleepy the way it used to, but it didn't. Still, it made me feel a little calmer, gave me a little peace. By now I paid no attention to Dr. Allen's taboo. I had never drunk very much, and I knew a couple of glasses of wine couldn't hurt me. I was waiting for our evening ritual to begin. Eric would come in with a glass of wine and sit down, ready to listen. And I would sit on the couch and talk. Eager for his comments, I would dive into the pool of my past and, like a trained seal, come up with the ball, another tidbit, something I knew would fascinate him.

That evening I told him about my grandfather. "I was only twelve years old, Eric. And my mother asked me to baby-sit with my brother, Eddie, one night. I refused. I wanted to play with my friends."

"Go on," he said, sipping from his glass.

"Early that evening we got a phone call. My grandfather had died of a heart attack. He had been on his way to our house to baby-sit with Eddie and he had died. It was my fault, Eric. My fault. I remember sitting alone in my room, hearing my mother cry. 'Papa, Papa, now I'm alone,' she said. 'First my mother, now my father. Papa, Papa, now I'm all alone.' I heard her through the wall; sitting in my room, I heard her crying and crying. What did she mean, she was all alone? She had my father, Eddie; she had me. Oh, Mama, I'm responsible for your pain, I thought. I killed Grandpa. I didn't mean to. I didn't mean to, Mama. I'm sorry, I'm sorry. And I cried myself to sleep."

"My poor baby," Eric said with a tender smile. "How painful it was for you."

"Eddie and I couldn't go to the funeral," I said. "We were too young. I knew my mother hated me for what I had done, even though she didn't show it. But I wanted to go to the funeral to tell Grandpa I was sorry. We lived across the street from the school. And I can remember looking out the classroom window to see the long black cars lining up in front of our house. I watched my parents and the rest of the family get into those strange black cars. Everyone had on dark clothes and people were hugging and kissing my mother. Oh, Eric, I wanted to be there with her and kiss her, too. I felt so left out."

The two of us sat in the living room silently. I had finished another painful expedition into my past. "I've never told anyone that story," I said, "not even Dr.

Allen." And then I began crying. Crying and crying as if the day my grandfather died were today, as if I heard my mother's voice, her cries of grief, through the wall of my bedroom today. As if I were twelve years old.

I looked up, waiting for Eric to come over and comfort me. He didn't move. Then he took a sip of his drink and said, "You are a brat." He said it just like that: "You are a brat," in the same voice he had used a few minutes before to say, "My poor baby." He didn't look or sound different, or make a face or scream or shout. He sat there with his eyes riveted on me and said, "You are a brat. What you did to your grandfather you're doing to me. You destroy everyone and you should feel guilty, you bitch."

He still hadn't raised his voice. He didn't sound angry, but he was calling me a bitch. Barbara, do something; Eric is calling you a bitch. He's calling you destructive. Do something, Barbara. But I couldn't speak, I couldn't do anything. I just sat there and stared at him.

He took another sip of his drink. "You are an evil woman, Barbara," he said in that same even voice. "An evil, evil woman. You are like most women. Evil."

I blinked. What an awful thing to say, I thought. How strange. We were both quiet for what seemed a very long time.

Then something even more frightening began to happen. I suddenly felt hollow. I looked up at him and said, "Eric, I'm scared. I don't know who I am. I can't explain it. It's a terrible feeling. I don't know who I am anymore. I'm scared."

My face must have revealed the terror I was experiencing. He got up and sat next to me on the couch. The awful words he had spoken just a moment before were forgotten and he became the Eric I knew. He smiled at me and held me close. "You're Barbara," he said tenderly. "You're my woman, you're Barbara Gordon."

At that moment, it was as if I were literally a heap of skin and bones, as if my blood were steel gray, as if a giant syringe filled with Novocaine had been injected into my head, as if Christiaan Barnard had removed my heart. Clothes hanging on a line waving in the air: it felt like that. If it had lasted only a moment, it might have been tolerable, but it didn't go away.

Sitting there, cradled in Eric's arms. I watched myself leave myself and I couldn't stop it. I was in a rowboat being swept toward the falls, powerless to turn around. I split. I watched myself go over the falls as I went over myself. Bad memories came flooding through my mind, taking me back, back, back to a past that shouldn't have been relevant, but a past that consumed my brain.

I remember thinking I was a little girl, a bad little girl. A very bad little girl.

When did the tantrums begin? I hadn't been out of the apartment for weeks. Eric had been urging me to go out, but I just couldn't do it. And then one evening, reaching for his jacket, he said, "Come on, babe, it's time for a walk. You've got to get out of here. You're getting phobic. Put some clothes on and we'll take a stroll through the park."

"I won't go outside!" I suddenly shrieked. *"Stay here with me. I'll be good, I promise. Please stay. Help the baby. Oh, Eric, stay with me, please!"* And I began to cry and stamp my foot.

I stopped, aghast. I couldn't believe what I had been doing. "Did you see what just happened, Eric?" I asked him in a panic. "Did you see me stamp my foot like a child, talk like a baby?"

He smiled at me knowingly.

I was confused. He didn't seem to want to help me. "Eric, you must take me to a doctor. I know I need help."

He kept smiling.

I ran to the bedroom and began searching for my keys, my glasses, my identification. If he wouldn't take me to a doctor, I'd go myself.

He followed me into the bedroom and stood there, still smiling. "You don't need a doctor, Barbara. I love you more than any doctor will. He'll put you in a hospital, and if a hospital sees the shape you're in, they'll stick you in a back ward and no one will ever see you again. With me, babe, you have love. You're safe." He was talking in a low, clipped monotone. He didn't sound like Eric at all. "In cases like yours," he said, "it's best to act it out. Get it all out of your system. I'll help you through it, babe. I'll help you. I love you more than anyone." And then he walked into the living room.

I was frightened by the slow, methodical, almost robotlike way he had spoken to me. Where had I heard that voice before? I remembered. That Sunday morning when he was talking on the phone to his ex-wife Catherine. But I still trusted him. He knew so much about everything—the law, house-building, fixing cars. He was a man who had learned to do everything himself. He read everything; he was smart. He loved me. He had to be right.

But he was beginning to look different. Somehow his face was fuller, his eyes seemed to pierce through me, he was drinking a lot of wine and he had begun to smoke cigarettes. He had seldom smoked before. If I was worried about who I was, I now started to think that I didn't know who he was either. He had been transformed from my lover, my friend, to some sort of authoritarian parent figure, and I was getting farther and farther from me. Whoever I was before, however neurotic or anxious, I had functioned. I was connected to myself and my world. Now I was connected to no one, not myself, not Eric, and my world had shrunk to the confines of the apartment.

Once I tried to call Edie just to talk, to hear another voice. I reached for the phone. "I wouldn't make that call," Eric said from the bedroom, pointing a finger at me. "Edie only makes you feel dependent. You shouldn't call her. Don't betray me, Barbara."

I listened to him as if I were hypnotized. Apart from the radio and the television, his was the only voice I had heard for weeks. What a strange thing to say, I thought. What does he mean, "betray me"?

One night we were sitting on the couch after dinner, talking. I was still consumed by painful childhood memories and I told him about Chatahoochie. When I was a little girl I remembered my mother saying to me, "If you're not good, you'll go to Chatahoochie, where all the crazy people go. That's where they put bad little girls, so be good." Years later, when I made a film in a mental hospital or even saw a movie like *The Snake Pit,* I would become anxious and frightened, and that fear had returned to haunt me the night Eric told me that I'd end up in some back ward and never be seen again.

"Eric, I'm terrified of mental hospitals," I said. "But I don't know what's happening to me. Everything looks so strange. Even you don't look the same. I love you. I trust you. But I think I need a doctor. I think I should go to a hospital."

He put his arms around me and smiled. Then he said softly, "You don't fear Chatahoochie, Barbara. You want it. It's really a secret wish you have, to go mad, to be dependent." His voice droned on, and I listened to him intently, looking up at his face, absorbing his words like a sponge. He leaned back, sipped his drink and continued in that strange new syllabic monotone. "In order to go sane, you must go insane. You don't fear it. It's a wish. You want it, you want it, it's a wish."

The more he talked, the crazier I felt. My mouth moved without sound and suddenly I had a compulsion to make guttural noises. I wanted to scream. The more hopeless he said I was, the more I felt I had to play the part.

Then he kissed me. I turned my head away. I felt no sexuality at all. That new, hollow sense of nonbeing had destroyed it. His lips felt cold, different. I didn't like it when he touched me. I didn't even want to sleep in the same bed with him. He wasn't Eric anymore.

He had been angry when I didn't want to make love before, but now, suddenly he was furious. He jumped up and started shouting at me. He accused me of withholding sex to punish him. I had punished my father and my grandfather, he said, and now I was punishing him. I didn't know what he was talking about. All I could think of was how odd he seemed. He didn't even smell like Eric anymore.

The first time he hit me, I felt no pain. I had been crying all day, screaming, clawing at my chest until my skin was raw. Eric just sat there for hours, talking to me, urging me to act crazy, to act like a baby. Then he suddenly said, "Oh, God, where's my adult Barbara? Where's my woman? She's nothing but a sniveling baby." I had been drinking some wine and he took the glass from my hand and called me a junkie. To be his woman, he said, I had to be drug and alcohol free. From now on, no more wine. And then he took his fist and smashed it into my cheek.

It didn't hurt, it really didn't. But I was shocked. Shocked that he hit me, shocked that I wasn't more shocked.

"You're a bad girl, Barbara," he said, "a bad girl who ruins people's lives. Your grandfather's, your mother's, and now you're ruining my life. People hate you. You hate yourself and you have to be punished."

Then he did a strange thing. He began to empty all the wine and liquor into the sink. And when that was finished, he tried to pull the chain lock off the apartment door with his hands. Finally he went for a screwdriver and I watched him with fascination as he removed the chain.

"I won't lock you out, Eric. Why are you doing that?" I said.

He gave me a long look and said, "You know why. You know." Then he went out, slamming the door behind him.

I sat on the couch feeling a paralysis of sorts. I couldn't believe what had just happened. I was confused. I didn't know what to do. I wanted to run, then I didn't. If I could only sort things out. But it was hard to think clearly. I felt so guilty and so sad. Everything he said was going through my mind. I hadn't known people hated me, that I had ruined people's lives. I thought about that more than I thought about his hitting me. All those terrible things. But if they weren't true, he wouldn't have said them. I hadn't known I was that bad, bad enough to be punished.

Days spinning through nights, nights spinning through days, my life was like a roulette wheel and I was the silver ball, whirling round and round, sometimes lodging at seven, then fourteen, then twenty-six, but always black, always a black memory of a different age of my life. Lost love, funerals, mean teachers: Eric urged me to talk about all my hurts and I did, forgetting the good times, ignoring the happiness. Day after day he told me to tell him more, tell him about other hurts, other disappointments. It didn't matter when they happened. Just tell him about them, experience the pain and maybe I would get better.

I had a grim determination to straighten it all out. Only by reliving each relationship, each year of my life, would I be able to make sense of everything. But I didn't know that I could get stuck, stuck at another age, with all the thoughts, emotions, personality and intellect of that age. And the more we talked, the more I felt my life was hopeless. I felt so sad. He said, "You *are* hopeless, but I'll take care of you forever. You are hopeless." I had loved life so much, so I cried and cried. It was over, I had ruined everything, and what's more, I was hopelessly ill. He nodded and looked at me sadly, saying, "It's too late, babe, too late. It's really a shame."

He often got angry with me now, but still he shopped, cooked and spent hours talking with me. Exhausted from my constant tantrums and his constant barrage of anger, I watched the weeks slide away. And every day he told me I was getting worse but that he would take care of me because he loved me. He would bring his face close to mine, look at me sadly and say that if he took me to a hospital now, they would lobotomize me. "Stay with someone you love," he warned me. "No one loves you like I do. Only, I sure miss my tall, beautiful Barbara, the independent woman. Where did she go, where did she go?"

He always answered the phone. "You're in no shape

to talk to people," he said. My friends Barry and Lisa Travis wanted us to come out to New Jersey for the weekend. "Barbara's too tired," he told them. "No, just exhausted from her last film. We're both taking it easy for a few weeks. We'll call you."

He let me speak to my mother whenever she called, but otherwise he waited for the service to answer, or he would pick up the phone and say that I was fine, resting, off pills forever, everything was super. I was embarrassed about what was happening, even if I didn't exactly know what *was* happening. But I knew that whatever it was, it was terrible. And what was worse, I felt powerless to do anything about it. I would watch Eric with amazement as he lied on the phone, telling everyone I was improved, resting, feeling fine. He did it so well, so naturally.

He told Edie the same story every time she called, but he never let me speak to her. I was always in the bathroom, or resting. "She'll call you back," he said. But I never did, even when he was out of the apartment. I was so ashamed—ashamed of the way I looked, the way I was behaving, ashamed of what was happening to me. I didn't want anyone to know, not even Edie. He was lying to my friends, but he was lying for me, I thought to myself, protecting me. I told my mother the same lies whenever she called. Part of me wanted everyone to believe those lies—I wanted to believe them myself. But part of me prayed, each time the phone rang, that it was my mother, Edie, anyone, calling back, demanding to know the truth.

Late one afternoon, I really was in the bathroom when the phone rang. Eric picked it up in the bedroom and I heard his voice through the door. "It's schizophrenia, Jonathan, acute schizophrenia. But she'll live through it. She's strong, and don't worry, I'm here. I'm with her." There was a pause and then Eric said, "Whose diagnosis? Mine. I don't need a second opinion. Why bring doctors into this? It's not necessary, Jonathan. It's not needed, not called for. Absolutely not. She's fine. She's doing fine."

I was stunned. Acute schizophrenia. When did I

become schizophrenic? How did Eric know what I was? How dare he tell my friends I was schizophrenic?

I walked into the bedroom. "Eric, I heard what you told Jonathan."

"Half the world's schizophrenic," he said. He was putting on his jacket. "I'm going out to get some things. We're going to have a celebration."

He left and I sat on the edge of the bed, dazed, unable to cry, unable to feel anything. A celebration for what? Because I was a schizophrenic? Because I was an evil, destructive bitch? Because I was hopeless? I looked at the telephone. I wanted so badly to talk to Edie and Jonathan. I wanted to hear a voice that wasn't Eric's. Someone to say I was Barbara, to tell me I was all right, to swear to me I wasn't hopeless. I needed help, but I wasn't crazy. I couldn't pick up the phone. I couldn't move.

I was lying down when Eric got back. He walked into the bedroom waving a bottle of champagne. "Come on, babe," he said. "We're going to celebrate."

I followed him numbly into the kitchen, blinking in the light. He had bought bread, cheese, fruit, a tin of caviar. There was another bottle of champagne on the counter. I watched him arrange everything on a tray and take it into the living room. I sat on the sofa as he opened the champagne. "Here's to Barbara," he said, lifting his glass. "You're off pills and bad shrinks. And now we're going to get married."

I couldn't believe my ears. I really must be crazy, I thought. He just told Jonathan I'm an acute schizophrenic, and now he says we're going to get married.

"Why not? Let's get the blood tests tomorrow and surprise everyone. We've proven our love by going through this thing together."

"Eric, I didn't need you to prove your love."

He put down his glass and began to glare at me. "You mean you don't want to get married, after all I've done for you?"

"Why now, for God's sake?" I said. "Look at me. I look awful. I feel rotten. Eric, I'm sick and you want to get married. Why?"

"Why the hell not?" he said angrily. There was no love, no tenderness in his voice. "Who loves you like I do? What the hell do I have to do to convince you?"

"I don't want to be convinced. I don't want to get married. I love you, you love me. That's all I want."

"God damn it, Barbara!" he shouted.

"Please, please, leave me alone," I cried.

I fled into the bedroom and shut the door. I sat on the edge of the bed and for the first time in weeks I began to think coherently. I was no longer a naughty little girl, crying and stamping her foot. I was no longer living in the past. I was in the present, here, now, in my own apartment. I was Barbara, and out there in the living room was Eric—not my father, not my analyst, but a man I had lived with for five years, a man I didn't really know. Why did he want to marry me now, right in the middle of this drug thing? Why does he keep telling me I'm sick, hopeless? Is this some kind of *Gaslight*? Does he want my money, the house at the beach? Is that what this is all about?

Stop it, Barbara, stop it, I said to myself. Isn't it bad enough to be schizophrenic without being paranoid, too? But I couldn't get the thought out of my head. I knew about the alimony payments, the child support. He hadn't been to the office for weeks now, and I had heard him talk to his secretary only a few times. Did he have any clients? Did he have any money at all? I had never seen his checkbook, but he helped me balance mine. He kept the records of the expenses on the beach house; he helped me get things together for the man who did my taxes. He knew what I had in my savings account. He knew about the trust fund my father had set up for me when he sold his business.

I got up quietly and opened the bedroom door. He was sitting on the living room sofa, reading. The bottle of champagne was empty and now he was drinking ordinary wine. He could commit me if we were married, I thought. He's a lawyer. He knows about things like power of attorney. No, it can't be that, I said to myself. It's not my money, it's not the house. Not Eric. He loves me.

Late one Sunday afternoon we were in the living room. Eric was reading a book and drinking wine. I was trying to read the Sunday *Times,* but I couldn't understand the words. I was unable to concentrate. I had repressed the thought that Eric was driving me crazy. He loved me, he was helping me. But why wouldn't he let me speak to my friends? Why wouldn't he let me leave the apartment? Why wouldn't he take me to a doctor?

I looked at him for a long time and then I began to talk. It wasn't my voice. It was a little girl's voice. Somewhere in the back of my head was the thought that if I acted crazier than I really was, he'd listen to me. "I've got to get out of this apartment, Eric. I know I'm sick. I know I'm hopeless. But I think I should see a doctor. Maybe there's a chance I can get some help." I started for the bedroom to put on some clothes, when suddenly I felt a crunch on the back of my neck. He was punching my neck. Then he turned me around and hit me in the stomach.

I began hitting him back, pretending I was doing it childishly, girlishly. I told myself he was kidding. To hit back, I had to pretend to be a little girl or else he would really hurt me. Why would he want to hit me? What did I do to him? I thought it was a game. I couldn't hurt him, but I had to vent my frustration, the confusion I felt, the anger somewhere, so I railed at myself, pounded my hips with my fist, and then began to claw at my own flesh. I watched myself as it happened and was helpless to do anything about it.

"You're insane," he said, and walked away, bored.

We no longer slept in the same bed, or even in the same room. I slept in the bedroom, and even during the day I spent hours in there, lying down, pacing, trying to think. Eric slept on the living room sofa, like a guard, a keeper. He no longer fed me fresh juice, vitamins. The food was just there and we ate in silence. I could have left the apartment when he went out to shop. I could have picked up the phone. But I didn't. I didn't dare risk his anger again.

One night I was sitting alone in the bedroom. I was no longer Barbara, I knew that, and I didn't know who

Eric was either, or when he had changed into this strange, sometimes violent person. I walked into the bathroom to wash my face. I saw someone in the mirror. Me. My neck was black and blue, my arms were covered with huge purple spots. Bruises! I reached for the faucet and then stopped short. I held my face with my hands; my eyes opened wide in surprise. Where had the bruises come from? Suddenly I knew. Eric has been beating me. And I felt a rush of blood to my cheeks, saw myself turn red. I was excited, and then filled with lucidity—the first time I had been lucid in weeks. *He's* insane, I said to myself. All this time I thought it was me, or the pills. Why has he been telling me *I'm* hopeless? The connections rushed through my brain. He's been threatening *me* with lobotomies and back wards. Me! My God, he *wants* me to be sick. It's *Eric* who is crazy.

Thoughts tumbled around in my head as I stared in the mirror. My breathing became rapid, and flushed with the excitement of recognition, I made up my mind. I had to get away from him. I had to. I thought he was helping me, but my God, he's keeping me a prisoner. He's torturing me. He was my love. Now he is my enemy. No time for second-guessing, no time for questions. I *must* get out of here. If I don't, I'll never get well. He'll kill me.

Quietly, ever so quietly, I tiptoed around the bedroom getting dressed. I hadn't worn shoes, hadn't even been dressed for weeks. I slipped out of the torn nightgown and wobbled around in shoes, getting used to the feeling of controlling my legs again. I put on jeans and a sweater. I needed my glasses and for some reason my keys. I don't know why I wanted my keys. Money. Where is the goddam money? To hell with it. Jonathan and Edie will pay the cab when I get to their apartment. Now, if I can just get out of here without waking him.

I was shaking with fright. I hadn't functioned in days, weeks. Walking was difficult, concentrating my thoughts was almost impossible. I kept saying, I'm going to Edie and Jonathan's, they'll help me. I must get away, Eric isn't my lover anymore, I must get away. I could still see my face in the mirror, my hands held to my cheeks, the rush of excitement when in what seemed like a second I realized what had been happening. Maybe my brain had gone to sleep, maybe I had suspended judgment for weeks. But now I had put it together. Barbara was back. *Gaslight* was over. I was getting out of there. I was sick, but he was crazy.

Slowly, straining to be quiet, I opened the bedroom door a crack. I just wanted to tiptoe through the hall and out the front door, then I would run down the sixteen flights rather than bring the elevator up, in case it could be heard inside the apartment. I opened the door farther and looked toward the dark living room. I relaxed for a second. He had to be asleep. It would be easy. I started to walk quietly through the hall. Then I saw something glistening in the dark: light from outside bouncing off something. His glasses. Eric's glasses. God, he was sitting in a dining room chair facing the bedroom, with his arms crossed. He was waiting. He knew! He had read my mind.

"Where are you going?" a strange voice said from the darkness. "Where the hell do you think you're going?"

It didn't even sound like him, I thought. I kept walking as he moved toward me in the darkness.

"Where are you going? I said."

"I just feel like taking a walk," I said. I knew that sounded implausible since I hadn't left the apartment for weeks. But I had to be very careful, had to weigh each word. He was violent; what could I say that wouldn't set him off?

I had reached the door when I heard him talking, only this time he was closer to me, close enough to touch me. He grabbed me from behind, grasping my neck. We began to struggle. It was no contest. But I fought hard. First I reached for his glasses. Somewhere, something had connected in my brain: without his glasses he can't function, he can't see. I ripped them from his face, shattering the glass in my hand, the pieces cutting my fingers. He tore at me, punching, hitting. I flailed at him like a wild beast. Then suddenly he turned to go to the kitchen. He put on the light.

He was looking for another pair of glasses. At last we could see each other, and I tried to make a run for the door. He ran after me and grabbed me from behind. It felt as if he was choking me.

"You're insane," he hissed. "You'll never go outside again, never, never. I'll take care of you. You're crazy; they'll only lobotomize you out there. You're insane, you bitch." And he knocked me to the floor.

I wrestled as hard as I could, but I was weak from not sleeping, not eating, from everything. He was too strong for me. He could have killed me. But for some reason he didn't. He dragged me into the bedroom and tied my hands behind my back with the sash of his robe. It's all over, I said to myself. My life is over.

I was lying on the bedroom floor, hands tied, exhausted, bleeding. What is he going to do with me? My thoughts were frantic, racing through my mind. "Please, I don't want to die," I said out loud. "I'll be good." He turned on the light and suddenly everything was clear. If I showed too much weakness, I knew he would feed off it. I knew he would hit me again. So in that humiliating captured state, I tried to look indignant, summoning up what I could of myself, some vestige of the old Barbara. I kept reminding myself he was violent, crazed. He could kill me.

Then I thought of a plan. Whatever was happening to him, I knew Eric wouldn't want people to see the mess I was in, a mess he had helped create. And I knew I could trick him. I had to get someone up here to see me, to help me. My plan had to work.

He had been pacing back and forth from the bedroom to the living room. Obviously he didn't know what to do next. I'd play sick, I'd have to play crazy to get away with this, I decided. I called out to him from the bedroom: "Jonathan and Edie are coming to get me, Eric, yes they are. They'll help make me better."

Suddenly he was standing over me. "When are they coming?"

I thought quickly. "Tonight," I said. "They're coming tonight."

He glowered at me, shook his head and smiled a

strange smile. "They are not," and he walked back to the living room.

"Oh, yes they are," I called out to him in my crazy, childish voice. "They are, too. I called them while you were sleeping." I started making my ugly faces, acting crazy. Please make him listen to me. Oh, God, please make him believe me.

He came back to the bedroom, looked at me for what seemed an eternity and then said, "I know everything you do. If you called them I would know. You didn't speak to anyone."

"You were sleeping," I said. "You're so tired from the cooking and the shopping, you can't keep track of everything." I watched him, pretending not to watch, and I could see that something inside him knew I had figured everything out. I was talking too lucidly, too logically, with too much authority. But he had to believe me. Please let him call Edie and Jonathan, I thought. Please. Then I'll scream.

He went to the phone. He seemed uncertain. He couldn't know I was setting a trap, he couldn't. He had to believe me. "What's their number—what's their goddam number?" he asked, sitting on the bed, the receiver in his hand. Please let him call. God, I don't want to die. I gave him the number.

He dialed slowly, staring down at me lying on the floor, still disbelieving, not sure. I couldn't look too proud or show the sense of victory I felt. I tried to look indignant, disinterested, angry, strong, crazy, all at once, and my expression must have betrayed something that angered him. He pushed his foot in my face. With my hands tied behind me, I couldn't fight back. Please be home, Edie. It was after midnight, and I knew Jonathan usually had surgery in the morning. They had to be home.

Someone answered and when I heard Eric talking into the phone, I began to scream. He swirled around and started hitting me with his free hand, the other hand muffling the receiver. He looked puffy, strange without his glasses. He was panting and I realized he was more afraid than I was. Again I screamed and again he hit me. The only thought in my mind was

Please, please let them hear me. All I could do was scream, scream and hope.

"Nothing's going on," he said into the phone. "That was just Barbara. No, she's O.K. I said she's fine, Jonathan. Better and better. She'll be going back to work any day. She's sleeping through the nights now."

I couldn't believe he could talk that calmly, but I kept screaming, "Jonathan, come get me, please! He's hurting me!" I knew what he was going to do to me as a result. But I also knew it was my only chance. If he kept beating me until they got here I could take it. He couldn't kill me now that somebody knew the truth. Please let them hear me. Please let them come.

I screamed again and this time he kicked me. "Barbara, will you please shut up," he said. "I'm trying to talk to Jonathan." Then into the phone: "She's trying this new primal scream thing to get rid of all her repressed anger. Listen, Jonathan, she has some strange idea that you're coming up to the apartment tonight."

"Please, Jonathan, hurry," I cried. "He's beating me!"

Eric said nothing. He was listening to Jonathan now. Then he began to protest. "I told you everything is fine, dammit. Barbara doesn't want you here. I can handle it, Jonathan." Finally he hung up the phone. "Do you know what you've done?" he yelled at me. "Do you realize what you've done, God damn you? Now they're coming here. You tricked me, you crazy bitch!" He grabbed my neck tightly with his hand and jammed his fist into my eye. But then he stopped and began walking around the apartment.

I said things, palliative things, quiet things, not vindictive, not abusive. I tried to calm him. I told him Jonathan and Edie would make everything all right. They were our friends. He ignored me and I thought, Oh, Jonathan, please, go to your car. Don't fail me. Bring the police. Come here and help me. I must get away from him.

The intercom rang from downstairs. They were here. It had been thirty minutes or so, minutes that seemed longer than my whole life. Then they rang the doorbell and Eric opened the door. I was struggling against the sash that bound my wrists, which only made the pain worse. I called out to them as they walked into the apartment. "Thank God, you're here, thank God. I need you. Please help me!"

They came into the bedroom and looked at me lying on the floor, hands tied behind my back, hair uncombed, bloodstains on my face, bruises covering my body. But whatever shock they felt, they disguised. They were calm and cool. They were amazing.

"She's hopelessly insane," Eric said to Jonathan breathlessly, trying to gain the advantage by talking first.

"No, no, no," I cried. "I'm not insane, Jonathan! I'm ill, but he's insane. He's been beating me."

"Ignore her, Jonathan," Eric said. "She's been hallucinating. I've been trying to help. I love her, Jonathan. I've given up everything for her. But I can't do anything for her now."

"Jonathan," I screamed. "Call the police!"

"Shh, Barbara," he said quietly. "It's two in the morning. Let's not wake everybody."

"Don't untie her, Jonathan," Eric warned. "She's violent. Look at my face."

"He was beating me!" I cried. "I'm not violent. I wouldn't hurt anyone."

Edie turned to Eric and said, "You two can't be together tonight."

"She's got to go to a hospital," Jonathan said.

I was exasperated, horrified, furious. I didn't know how to make anyone believe me.

Edie stood there looking at Eric, looking at me. She began to kneel down to calm me, to help me, but Jonathan restrained her. "I think you're right, Jonathan," said Eric. "Where's the phone book? We can call some hospitals. We don't have to call the police."

I began to scream again. "No, no! Can't you see what he's doing? He's crazy. He hates me!"

Eric went into the living room to look for the phone book. Jonathan knelt beside me. "Help me, Barbara," he said softly, looking deep into my eyes. He lifted me to my feet and led me to a chair. "Help me, please."

I knew what he meant. He was asking my help to placate Eric, to make it seem that he agreed with Eric. He knew what was happening and he was trying to defuse the situation and separate us. I stopped struggling against the sash. "Yes, Jonathan," I whispered. "Yes, I understand."

Eric came back to the bedroom and started dialing hospitals. I heard him say into the phone, "No, she's been violent. I guess she probably should be put in a locked ward."

"Jonathan!" I started to scream again.

"Barbara, Barbara, you promised," Jonathan said.

"She will probably need long-term care," Eric was saying to some nameless attendant. Some faceless clerk was being told I was hopelessly insane. I was filled with rage and indignation, but I knew I had to remain quiet.

I tried to get Edie's attention with my eyes. She was standing next to her husband, watching Eric, looking at me. Still, they both kept their composure. They acted as if everything were under control. "He's crazy, Edie," I said, only mouthing the words. "He's been beating me. Don't listen to him. I don't need long-term care." I tried to say all that just by moving my head, fluttering my eyes, whispering.

Eric was talking to someone at Mount Sinai Hospital. "Can you take her tonight? She's violent."

I shook my head with rage. Edie took a step toward me and with her arm at her side, she gave me a sign, making a circle with her thumb and index finger to show me that she, too, had figured out what was happening. Thank God, she believed me. She believed me.

Eric called Lenox Hill, Roosevelt, St. Vincent's. He went right down the list. "We must have a room for the night," he said. "Yes, yes, yes. She's violent."

The answers were always the same: bring her into emergency, call your doctor, call the police. Eric shouted into the phone, he slammed down the receiver.

"God damn it," he said. "We've got to get her into a hospital!"

"It isn't like checking into a hotel," Jonathan said. He was trying to calm Eric down, to keep him occupied. I could see that, but I couldn't stand it. I was too agitated, too excited to stay quiet. "Jonathan," I screamed again, struggling in the chair. "He's the crazy one. He threatened me with lobotomies!"

"Help me, Barbara. Help me, please."

Over and over it happened as I sat there with my arms bound behind my back while my best friend and her husband listened to my lover trying to commit me for the rest of my life. We tried to say everything with our eyes, but it didn't help me. It couldn't put an end to the frustration I felt.

Finally Eric collapsed on the bed and began to cry. "Oh, Jesus. Jesus. My beautiful Barbara. I tried to help, Jonathan, I did everything I could."

"I know, I know. But sometimes these things happen. It's nobody's fault." He was talking very quietly. "I know a very good hospital right outside the city called Longview. Let me try a call there, Eric."

"I want to do it myself," Eric cried. "I'll do it, Jonathan."

"Eric, give me the phone. Please let me help. You're tired."

Reluctantly Eric handed the phone to Jonathan and within minutes he was assured of a bed in Longview.

"I'll drive her," Eric said when Jonathan put the phone down.

"Wait a minute," said Jonathan, now firmly in control. "First of all, Edie, get Barbara some milk. She's hyperventilating. She must have some milk."

"And untie me, Jonathan," I said. "My wrists are bleeding."

"Will you be all right, Barbara? Will you hurt anyone?"

"Jonathan, goddammit, this is Barbara! I won't hurt anyone. Untie me now," I cried.

"You better not, Jonathan, you better not," Eric said. "She's violent. I've warned you." He got up and started pacing from the living room to the bedroom.

Jonathan had to calm him down all over again, and I tried to stay quiet as Edie untied my wrists. She poured me a glass of milk and I gagged it down.

"I'll drive her," Eric said again. He put on his jacket, looking at me with disdain, hatred, contempt, as if he had never known me, never loved me. I watched him with amazement. What had happened between us? What had happened?

"I won't drive in a car with him, Jonathan," I said. "I'll only go with you. Eric wants to hurt me. You must take me."

"It's all right, Barbara," he said. "Everything is going to be all right. Edie, help Barbara get dressed."

I was so weak I could hardly stand. I went into the bathroom to wash my face. And then Edie helped me change into clean clothes. I put on a coat and tied a scarf over my hair. I tried to look normal.

Jonathan took me by the arm and led me down the hall into the living room. I tried to speak, to explain, to thank him. But the words wouldn't come. Who was I? Where was I going? I felt I was just drifting.

"Hold on, Barbara," Jonathan said, giving my arm a gentle pressure.

Eric was waiting at the door. I tried to look at him, but my eyes wouldn't focus. Who was this man? Why did he do this to me? Why did he want all this destruction? Why didn't he help me?

Eric insisted on coming to the hospital with us. The four of us waited for the elevator, and when it arrived we were straining to look calm, to look ordinary. The elevator man smiled a hello at me as if he had taken me down only yesterday. How long had it been? Weeks? Months? I smiled back, a weak smile. No one in the building would know what had happened in that apartment. We looked like four people leaving a party.

5
Longview

I rode to the hospital with Jonathan and Edie in their car. Eric followed us in old Sammy; it would be the last time I ever saw that car. Jonathan cut off my talk of the police. He wanted no talk of violence or the police. At first I was angry. Then he explained that on their way to my apartment, he and Edie had decided that if they called the police, it could ruin my career. They hadn't known what was going on; they feared something terrible, but they didn't expect the horror they found. Still, they knew that with police there would be reporters.

I was stunned. I hadn't thought of that. I could see the headlines: "CBS Producer Arrested in Sex Love Prison on Central Park West."

"Oh, Jonathan, you're so right," I said. "I just wasn't thinking." My friends had come through even more than I had expected. I had outwitted Eric, sick and hopeless as I was. I had outwitted him and saved my life. But I knew my brain still wasn't working right.

"How did it happen, Barbara?" Edie said. "How did you let it happen?"

"The pills," I said, and began to cry. How could I explain that after going off the pills I couldn't think anymore, reason anymore? I didn't know right from wrong.

It was a long drive. Longview was in Suffolk County, and when we arrived, the four of us sat in silence in the waiting room until I was called into the admissions

82

office to fill out forms. An Indonesian woman began to ask me questions. "What does the following mean to you, Miss Gordon? People in glass houses shouldn't throw stones." I thought and thought, straining to make my brain work. I didn't know what it meant. The doctor smiled and continued, "How do you interpret: A rolling stone gathers no moss?" I couldn't figure that one out either. I ran back to the waiting room and grabbed Edie.

"Edie, Edie, I can't think. Tell me, what does it mean: A rolling stone gathers no moss?" I saw Edie's eyes fill with tears. Jonathan was staring at me, and Eric looked away. Edie started to explain, but the doctor came out of the office and led me back to her desk.

Sitting across from her, watching her fill out forms, I knew she thought she had a bad case. I could tell by the way she looked at me. She asked me how I felt. She asked me about the bruises on my arms. My answers were incoherent. I was still thinking about glass houses and rolling stones. But somehow, in all the confusion of my mind, I saw that she was trying to find out how sick I was, and if I might to violent to myself or to someone else. Finally she looked up and said, "I think we'll be able to help you, Miss Gordon."

I went back to the waiting room and things were said about bringing me more clothes, checking to see what kind of insurance I had, and then there was talk about a tennis racket. Longview had marvelous outdoor courts, Edie told me. It was four in the morning. Jonathan had surgery at eight. Still, he and Edie did not leave my side.

Then it was time to go. I glowered at Eric as a nurse from the ward came to take me away. I kissed Jonathan and Edie and then I looked again at Eric. I felt a burst of sadness when I said goodbye. I thought to myself, I don't know how this happened. I loved him and now this. He was my life; what happened?

The nurse and I left the admissions office and walked across a patio to a one-story building nearby. It was dark and I couldn't tell what season of the year it was—spring, summer? I started talking to her. "I took pills," I said, "I went off pills, something happened to me, the man I loved changed." I was rattling away and the nurse just nodded and told me that everything would be all right. I just needed some rest.

What happened to me? God, tell me what happened.

The next day I found myself in something called Tyson Cottage. It was not a locked ward like some of the others, my roommate, Yvonne, explained. We were lying in forced intimacy on two cots in a tiny cell-like room while she filled me in on hospital life. Yvonne was a heavy-set black woman who wore baggy pants, loud floral-print blouses and very high heels. "You can't be very sick," she told me, "because you're in an open ward." Obviously, the fact that I hadn't known the meaning of "A rolling stone gathers no moss" hadn't sent me to the violent ward. Yvonne continued her briefing. "Once you work yourself from the lowest status to a higher one, you can come and go as you please, like I do." Why, she spent weekends home and only weekdays at the hospital!

Sometime earlier that day I had met my doctor. Dr. Alex Robertson. He smoked a pipe constantly, wore tweedy jackets and light-blue oxford shirts, and carried an attaché case. He looked like a college professor. He was responsible for Tyson Cottage and would be my therapist. Yvonne thought that was wonderful. "Most of the other patients have social workers or psychologists," she told me. It seemed the hospital had only enough money to pay for one medicine man per ward. "Right now, because we're sort of short on space, you'll have to share a room," Dr. Robertson had said. "We don't have any private rooms, and of course you'll share the bathroom with the other patients." Business must be great, I had commented wryly.

My "primary nurse," Marie, brought my things to Tyson Cottage and introduced me to Yvonne. I thought it was strange that Marie was wearing jeans and a sweater. The air of the cottage had a thick, dense smell, but it wasn't the smell of a *hospital*

hospital. I was confused. I *thought* I was in a hospital, but where were the nurses and the bedpans?

Longview was a "short term" facility, not one for the chronically ill. Yvonne, an old hand at the Medicaid game, explained the set up. The hospital had a ninety-day limit because Medicaid would pay for only ninety days. After that, if you didn't have insurance or couldn't afford the bills, then it was state hospital time. And every mental patient knew what that meant. The end.

I don't remember everything Yvonne said, but I know that I wasn't concerned about money. I was just happy to be in a short-term hospital. That made me feel better. And despite all of Eric's dire threats, no one had mentioned the dreaded word "lobotomy." So the policy of mental hospitals was dictated by the rules of Medicaid. How odd. What would Freud have thought of that? What if it takes you 102 or one thousand days to get it together? Too bad. You have to do it in ninety or it's the pits in the state hospital for you. That wasn't my problem. I knew I would be out of here soon.

Yvonne took me around, pointing out the tennis courts, the cafeteria, the infirmary, as if she were conducting an official tour. There were eighteen patients in Tyson, she told me, most of them depressed. She took me into the day room and there some of them were sitting. They didn't look crazy. They all just sat there, some of them smoking cigarettes and listening to records. Judy Collins singing "Both Sides Now" was the house favorite. I wondered if that had something to do with schizophrenia. Still others were staring at the TV or sat numbly doing nothing at all.

Yvonne had been in and out of hospitals for years. She told me that whenever things got tough, she'd just sign herself back in. She was the president of the cottage and served on many committees at the hospital. She was an active member of the hospital world. Later I realized the hospital gave her an identity that she had never attained in the crowded Jersey City ghetto where she lived. And thanks to Medicaid, which paid for ninety-day visits every year, she was able to straighten out her life. We sat down together in a corner of the day room. Yvonne hadn't stopped talking. "Robertson is a terrific shrink. He's better than Goldberg, who's better than Ira. You're lucky to have him. The hospital works on a team approach," she explained. Sure, each patient had one primary therapist. But Longview adhered to "milieu" therapy, meaning therapy that goes on while you eat, talk, rest, watch TV. You're observed all the time. The staff held constant meetings and the social workers, psychologists and nurses reported to the primary therapist on how each patient was doing, how he was acting, or interacting, sleeping, eating. "Robertson might be your doctor, but everyone on the staff knows your story," Yvonne said. Terrific, I thought, that's just wonderful.

She had to go to a patient-nurse meeting in another building, and I just sat there after she left, staring into space like the others. Welcome to the club, I thought. Then I looked up and there was Edie. She was carrying a small suitcase packed with some clothes she thought I'd need. "Here are scarfs—I know you love them—and some paper and pens, some clean underwear, perfume. The works, kiddo. How are they treating you, Barbara?" she asked me nervously.

"I'm getting ready to play Jack Nicholson and lead a revolution in this place," I said. "Just as soon as I get my act together." I smiled and gave her a big hug.

"This is called the day room," I said, taking over Yvonne's role as tour guide. "Does that mean I can't sit here at night?" She looked at me apprehensively. "I'm kidding, Edie. Really. How is Eric?"

"I don't know. He hardly said a word when I went to your apartment to pick up your things. I still don't know what happened, Barbara. You loved him so. We all thought he loved you." And she gave me one of her inimitable penetrating looks.

"I don't know either," I said. "The pills, terrible things happened to me, and then to him." I knew I wasn't making any sense. "I can't talk about it now, Edie. I'm so frightened."

"You're going to be fine, Barbara," she said lovingly. "You're stronger than you think."

Marie interrupted to say Edie could stay only a few minutes longer. We looked at each other, my dear friend and I. We tried to express all the fears we felt, all the hope, all the gratitude, all the love with our eyes. "Will you call my parents?" I said. "Just tell them where I am. I want them to hear it from you, not Eric."

After we said goodbye, I went back to my room and tried to find space for my things among Yvonne's belongings. Then I decided I wouldn't unpack at all. I didn't want to get too comfortable in this place. I just left the suitcase on the floor under my bed.

Edie had brought me a notebook. I sat down on the edge of the bed and began to write. I wanted to keep track of things. I smiled as I remembered being a small child in Miami, baby-sitting with my brother when my parents went out to visit or play cards. Or nights when my favorite radio programs were on the air, I would write down all the funny jokes from *Duffy's Tavern* and *It Pays to Be Ignorant* so I could share them with my parents the next morning at breakfast. Writing things down would help me connect, I thought.

That first day, I was given a cursory physical examination. Since Dr. Robertson was a medical doctor, he gave me the physical himself. I had never been examined by a psychiatrist before. It felt strange. He looked at the bruises on my arms and scowled. "Who did this?"

"Eric," I answered softly, hiding my face from his. I was dying of humiliation. I didn't know how to begin to tell him what had happened. How could I tell him I had been beaten but I hadn't even known it until last night? How could I tell him that it wasn't me who had been beaten, but some little brat. That it wasn't associated with sex.

"You have multiple contusions," he said flatly. I saw Marcus Welby saying "contusions," Ben Casey, Dr. Kildare. I never knew what a contusion was. I looked at the bulging purplish-yellow bruises that covered my arms like grotesque tattoos. "They will go away," he told me, "but he could have broken your arms."

Dr. Robertson weighed me. One hundred and eighteen pounds. I had lost ten pounds. Then he took blood and urine tests, and those I could understand. Now it seemed like a hospital, and that made me feel more comfortable. Now I knew where I was.

While he did the tests, Dr. Robertson told me about occupational therapy and the tennis courts, urging me to participate when I felt better. "And I want you to start eating. Marie will bring your meals to you the next few days, but then you'll have to go to the cafeteria in the main building. We don't have room service here."

He was so matter-of-fact, so impersonal. I wanted to talk to him, to explain about the pills, about Eric, but I couldn't think straight. Please listen to me, please. I haven't always been sick. Please don't be so abrupt. But I couldn't say a word. Suddenly my scalp was burning and I began to experience that same terrible hollow feeling of unreality that had so frightened me in the apartment. It was a terror. I tried to tell him about it. But he wouldn't listen. He had to rush off to a meeting. I went back to my tiny room and wrote in my notebook, "I'm Barbara, I am, I am, I am."

I was in Chatahoochie after all. But how had it happened? All I remembered clearly was my decision to go off Valium. That was the last adult thing I had done feeling whole, feeling clear and decisive. I remembered Saint Patrick's Day. It was now the middle of May. I had spent fifty-seven days in that apartment, fifty-seven days that I could scarcely remember. Fifty-seven days that I would never forget.

For the first few days at Longview, I couldn't sleep, couldn't control my body at all. I spent hours pacing up and down the brightly lit yellow corridor, pacing to ease the feeling of agitation I was experiencing. I thought of Eric, Edie and Jonathan, but I still couldn't think clearly, so I just kept pacing. Besides, I couldn't let myself sit and do nothing like the other patients. Friends and my parents called. Edie had told them I was in the hospital. I tried to return the calls, but I was too agitated to talk. I couldn't taste food, couldn't cry, couldn't feel. I wanted to make sense out of everything. Eight weeks ago, I had a job, I lived with a man I loved, I had a nice life—except for those damn anxiety attacks. Now I was in Longview Hospital living with eighteen other men and women, most of whom were suffering from deep depression. What was I suffering from?

There was only one thing I looked forward to all day—my session with Dr. Robertson. He would explain what had happened, help me get my life back together. He wasn't an unattractive man, rather handsome, in fact, with his tweed jackets and his pipe. I was in wonderful hands; I knew it.

"What's wrong with me? Please tell me what happened." I was sitting in his small, uncluttered office, facing him across a giant desk with file folders spread everywhere. There was not a plant, not a picture, not a sign that the office belonged to anybody. "I don't remember anything very clearly after the Valium," I said, moving closer to the desk as I talked, as if being close to him would force him to become engaged in what I was saying. I wanted to be understood, desperately. I wanted to talk about how I had loved my old life, how I loved Eric, what happened. But Dr. Robertson wanted to know about my past: had I had chicken pox, mumps, were my parents alive? He just sat there asking questions and writing down everything I said in a large black loose-leaf notebook. I had expected therapy sessions, but it was more like fill up the pages in Dr. Robertson's notebook.

"I must write everything down," he told me when I complained during our second session. "It's necessary for the hospital's records."

The phone rang and he picked it up. He was constantly being interrupted for consultations, and it was also his responsibility to prescribe medication for the patients of all the other therapists. "Where were we?" he said when he hung up.

"How can this be therapy," I said, "when you spend all your time writing or talking on the phone?"

"It's procedure. Rules are rules," he replied. "Really, you are so neurotic, Barbara. Be a good girl and don't complain. Now, as I was saying, do you have any brothers or sisters? Where did you go to school?"

I felt like screaming. "I want to talk about now—going home, going back to work, how I will live," I said, trying not to sound too neurotic, too crazy.

"Rules are rules," he said, shaking his head. "Now our time is up. I'll see you next after the nurses' meeting on Friday. I think we can have thirty minutes."

That Friday, Dr. Robertson announced his diagnosis. "You are a cyclothymic personality," he said, "not a manic-depressive. You have wide mood swings within a twenty-four-hour period. Classic manic-depressives have cyclical ups and downs."

I sat there listening intently. At last he was talking about me. A cyclothymic personality, I thought. I've never heard that before. Well, at least it wasn't schizophrenia.

"You are deeply depressed and have far too much anxiety," he continued briskly. "I'm going to give you something to make you feel better. It's called Sinequan. It's an anti-depressant and an anti-anxiety drug."

"Will it help this terrible hollow feeling I have all the time? Will it stop the burning? Will it give my self back, Dr. Robertson? I pace up and down the halls of the cottage all day. Will it make me feel quiet, so I can sit quietly, so I can stay in one place without moving?" The questions were pouring out of me. "I didn't know that anxiety can be a symptom of depression," I said. "Why did Dr. Allen give me a depressive drug for depression?"

"He was wrong," Dr. Robertson said matter-of-factly. The phone rang and I heard him rattle off the names of drugs he wanted patients to get that night. When he hung up he said, "Where were we? Oh, yes, I remember. What I don't understand, Barbara, is why, after you began to experience withdrawal symptoms, you didn't take at least a small dose of Valium. That would have helped you."

I struggled for an answer, forcing my brain to think. It was still difficult for me to absorb what other people said to me. Then I remembered. "Because Dr. Allen said, No matter what happens, don't take any. I listened to my doctor."

"I have a patient right now, Barbara, who's here to withdraw from Valium. Her own doctor sent her. We're decreasing her dosage by five milligrams a week to avoid a psychotic episode."

Smart. Lucky, I thought to myself. "But heroin addicts always withdraw cold turkey, don't they?" I said.

He stared at me incredulously. Then he just shook his head and left the room. Our time was up.

So Dr. Allen was wrong, I thought. It's that simple. Wrong doctor, wrong disease, wrong pill. And now I have a new doctor, a new disease, a new pill. That's progress.

I went back to my room and lay down on my narrow cot, trying to hold on. I'm Barbara, I said to myself, I'm Barbara, my mother is Sally, my father is Lou, I loved Eric, I worked at CBS, I am, I am. I chanted the litany over and over again, hoping to spark a sense of recognition of myself.

"Our session can only be twenty-five minutes today, Barbara," Dr. Robertson said as I walked in the door. "You're looking better, much better."

It's amazing, I thought. I put on a little lipstick and he thinks I'm better. It's so easy to deceive him; too easy.

"I think the Sinequan has really helped," he said, sitting back in his chair and filling his pipe. "What do you think?"

"I guess so," I said nervously. "At least I'm sleeping three or four hours a night now and I don't pace as much. But it's still hard to concentrate, and the burning in my head doesn't go away. I still feel like a skeleton with flesh. I can't feel my soul."

Dr. Robertson gave me a quizzical look and then began to speak. "That's to be expected, Barbara. Going off Valium so rapidly precipitated a psychic storm in your head. You are still having withdrawal symptoms. It will take time, but you'll get over it."

"But what about my life? What about Eric and me? I still don't know what happened. I loved him so."

I sensed that Dr. Robertson was always a little uncomfortable when I began to talk about Eric. After we had finished with childhood diseases and my cyclothymic personality, he finally let me tell him about our relationship and what I could remember of the weeks we spent together in my apartment. My memories were jumbled, my words sometimes incoherent, but he jotted everything down dutifully in his notebook, puffing on his pipe, nodding. Did he believe me? Did he think I was making it up? I sometimes wonder myself. The whole thing sounded like a porno movie, a trashy paperback, the ravings of a real lunatic.

"I don't know what happened either, Barbara," he said. "I've heard only your side of the story. But you must have driven Eric crazy with your demands for attention and your infantile behavior. Poor fellow."

Poor fellow! I looked at the bruises still visible on my arms. Eric was sitting in my apartment, reading, listening to music. I was in a nut house.

"Love sometimes expresses itself in peculiar ways," Dr. Robertson said. "I'm sure if Eric goes into therapy, you two can still have a life together."

I couldn't believe it. He was saying that Eric and I could have something together again. I had thought it was all over. Maybe I won't be alone after all.

"You're getting much better, Barbara," Dr. Robertson said, "but I cannot discharge you as long as Eric is living in your apartment. It's still a potentially dangerous situation. But with a little help, you'll both be fine."

Eric and me together? I went back to my room and lay on the cot, remembering Eric as I had loved him. How he smelled, how he smiled, how he made love. I turned over and buried my face in the pillow. Why did you do it, Eric? Why did you let me stay in the apartment? Why didn't you get me to a hospital? And then, from a very deep part of me, I asked myself another question. Why did you let him do it? Because I loved him. That was the only answer. I loved him.

I was sitting in the day room trying to read the paper. What had once been a normal, spontaneous part of my life was now a difficult chore, like reading Sanskrit or Arabic. I was mouthing the words out loud, like a child in the first grade. Marie tapped me gently on the shoulder. "There's a phone call for you," she said, then paused. "It's a man. It might be Eric." Marie knew everything that had happened to me; it was on my chart. Besides, I was beginning to talk to her a little each day. We were becoming friends. "Do you want to speak to him?"

I nodded. I hadn't returned his previous calls. I hadn't spoken to anyone, not even my parents. Eric and me together again? We might as well start somewhere. I went to the pay phone in the hall, where all the patients took their calls. There was no privacy, but usually everyone was too locked in his own misery to care.

"Yes," I said, feeling my heart pound.

"It's me, Barbara."

It *was* Eric but his voice sounded flat and mechanical, the way he had talked in the apartment. When did he start talking like that? I couldn't remember.

"How are you doing? Are they treating you all right?"

"Fine."

"Do you want me to visit?"

"No, not now. Not yet, Eric."

"Your friends are cutting me off. They're turning me into a nonperson. You are ruining my life, Barbara. Edie and Jonathan have ostracized me. Your parents have arrived in New York and they don't want to see me. They're in collusion, everyone is in collusion against me. I only gave you love and do you know what?" He was beginning to shout. His voice almost pierced my eardrum through the phone. "You took, you took, you sick bitch! I gave you everything. *Everything!* And now you're destroying me!"

"Please, Eric. Please," I said. "Don't talk to me like that. You need help. We both need help. Go to see someone, please."

"No," he screamed. "I'm fine!" Then, abruptly, his voice was under control. "But if it will make you feel better, I'll consult a doctor. Just to make you happy. Anything to make madam happy."

I hung up the phone and went back to my room. I felt empty, sad. I never wanted to ruin you, Eric. I'm not trying to punish you. And I lay down in the dark room with my hands across my forehead until I fell asleep.

He called again a few days later.

"Babe, how are you? I miss you. This apartment is so quiet without you."

"Hello, Eric. What do you want?" I said, straining to stay calm.

"I've done it. I went to a shrink. A good one. And you know what he said? Never, never have I heard of such love and devotion as you have shown to that woman. That's what he said exactly. He said I gave up so much of my own life to go through the storm with you."

I held the receiver in my hand, not knowing what to believe. "Did you tell him everything, Eric?"

"Of course, and he says I'm one hundred percent terrific. Diagnosis: marriage. He thinks we make a great team."

He's lying to me, I said to myself. Why is he doing this?

Later, when I told Dr. Robertson what Eric had said, he remarked that it might be true. "I spoke to him myself this morning. He wants to come to see you. You know I won't release you until he is out of your apartment."

"I can't see him," I said. "I can't even bear hearing his voice." How could I get him to move? I had to find a way, but if I asked him to do that, I was frightened that in a burst of anger he might destroy the apartment or wreck the beach house. Nervous breakdown or not, I didn't want to lose my rent-controlled apartment on Central Park West.

It was a bright June afternoon. My parents had been in New York for several days. They had flown up from Miami after talking with Edie and Eric. Though I had spoken to them a few times by phone during the Valium withdrawal, they had had no idea of what was happening to me. Later they would say that I hadn't sounded like myself at all during those weeks, but obviously I had been very careful to conceal what was going on. It must have been a terrible shock when they learned I was in a mental hospital.

I refused to return their calls at first, but now I had spoken to them on the phone and they were coming to visit. Today was the day. I was humiliated, embarrassed and excited all at once. I didn't want them to see me, here, looking like this, but they would talk to me, confirm my sense of existence. After all, they were where I came from. One look at them and I'd know who I was. That hollow feeling would go away. I'd connect—instantly.

When Dr. Robertson told me they had arrived in the main building and were coming over to Tyson Cottage, I forgot my humiliation and ran down the path to greet them. I knew they would try to hide whatever nervousness and apprehension they felt. They would have to act as if I were in a hospital with a broken leg. I wanted to make it easy for them, as painless as possible.

We sat on folding chairs on the lawn in front of the cottage. I looked at the two of them. My mother, petite, attractive, perfectly dressed. How frightened she had to be. My father, his head of hair shining like patent leather, the perfectly trimmed mustache, the colorful clothes. They both looked the same. Nothing changes, nothing really changes.

"It'll be all right," I began. "I don't know quite what happened, but I want to assure you both it will be all right. I'll be out of here in no time. How much do you know?"

"Well, darling," my mother said. "Edie called us, then Eric did. So naturally we rushed right up. Is this a good place? Your doctor sounds very nice over the phone."

"Yes, he's very nice. What did Eric tell you?"

My mother began to speak, but my father interrupted her. "Let me talk, Sally, let me talk."

"It was a very strange call," my mother said.

"He told us he saved your life," my father said. "He told us that when you first met, you didn't have any friends and you were in way over your head financially and your career was dying. He said he introduced you to the right people and gave you ideas for your films. He gave you everything. He said he loved you and you were going to get married, when this happened. Then he saved your life by bringing you to this hospital."

I shook my head in disbelief. My parents were staring at me, waiting for my response.

"Tell me again," I said slowly. "Tell me everything. It's important that I know it all."

They both started talking, repeating the details of Eric's call. My career! Not that, too, Eric! "It isn't true," I practically screamed. "I got *him* clients, I loaned *him* money, I introduced him to *my* friends. Why is he doing this?"

"Now dear, I'm sure it isn't good for you to get so upset," my mother said. "We didn't believe him, did we, Lou? Edie said you'd tell us what happened, so we haven't talked to Eric since."

"What *did* happen, baby?" my father said.

"I don't know," I said. "It started with some pills I was taking for my nerves."

"You always were so high-strung," my mother said. And then she began to talk about my brother and his wife, her grandchildren, family news. If she was so concerned about having an unmarried daughter, I wondered how she was going to explain to her friends that I was in a mental institution.

"What do you need, baby?" my father asked.

"Nothing, nothing."

"Barbara dear," my mother said, "we know everything is going to be fine, so don't worry about anything. I'll stay in New York as long as you need me. Daddy's going back to Florida in a day or so, but I'll stay. I want to help you get settled back in the apartment. How much longer will you be here?"

I told her I didn't know. But when she said "the apartment" my insides turned over. Eric was there, among my things, our things. How and when would I sort it all out?

When our visit was over, I kissed them goodbye and watched them walk together to the main building. My mother took my father's arm. I had never seen them so close. They seemed more like a couple, a loving couple, than I ever remembered. Had they always been like that with each other, tender, considerate? Perhaps my crisis had brought them closer together than they had been before.

I felt sad after they left, sad and confused. I loved them. I could see that they loved me, that they were concerned. But I was disappointed that our visit had not made a lasting impression on me, hadn't made me connect with reality once and for all.

I never really got into the hospital routine. Occupational therapy and volleyball games weren't for me and I didn't want to become a hospital gadabout like Yvonne. I wanted to get out, get back to my life, get back to work. The problem was it was still difficult for me to think clearly or to concentrate. But I had finally managed to go to the main building and have my meals in the enormous and noisy cafeteria filled with hundreds of other patients. I had fought my apprehensions, walking stiffly with my tray, enduring the insults of the kitchen staff, feeling the rudeness, the hatred, seeing them flaunt their higher station in life over me. I felt the intensity of their superior attitude keenly, and I had to suffer through that as well as the overcooked gray meat, the soggy vegetables, the lifeless salads. It was then I realized that there is nothing lower than being a mental patient.

I was at my lowest one Saturday night. All the other patients were in the activities building, listening to music, watching a movie or playing games. I had opted to stay in the cottage, which frustrated Pat, the night nurse. Had I gone to the activities building, she could have gossiped with her friends. Now she had to stay behind with me. I sat in the empty day room and turned on the television, forgetting it was Saturday night, just wanting some diversion from myself.

The newscast was coming to an end, and as the commercials went on, I found myself staring into space. Then I was jolted by familiar dialogue, words I had heard before, music I knew intimately. I stared at the screen. A woman was lying on a psychiatric couch, and a narrator's voice was talking over the picture. I knew what he was going to say before he said it, but I must have stared at the set for two minutes before it clicked. It was the opening of a film I had written and produced for CBS, a film about the psychiatric profession that I had made with Steve and Fran not more than five months ago. It had been a difficult film which tried to illustrate that psychiatry was often being used as a form of political punishment in segments of American society just as it was in the Soviet Union.

The end of the opening segment of the film appeared and then I saw my name on the screen: PRODUCED AND WRITTEN BY BARBARA GORDON. I became very excited. "That's me, that's me!" I said. "Pat, come look. This is my show, I did it." I desperately wanted someone to see my name on the screen. I wanted someone else to see that I did exist, I wasn't dead, I had a history, a life before this place. And I could return to it. But Pat simply stared at me from behind the glass walls of the office, and continued talking on the phone.

I sat there watching a television show I had produced about the abuses and conflicts of interest in the psychiatric profession in America, about psychiatrists whose allegiance is sometimes not to the patient but to the system they serve, about mental institutions that are used as detention camps, prisons, for the old, the handicapped, the undesirable. And now I was sitting in the darkened day room of just such an institution, both a victim and a captive of the psychiatric profession. Who would believe it? I had to tell someone, but by the time Pat came out of the office, the titles were gone, the show had begun, and my attempt to explain why I was so excited must have seemed crazy to her.

"Sure, Barbara," she said. "Of course you produced that show." She was pacifying me and there was no way to prove that I was not mad, that it had been my show. She walked away, shaking her head and muttering to herself, and I knew she would write on my chart that I was hallucinating and delusional. I laughed in spite of myself.

The problem of Eric and the apartment haunted me. I told Dr. Robertson I couldn't ask Edie and Jonathan to get him out; they had done so much for me already. I didn't want my parents to get involved. Finally Dr. Robertson volunteered his help. "You have to meet sometime," he said. "Why not here? I'll speak to him and ask him to move out diplomatically."

A day or so later, Marie told me there was a call for me and she thought it was Eric. I dreaded hearing his voice; I always felt so confused after talking with him.

"Barbara, you have some decisions to make."

I held the receiver, trembling. What did he want?

"The tennis club closes its membership list at the end of the month. Don't you want to send a check?"

"Eric, I can't think about that right now." What an odd thing, I thought. Tennis, at a time like this.

"I'm just trying to plan ahead," he said. "And I really want to visit you. I'm feeling excluded." He wasn't shouting. He wasn't angry yet. He was trying to keep in control. "Edie has visited you, your parents. What about me? Everyone but me. That's why I wanted to marry you. I knew this would happen. I knew I'd be left out. In marriage one has rights." Now his voice was growing angry, loud. "All my life I've feared being a nonperson, and now you are trying to destroy me. What about our trip to Europe? What about our life? What have you done to our life?"

I listened without saying a word. Would I ever get used to the sound of his voice? "Dr. Robertson wants you to come visit on Monday, if that's all right," I said finally.

"That's great, babe. Great. I'll be there."

I was agitated on Monday. Just the thought of Eric stirred up such a mixture of emotions in me, I couldn't imagine what it would be like to see him again. I could hardly sit still all morning, and that afternoon I was trying to read in the day room, when I looked up and there he was sitting next to me, smiling that strange smile, staring at me. I hadn't even known he had arrived. Suddenly I was frightened. I felt trapped like an animal. I was afraid he would hit me. Part of me felt instinctively the old love and tenderness I used to feel when I saw him. And part of me felt anger and hatred for what he had done to me. I knew I could never be sure who I was or what I felt if I continued to have such conflicting emotions.

I got up and ran to Dr. Robertson's office, like a frightened child. I needed protection. I couldn't be with Eric alone. I was terrified of him. I saw the face that had kissed me, had loved me, that I had adored, and then I remembered the look on that same face when he struck me, when he called me a junkie, when he said I was a sniveling brat who had destroyed his world as his mother had. Which Eric was he? Who had destroyed whom?

I sat shaking in Dr. Robertson's office while he went out and brought Eric in. He was dressed as usual, but he looked fatter, flabby; his glasses were dwarfed by the puffiness of his cheeks. I couldn't remember exactly how he had looked before, but it wasn't like that.

"Well, it's about time you two decided to let me visit," he said as soon as he sat down. I could see he was struggling to remain calm. "Everyone can visit you but me. Is that it, Barbara? You made me a nonperson. I knew it would happen. If we were married, I'd be a person. I'd have rights."

I looked toward Dr. Robertson, hoping he would help me. I didn't know how abusive Eric would get and I was frightened. But Dr. Robertson was sitting back in his chair, smoking his pipe, looking straight ahead at Eric, not at me.

"Now, Eric, old fellow," he began, "no one wants to isolate you. But you must admit Barbara was in pretty bad shape when she arrived here, and I can't discharge her if you're still in the apartment. It will only be a temporary move. I'm sure you two will work something out in the future. But for the present, I think it's best that you live separately."

"What do you mean, temporary?" Eric shouted. "It's my life, too. Why are you separating me from the woman I love?"

Dr. Robertson took a long puff on his pipe, and I could see that he was trying to choose his words carefully. "No one is separating you. It's just that for the time being I think it's better that you and Barbara were apart. Two or three months, that's all. By then you'll both be stronger. You will have had help. Then there can be talk of a reconciliation."

I remembered the look on Dr. Robertson's face when he saw the bruises all over my arms; I remembered the disgust, the anger. Now he was saying that Eric and I could be reconciled. I was bewildered and frustrated because I felt my life was out of my control. I didn't know what was right, what was wrong, or even what I wanted. I heard these two men talking about me as if I weren't there. I heard them saying *she, she.* I was Barbara! Why didn't they talk to me?

Finally Dr. Robertson suggested that Eric and I talk together alone and make plans. He walked out of the office and the two of us just sat there staring, not saying a word. The tension was unbearable. Suddenly I got up and left, heading for the day room, where there would be other people. I was still afraid to be alone with him. I didn't like that cryptic smile, the unfocused eyes, and the strange robot way he had of speaking. He followed after me and asked me to walk with him on the grounds. I was frightened, but I agreed. He wouldn't dare hurt me when other people were around. I knew he could be violent, but he was terrified of others' seeing that side of him. He had hidden it from me for five years. Or had I hidden it from me? I wasn't sure.

We walked outside the cottage and sat down underneath a maple tree. We were two different people; we were no longer Eric and Barbara. I looked at him, stared at him really, hoping that his face would reveal the answer to my loss of identity. There had been so much happiness with him—and so much terror. If my parents couldn't provide the clue to my identity, Eric would. He had to. I was sure of that.

But before we could talk, he suddenly began to sob. I had excluded him, he said; my parents, Edie and Jonathan had excluded him, and now he had nothing. I had robbed him of himself. I had destroyed his world. Didn't I know the pain he was enduring, living alone in my apartment with memories of me everywhere? He didn't ask how I was, he didn't say a word about the terrible weeks we spent together in the apartment. He only said how much he loved me, how much he needed me to keep his world from shattering.

I should have expected it. I had heard it all before on the phone; he had said the same thing to Dr. Robertson. But I was confused. I thought I had been the dependent one in our relationship. Eric had called me dependent, so had Dr. Robertson. And I couldn't deal with his tears. I didn't know what to say. Finally I mumbled something about the move being only temporary. Everything was going to be all right. We'd be back together soon.

He stopped crying. "All right," he said. "I'll start looking for a sublet for a few months, but are you sure that's what you want? You're not just appeasing Dr. Robertson?"

"Yes, that's what I want," I said. "I just can't live with you right now."

Then we started to talk about the beach house, prospective tenants, work that had to be done there, and he gave me messages from friends who had called. It all seemed so normal, so ordinary, just as if nothing had happened. I stood up and looked at him. He was Eric. Had he really changed? Or was it all me? "Why did you do it?" I asked flatly. I struggled to control my breathing, to regulate my voice, which tended to go too high or too low. That's all I said: "Why did you do it?"

He reached for his jacket, stood up close to me, looked at me tenderly and smiled. "I did everything out of love for you," he said. "Don't be afraid of me,

Barbara. I'm Eric. Kiss me." He didn't say it, he commanded it.

I didn't want to kiss or touch him.

He stood there rigidly, his face contorted with the enigmatic smile that was now twisted into a sad lost look. "Kiss me, Barbara. I love you," he said again.

I kissed him childishly on the cheek and ran back to the cottage. Looking through a window, I watched him disappear into the admissions building. I tried to remember happiness, laughter; I tried to remember the pain. But I couldn't remember. I couldn't cry. I felt nothing. Not anger, not fury, not rage, not love, not hate, not loss. Nothing. And nothing is worse than anything. Nothing is the worst.

I stayed at Longview for seventeen days. During that time I saw Dr. Robertson nine times, listened to his soothing voice and watched him fill countless pages in his big black notebook. After our sessions I would return to my room and write in my own notebook, trying to remember, hoping to connect. I was looking for answers to questions I didn't even know how to ask. They all came spilling out when I spoke with Dr. Robertson, but I would see a look of incomprehension across his face. "Really, Barbara," he said, "you are so neurotic. Now just take your pills, like a good girl, and you'll be out of here soon."

I spent my days talking with other patients, like Jenny, a young nurse suffering from manic depression. Lithium would straighten out her life, even out her highs, elevate her lows. With her Dr. Robertson would look like a miracle man. Then there was Dennis, a young student, who while traveling in London found himself crying in a department store, crying at the age of nineteen when he couldn't decide which book to buy. He had tried to take his own life. Depression was a killer worse than cancer. Though each patient was in the hospital for a different reason, I discovered we all had one thing in common. Schizophrenia, depression, manic depression, anxiety neurosis—it didn't matter. All of us had been in therapy for years. Each of us had sought help, and all of us came from New York, one of the great medical centers in the world. Dennis, Jenny, me—our doctors had given us pills: the wrong pills, the right pills, but too many pills. They had treated the symptoms and not the cause of our illness.

One night, on an impulse, I decided to call Dr. Allen. I was still angry at him, but maybe he had a clue to what had happened to me; he would definitely remind me who I was. I told him where I was and then said I was on Sinequan. "You're in a fine hospital and Sinequan is an excellent drug," he said. "I'm sure you'll do fine."

"But don't you think you should see me?" I asked. "You know me so well. I could go to your hospital."

"No, I'm afraid I can't arrange that." Click. He was gone. He had hung up.

After ten years and thousands of dollars, after telling me to do the wrong thing by going off Valium cold, he hung up. He phoned me once later while I was still in the hospital to say hello. After that I only heard from him periodically when he called to complain that I owed him seventy-five dollars and please would I settle up the bill.

I wasn't at Longview long enough to make any lasting friendships. In this mental hospital, we were like passengers on a ship brought together by circumstance, eating, sleeping, living together for a short, intense time. Unlike passengers, we had no destination. I knew now that my world would be an empty apartment. I watched as other patients went home on overnight passes, then for weekends. I did none of that. Edie would just come and get me when I was ready to leave and that would be that. No, I didn't want to go shopping in the neighboring village; no, I didn't want to go to the movies with Jenny and Dennis. I would only walk out of the door of that hospital when it was time to go home.

Months later I would regret that. Only then would I realize how unprepared I was to begin living outside again. And besides, I still thought I wouldn't be alone for long. Maybe Eric would get help, maybe it was all my fault, maybe he would apologize, maybe he would explain to me what had happened to him, to us. After a few months we might meet for a drink and things would be good again. Perhaps we could make a life together out of this hell. I remembered what Dr. Robertson had said about Eric: "He's a nice chap; a little argumentative, but a nice bright chap." He was a doctor. If something was wrong with Eric, he would have told me.

Edie was coming at last. I had packed the night before. I was bored as hell in the hospital. I wanted out and Dr. Robertson had finally agreed. But who would be my doctor when I got home? I asked him. He promised to give me a few names. "But other patients have a doctor waiting when they're discharged, someone they've seen or called," I said. "I can't go home to no Eric, no job, no doctor. Please help me." I pleaded with him to recommend someone specific. I couldn't possibly go back to Dr. Allen.

"Really, Barbara, don't be so neurotic," he said. "I'll get you a list of doctors before you go and everything will be fine."

On the afternoon Edie was due to arrive, I took a walk with Marie, my primary nurse. She had sat with me, talked with me, had helped me time after time when I needed someone. When I was on the verge of regressing, acting like a little girl, Marie would look up at me and say: "When the adult Barbara Gordon wants to talk, come see me. I will not talk to the child." She had been cool, firm, professional and kind. She would sit with me, urging me to repress the impulse to act out, to throw a tantrum. She would frown and tell me Eric had reinforced that kind of behavior. He had made it acceptable and now I had to unlearn it. One Sunday afternoon I had been lying in my room, unable to think, able to feel only rage at Eric. I thought I would jump out of my skin. Marie sat with me on my cot, talked to me, suggested a long hot shower, then brought me a lemonade. She was a person.

We were walking around the grounds saying goodbye. "I can't cry, Marie, I can't even cry," I said. "Will

I ever be able to feel again, love again, feel sadness, anger, anything?"

"You must learn," she said coolly, "to express what you think."

"But I didn't discover anything here, why what happened happened, and I still don't have a doctor to see when I get home."

"Dr. Robertson will get you someone," she said.

"Marie, what's your opinion?" I asked. "Dr. Robertson says he thinks I can still have a life with Eric."

She looked surprised. "Well, only you can decide that."

"We had so much love, Marie, so much love," I said, looking at her earnestly. "We should be able to salvage something. He had never hit me before. Dr. Robertson says my sickness made him sick, that the two of us couldn't cope with the intense passions that were evoked by my going off the Valium."

"You'll have time to decide," Marie said. "The most important thing is that he has moved out and you can go home and not be frightened. Everything will be all right."

"But I want to be able to cry, to feel," I said. "I'm just beginning to be able to taste food again."

"You will," she said confidently.

As we walked back to the cottage I saw Edie's blond head in the distance. There's my friend. Home —I was going home! I ran to get my suitcase, said goodbye to Yvonne, Jenny and Dennis. I went to Dr. Robertson's office, to ask him for the list of doctors he recommended. Absently, he handed me a crumpled piece of paper with five names on it. "They're all good for phobics like you," he said. Then he added, "Good luck, Barbara. Don't send me any presents." What a strange comment, I thought. Why would I send him a present?"

Edie was waiting for me, smiling. We hugged each other and practically ran to the car. I threw my canvas suitcase in the back seat. Edie looked pensive as she drove onto the Long Island Expressway and we headed for the city.

I was telling her what Dr. Robertson had said. "He

says if Eric gets help, we can have a life, that I'm so nutty I made Eric angry. Edie, maybe it *was* all my fault and maybe I won't be alone after all. I loved him so."

Edie bit her lip, gave me a nervous smile and kept her eyes fixed on the highway. "You're going to go back to work," she said. "You'll meet new people. You'll be fine, Barbara."

"I don't want to meet new people, Edie. I want my old life back."

Edie said nothing. She concentrated on her driving. She was treating me gingerly, I could see that. She must be nervous, I thought. This isn't like a broken leg at all.

I chose to ignore her all too obvious skepticism. I was praying that there was a chance to salvage something of my old life. I had hope.

We were crossing the Fifty-ninth Street bridge. I looked out at the spectacular view of the city from the upper level and I immediately thought of the hundreds of summer Sunday nights driving over this bridge, coming back from the beach with Eric. There was the restaurant on the corner of Second Avenue where we sometimes had dinner, the gallery on Madison where we had bought a picture for the apartment. I couldn't seem to look at anything without associating it with a recent memory of Eric. That's natural, I thought. You have lived in this city with him for so many years. It's natural.

6

Summer Alone

When we arrived at my building, Edie, remembering how impossible it had been for me to go into stores, asked me if I wanted to pick up some food for the apartment. We went into a little market around the corner. Then it was time to go home. Edie rode up in the elevator with me. Carrying groceries and suitcases, the two of us stood in front of my door. I fumbled with my keys, almost afraid to go inside.

I don't know what I expected to find. It had only been seventeen days; still, it was a shock to see the apartment looking so sunny and bright after the harshly lit corridors and the gloomy day room at the hospital. Eric had not destroyed it. I collapsed on the couch with a sigh of relief and Edie and I said our goodbyes.

I was home. Eric had moved out, but after five years of living with him, it was eerie being in the apartment alone. It's like having a nervous breakdown *and* a divorce, I thought. I forced myself to think of the time I had lived here alone before I met Eric. I could remember it as a fact, but I couldn't experience the feelings. Part of me wanted the Eric I loved to surprise me and come walking out of the bedroom saying, "Hi, babe. How ya doing? It's all been a bad dream. We're still together. We're intact." And another part of me felt a glacial terror at the very thought of being in the same room with him.

I began to look around the apartment. There was nothing to reveal the insanity or the violence that had taken place here. Although Eric was gone, some of his things—his winter jackets, his boots, his books and records—were still where they had always been. They were both alarming and comforting. He will be coming back, his things told me; he will be coming back and everything will be good again. It will just take time. It will be a purgatory, this being without him, I thought, but today I must start living as a woman alone.

I unpacked, trying to busy my mind with tasks. I bathed, watered the plants, sat on the edge of the bed. I didn't know what to do with me. Whom do people talk to, how do they do this alone? I thought. But I'm not alone! I ran to the telephone and called my mother. She was at a nearby hotel. We made plans for dinner together that night. Then I started phoning some of my friends to announce that Barbara was back. But they sounded strange, cool, put off, not very happy to hear from me. I couldn't imagine why. "Oh, Barbara, we must have a drink sometime," was all one of them said. What was going on? A drink sometime—they're talking to me as if I'm a stranger. Then I decided that my being sick had made everyone a little nervous. Still, I wasn't comfortable with that coolish, distant tone I heard over the phone.

I walked down to Central Park South to pick up my mother in the lobby of her hotel. She was sitting on a sofa near the door, waiting for me. I wanted to say, I know how frightened you are, but I think everything is going to be all right. I wanted to say I'm sorry I botched things so. I don't know what happened to me, but I'll fix it, you'll see. And I wanted to say that Dr. Robertson thought Eric and I could have a life together again. But I didn't say anything. Will I, all my life, push aside what I really want to say? But I was feeling so light-headed—not good light-headed—so selfless, so fragile that I thought anything I said right then might be wrong, or would be interpreted as craziness. I hugged her. "Come on, Sally, let's go have some good food. I've had it with that hospital crap." She gave me a big smile. She looked relieved. I was Barbara; I looked like Barbara, talked liked Barbara. I was her daughter and I was alive.

We sat in the back of a small Spanish restaurant near the hotel. I ordered a Margarita and my mother her traditional Canadian Club and ginger ale. One was her limit. More than that and she was looped. So we sat there nursing our drinks.

"And Daddy says Eddie and Melinda are dying to come up and see you. And Eddie wants you to know if you need him, he's there for you."

"Yes, Mother, I know he's there. I don't need any help, really. But I'm so grateful you're here. I know you can't stay long. Dad will miss you." It was true. He needed her, too. But now she was my mother, she was Sally, always there for me. I was grateful, but not at all surprised.

"And did I tell you, Barbara, Marge is going to Russia and the Irvings back to Capri for the summer? Why don't you come to Europe with Dad and me? We'll feel so much better if you're with us."

"I have to get a job, Mother. I must talk to Alan about going back to CBS, work things out with Eric, get my life together. I can't go."

I saw the almost imperceptible frown that she tried to disguise at the sound of Eric's name and I realized immediately that I shouldn't have mentioned it.

"Eric?" she said. She didn't yet know the whole story of what had happened between us. I couldn't bear to tell her. But she knew enough to be alarmed.

"Dr. Robertson says he thinks Eric is all right, Mother," I said, wanting to believe it myself.

"But, Barbara, after what he did, after all those lies he told us, how can you even think of going back to him?"

"We'll see, Sally. We'll see."

I saw the look of concern on her face and I reached across the table to pat her hand. "Really, Mother, everything is going to be fine. I feel wonderful." I had to reassure her, but even as I uttered the words, I knew I was overplaying my hand.

During the rest of the dinner, Mother went on about her friends, their children, their illnesses, their funerals. It was such a relief just to sit there and listen while she rattled on and on about life in Miami Beach. We couldn't talk about cosmic things, we couldn't talk about my children, my husband, my work—so we talked about other people's lives. On that night it was safer.

"O.K., Sally, it's past my ten o'clock curfew," I said finally. "I've got a hard day of psychiatrist-hunting tomorrow." Again I saw that look of concern. Psychiatrists were doctors and doctors meant illness. "Don't worry," I said. "This time I'll find a good one. Go shopping tomorrow, Mom. Do something. I don't want you sitting around the hotel all day worrying or doing errands for me."

"I'm just going to get you a new filter for your air conditioner—yours is filthy—and a few things for the kitchen. Will I see you tomorrow for dinner?"

"I'd love it," I said. We walked back to her hotel, arm in arm, chattering like schoolgirls. Was she buying my self-confidence act? She looked less pensive, less worried, when we kissed good night. I almost believed it myself. I was almost certain I had silenced the little demons saying nasty things in my head.

The next morning the phone rang as I sat having coffee and looking out at the day. It was Edie, of course. It was just a check-in-to-see-if-you're-still-alive call. She tried to sound light and cheery. She knew I would be frightened my first morning in the apartment alone. And I was. We made a date for later in the week, but first, somehow, I had to get through today.

As I started for the elevator, I thought of the old creeping terror that came over me whenever I went outside. Agoraphobia, Barbara, fear of the marketplace. Remember what Dr. Robertson said: we only fear what we hate. Oh, someday I want to live without holding on to the homilies of shrinks. Someday I want to be on automatic pilot. Why should I hate the marketplace? Forget it. You have nothing to fear. Move. I will function. I told myself. I will.

I went to the bank, bought newspapers, but as I headed back to the apartment I was suddenly flooded with memories of Eric, of all the good years, then the

horrible weeks, the love and the terror. I felt so sad
that I was crying as I walked into the apartment. I
remembered Marie's words: "You'll cry. You'll feel
again." And at first it felt wonderful to cry, just as it
was wonderful to taste food again. But I was crying so
hard that I felt as if my heart were one giant tear. I
was crying for the loss of Eric, the loss of love, the loss
of me. And I couldn't stop.

That afternoon I sat staring at the crumpled list of
psychiatrists Dr. Robertson had given me. I didn't
know one from the other. I looked up their addresses
and phone numbers in the book. East Side, West
Side—it didn't matter, as long as it wasn't on Riverside
Drive.

I dialed the first number. The voice on the answering machine sounded cheerful and authoritative. "This
is Dr. Robert Steinberg. I'm not in right now, but if
you leave your name and number, I'll phone when I
get back. Talk after the beep."

Dutifully I left my name and number, and then
proceeded to leave my name and number with two
other mechanical shrinks. The fourth call was more
productive. I spoke to a human being: Dr. Marcus
Popkin. "No, I'm not in session right now, so I can
talk."

If you're not in session, I thought, you can't be very
good or very busy. But I censored my hostility and
gave him a précis of the past seventy days of my life.
This script needs work, I kept thinking to myself. Cut
a little bit here and there, beef up the characters.

"That sounds most interesting," Dr. Popkin said.
"I'm certain I can help you. When are you free for an
appointment?"

When am I free? Didn't he hear me? "I'm *always*
free, Dr. Popkin."

"What about this evening?"

I knew Mother wouldn't mind breaking our date for
dinner, so I agreed to an appointment at eight that
evening. Then, not wanting to put all my neuroses in
one basket, I dialed the last name on Dr. Robertson's
list.

Dr. Tom Rosen answered the phone himself. No

nurse, no machine. That's a good sign, I thought. I gave him a much more polished version of my story and I made an appointment.

I knew that searching for a psychiatrist in the summer would be fraught with disaster. They are either in Europe, or the Cape or out in the Hamptons. No one wants to take on a new patient in June. If people on the street in New York during the summer look drawn and anxious, it's because every shrink worth his Valium has disappeared. But Dr. Robertson had said these were five "top men." That sounded like my parents' comments about doctors: a top bone man, a top eye man, a top head man. Well, I'd fine one, dammit, even if it took all summer. This time I wasn't going to rush in and grab the first thing I saw on the rack. I was going to look at the label, try it on. This time I was going to *shop*.

Dr. Popkin's office was on East Seventy-second Street and he was about thirty-five, dressed in a sports shirt and slacks. That was refreshing. Dr. Allen and Dr. Robertson had always worn jackets and staid ties. It was a cheerful office. It had a few plants, lots of books and the required medical degrees hanging on the wall. He asked me to sit on a chair in front of his desk, and I proceeded to give him an expanded version of the recent trials and tribulations of Barbara Gordon. I think I did it in twenty minutes.

Dr. Popkin listened intently and then turned away to stare out his window. "I am both saddened and excited by you," he said finally, with a note of solemnity.

He was saddened and excited!

"I'm very ambivalent about what happened to you," he continued, "but I feel sad, sad and excited all at once." He paused. Was he waiting for me to interpret *his* feelings?

"Why are you sad?" I said. "I don't want pity. I don't want your pity."

"It's not pity," Dr. Popkin said. And then before I knew it, I had lost the ball and we were embarked on a thirty-minute analytic discussion of why Dr. Popkin felt sad. I mentally crossed him off my list. I couldn't afford either financially or emotionally to help Dr. Popkin with his problem.

I was gathering my things at the end of the hour when he said, "Wouldn't you like a prescription for some tranquilizers?" That did it. They're crazy, these drug-pushing shrinks. I must get out of here. "I'll continue taking the Sinequan they gave me in the hospital," I said. "Thank you, no more pills."

"A little Librium, perhaps? And what about an appointment for a consultation in a few days? You really should see someone regularly and be on heavier medication after all you've been through."

"I'll call you," I lied. "Right now I must run and meet my mother for dinner."

"Your mother—you didn't mention your mother." He was grasping at straws now, trying to inveigle me into his psychiatric net.

"I must go," I said, and hurried out to the elevator.

One down and four to go, I thought in the cab as I headed back to the apartment. I started to laugh. Who could I tell about Dr. Popkin's sadness? There was no one, no one to share that with, no one to share anything. And now *I* felt sad. Self-pity began to well up in me. I hated that, and I knew that along with everything else, I was going to have to fight self-pity, too. But I'm afraid it got the better of me that night.

A day or so later I had lunch with my boss, Alan Newman, at the Edwardian Room of the Plaza. I walked from my apartment to the hotel, thinking, You are Barbara, you're going to see Alan, you've known him for four years, you like him, he likes you, just be yourself. But after having been in a mental hospital, I felt ashamed, embarassed. Would he be nervous about seeing me? Would he think I couldn't work again? No. I love my work. He knows I'm good at it. I can have that part of my life back. I can't have lost that, too.

When he saw me walk in, he got up from the table and I found myself running to hug him. We ordered and Alan began to fill me in on what was happening at the office. "We want you to come back now, Barb.

We've got this new consumer show, and Greg says you're the only one who can produce it."

I smiled at him. I had been afraid he wouldn't want me back. I knew all about the stigma of mental illness. But there it was, a job. Why wasn't I excited about it? Why didn't I tell him I'd be there tomorrow? I wanted to say yes, but instead I started to tell him about the symptoms of Valium withdrawal. I said I had come apart in a thousand pieces and I still wasn't whole. I told him about the hospital. I wanted my friends to be able to talk about it. I didn't want to hide it, but I didn't want it to become *too* important. So I made jokes about my being a revolutionary, about the kitchen help, about milieu therapy.

"Well, your milieu is CBS," Alan said. "So come back next week."

"I'll let you know. Just give me a few days to make sure who I am."

"And Eric?"

"We're separated now, Alan. I can't begin to tell you all that happened between us. Someday, someday when there's distance, more time."

The waiter wheeled up a cart of beautiful desserts —strawberry tarts, éclairs, napoleons. It's all there, Barbara, I said to myself. Just take your pick. Why can't you decide? But for some reason I thought of the Swedish restaurant where my five-year affair with a married man had ended. Bill. We were both married when it began. I got a divorce and now it was his move. He had come back from Europe, after sending me telegrams promising marriage, telling me to look for an apartment. We were having what I thought was a celebratory lunch. And instead he said he couldn't leave his children. He couldn't get a divorce. I sat there staring at the huge smorgasbord carrousel in the middle of the dining room, watching it go round and round. I heard Bill's words and all I had been able to do was look at the lobster and the shrimp.

"Barbara, please say yes," Alan said. "We all need you. You're one of the best producers we ever had."

Alan's words brought me back to the Plaza. Funny, I had been thinking about Bill, not Eric. But it was all the same—loss, sadness, learning to live again. Twice, everything I wanted in life had been spread out before me. Twice it had suddenly been snatched away. "Thank you, Alan," I said with genuine gratitude. "I'll think about it. I'll probably say yes." And we left it like that. We hugged goodbye. I told him to kiss Steve and Fran and everyone and say hello to Greg. I walked back to the apartment buoyed by his words. A job, I had a job again. I'll decide tonight. I just want to be sure I don't fuck it up.

The next afternoon Eric called, finally. I had waited for it, dreaded it, anticipated it, counted on it, ever since I had been home from the hospital.

"Well, babe, I'm in my new pad. And I've got a couple of new clients. Everything is going great."

I held the receiver tightly. I wanted to hear everything.

"But I'm glad this is only for a couple of months. I miss the apartment. I miss you. How are you doing? How do you spend your time these days?"

"Busy, Eric, I'm very busy. I have lots to do. They want me back at CBS. I'm looking for a new doctor." I tried to control my voice, but I just couldn't pretend that nothing had happened between us. I had to know why. The words came pouring out of me. "You've got to see a doctor to find out why you wanted me to suffer, why you encouraged all this sickness instead of helping me. Please, Eric. I've got to know why."

Breathing rapidly, trembling, I waited for him to answer me.

"I told you I went to one," he said. "I have no intention of spending the rest of my life talking to shrinks, even if you do. Besides, I'm well. You're the sick one. And now I suppose you're spreading it all over town that I destroyed your life. Well, I've got news for you, babe. Your friends know different. You're a sick, manipulative bitch, and you destroyed my life just like you destroy everyone. But don't get me wrong. I still love you."

I hung up. He was starting all over again. I hate you, I love you, you're sick. I couldn't stand it. I walked around the apartment, looking at the paintings, watering the plants, trying to make my brain concentrate on something, but I was unable to deal with all the conflicting emotions I felt. I decided I had to call Edie. I had to talk to someone. She was at home. I told her how agitated I was. And then when she heard about Eric's call, she wanted to come see me. There was something important she had to say.

When she walked in the door she looked almost pensive, not at all the self-assured lady I had seen a few days before.

"Don't lose the strength you've just gained," she began, "but I suppose I'd better tell you. You're going to wonder and eventually you'll find out yourself. No one understands Eric."

What was she talking about? I wondered. I went into the kitchen and poured us both large glasses of grapefruit juice. Then the two of us sat on the couch and I waited, waited for my friend to tell me what was so urgent.

"While you were in the hospital, Eric did some outrageous things." She paused, wanting to be sure I knew nothing of what she was about to say. "I've been getting some really crazy phone calls. Sue called and told me that Eric said she was a lesbian."

"Oh, Edie, stop it. That's ridiculous."

She looked at me solemnly. "He did, Barbara. He told Sue you said she was a lesbian and that she had made a pass at you."

"Edie, that's preposterous. Sue's not a lesbian, and even if she were . . . Oh, Edie, I don't believe it. That's nonsense!"

"It didn't end there. He went to Lynn's office and told her that Irv was being unfaithful to her. He said you had known about it for months and it was time she knew. He said he wanted her to hear it from him."

"But that's not true!"

I sat there dumfounded, speechless, as she went on, telling me things Eric had told other friends, things he said had come from me. Some of the stories had a grain of truth, stories I had told him in moments of intimacy, that he had transposed into vicious gossip. But most of them were lies, total lies. My brain was racing, trying to figure out why he would do something so terrible. "Edie, why? Why did he do this?"

"Jonathan and I have talked about it. It doesn't make sense, but we think he's trying to undercut your friendships so you'll have to go back to him, so you'll have no one to lean on for support. So you will need him after all. It must be part of some crazy plan, Barbara. And by telling these terrible stories, he's also protecting himself. He probably thinks that when you tell anyone the truth about what happened, about him, they won't believe you."

I was numb with disbelief. "Edie, please tell me you're making this up."

She shook her head sadly. "No, Barbara, I wish I were. People have been phoning me. He's done terrible things. I wanted to protect you at first. I didn't think you could handle knowing this now. But it explains why some people don't want to see you. They're confused, hurt and angry, and they don't know what to believe. Remember they liked Eric, too. And they haven't seen the dark side of him. They almost believe him."

Yes, I could see his crazy logic now. Destroy my friendships so I would have no one to turn to but him. All in the name of love. How can you destroy someone you love? But it had to be true. "Oh, God, Edie," I said.

The phone rang and I answered it woodenly. It was Eric. He sounded like the old Eric, sweet and tender. "How are you, babe? Just checking in. How's it going? Back to work yet?"

I listened to his voice, thinking of what he had told my parents, of all the things he said to my friends. And something inside me broke in two. I listened, hoping his words would confirm what Edie had said. But he was making small ordinary talk. What will your next show be about? Why don't we have dinner with your mother before she goes back to Miami? Hurry and find a good doctor so we can get back together again. I trembled as I listened. I was in the bedroom and I remembered myself lying there on the floor, a prisoner in my own apartment, and now Eric was asking me if I wanted to play tennis. I hung up.

I went back to the living room and Edie and I sat silently, unable to say a word. It was over. Whatever had happened, I knew at that moment it was over. Whatever magic we had had, it had ended. There was no respect, no tenderness, no sanity; there was nothing on which we could build a life. He hated me too much. Yet I still felt numb, unable to hate him. I only felt shock and wonder that he didn't even know how much he hated me.

I could tell that Edie knew what I was thinking. It was over, Eric and me. I nodded and her clear blue eyes suddenly filled with tears. We held each other, watching the late afternoon sun pour through the living room windows. "I will forget him," I said. "It wasn't all my fault. I know that now. But I've got to find out what happened to me. I've got to find a good doctor and get some proper medication. If I can't have my old life back, then dammit, I've got to start making a new one."

I continued the great shrink hunt for the next few days and I met one psychiatrist who told me that if I gave him a check for ten thousand dollars, I could join a privileged group of patients. He had assembled a number of former drug-takers and alcoholics who had all worked in "the arts" and he thought I would be a very valuable addition to the group. During our consultation he showed me how the therapy worked. "Touch the wall, Barbara," he said.

I touched the wall.

"Thank you, Barbara, for touching the wall." Then he walked closer to me. "Touch the lamp, Barbara." I touched the lamp. "Thank you, Barbara, for touching the lamp."

And so it went for fifty minutes, and I realized I was talking to a lunatic. He pressed me for the ten thousand dollars at the end of the session—a certified check, at that—and I went flying out of that office, too.

These guys are beginning to make Dr. Allen look like Erich Fromm, I thought. Have faith, Barbara, you're in the medical capital of the United States. But what I needed was a Michelin guide to Manhattan shrinks. Why couldn't somebody figure out a system of stars and little symbols for the quality of the service, the comfort of the waiting room, the adequacy of the bathroom facilities? If only I had felt stronger, I might have enjoyed all this craziness.

I went right down Dr. Robertson's list, and although I felt that one or two of his recommendations were themselves candidates for Tyson Cottage, I finally settled on Dr. Tom Rosen. He was young, energetic, smart, and he wore jeans. I had opted, I suppose, for the anti-establishment route. But he was associated with a good hospital and during our first two consultations he hadn't displayed any neurosis that was very apparent. He seemed genuinely confident that he could help me, but said I would need different medication. He recommended lithium, a salt that was used in the treatment of manic depression. "Am I a manic-depressive?" I asked. "No," Dr. Rosen said, "but it's useful in cases like yours." Maybe one day, I thought, somebody will give me a pill for a disease I really have.

My mother returned to Florida, knowing I was settled back in the apartment and seeing a good doctor. The relief on her face was touchingly visible the evening I told her I was certain now that a reconciliation with Eric was impossible. "Well, don't you worry," she said with a bright smile. "We'll find some nice man for you to marry yet."

He called one afternoon just after she left. I braced myself for the usual diatribe. But no; this time he was gentle Eric. He was leaving for Boston. He would be taking the Massachusetts bar exam. He told me he had a friend from law school who had a practice in South Boston. "It's the opportunity of a lifetime, babe. I've had it with New York. It's a bureaucratic nightmare. I can really help people up there."

Is he lying again? I wondered. And if he's telling the truth, why has he decided to leave so suddenly? He had never once referred to the stories he told my friends. But I had seen or spoken on the phone to most of them, and they were rallying around me. Maybe he had finally accepted the fact that we were finished.

He wanted to come to the apartment to pick up the things he had left when he moved out. "No," I said. "I'll pack up everything and leave it downstairs with the doorman." I was frightened to be in the apartment alone with him. Just the thought of being close to him again sent a chill right through me.

"Okay, babe," he said. "We'll do it your way."

The next afternoon the phone rang. It was Eric again. "Listen," he said, "I've been checking up on you. You were in hospitals before. You went crazy before. I called Stan. You were sick when you were married to him. He had to take you to a hospital, too. And I called your friend Bob, your old film editor. He told me you freaked out right on the job. So listen, honey, you've been in Chattahoochie before. You're one sick lady. Ask Stan, ask Bob. And I found out you left NBC to go to a hospital, and not because of your old boyfriend Bill. I checked with him, too."

I swallowed hard, trying to keep my composure. I couldn't believe it. He was talking fast, earnestly, in that strange robot speech. "You've been crazy before," he said. "You've been sick all your life. All I did was love you. All I did was help you. I'm going to Boston. Your friends in New York will desert you one by one. And you'll need me, you'll want me, you'll come to me. You'll see!"

He would never stop, I thought. This was worse than being hit physically. It was more brutal, more barbaric and infinitely more destructive. I put the receiver down. *Gaslight* was still going on, and I didn't know when it would end.

I began to pack up his things. I felt anger and sadness, and a terrible anxiety, as I pulled his books and records from the shelves. I was taking his clothes out of the closets, when I remembered what my mother had said: "Just think, darling—with Eric gone, you'll have so much more room for your own things." And I had snapped back, "I'd rather be crowded. Don't you understand I'd rather be crowded?" I knew she was only trying to make me feel better. Still I had hated her saying that.

This is it, it is over, the nightmare is over, I thought as I packed everything in the large cardboard cartons. But for some reason I was more depressed than ever. He had fooled everyone. But how could I have loved someone who would go to such depths to hurt me? Had it always been there in him? I still had no answers to those questions. But maybe, I thought, just maybe, if he goes to Boston, I'll be able to breathe again. I'll get my life together.

I told Alan I didn't want to produce the consumer show. I said I'd rather wait and do a documentary in the fall. Why? I don't know. Compared to the films I usually made, a consumer show would have been a snap. But I was terrified to go back to work, terrified that I wouldn't be able to handle it, and I knew that if I failed on the job, it would do more to destroy my career than anything that had happened in my personal life. Had I lost the part of me that loved my work, along with everything else? I was too frightened to find out.

It was a mistake. I should have gone back and started to do something. Produce, direct, write, edit, empty wastebaskets—anything. Now my days were completely empty. I had nothing to do.

I sat on the edge of my bed after making coffee one morning. It was going to be a steamy, hot July day, the radio said, and I was shivering in an air-conditioned bedroom. Jimmy Carter and the Democrats were holding their convention at Madison Square Garden. It was only ten o'clock. I had no appointment with Dr. Rosen that day. I had nowhere to go, nowhere to be. I knew I had lived alone before Eric. I had lived without this hyperawareness, this watching and monitoring of myself, something I had to do to keep myself from disappearing. Should I meet someone for lunch? Who? Why? What would I talk about? What should I do with this day that was stretching before me? There had to have been a time in my life when I didn't work or didn't live with someone I loved, a time when I just *was*. No one could be productive and loving twenty-four hours a day. What do you do in the meantime?

I looked at the newspaper. The *Times* was filled with reports of art galleries, plays, movies, concerts—all the things I had loved before. But I didn't want to go anywhere alone. Besides, I wasn't interested. I decided to go out for a walk. I'd see people, buy some food. But when I reached the street I felt like a Martian, a creature from another planet wandering along Central Park West. "Come Meet Jimmy Carter at Fifty-second and Broadway," the placards read. Jimmy Carter? Who was he? How had it happened that he was the front runner? I had missed the primaries during my drug withdrawal. I felt so out of touch with things. I was disconnected from this political year.

I returned to the apartment, grimy from the hot summer air, and soaked in a tub while I listened to the speeches on television from Madison Square Garden. I had nothing to do until tomorrow at three, when I would go to Dr. Rosen. I lay on the bed, trying to take a nap. But I couldn't sleep. If I closed my eyes I saw scenes of the past months, the good times and the bad. I told myself, No one understands how hard this is. It's not as if Eric and I had been quarreling for months and decided to part. No, we had been in love and happy one day and then madness the next. No preparation. We were and then we weren't. There was love and then there wasn't. There was a life and now there is emptiness.

I got up and watered the plants again. They'll drown if I don't get well soon, I told myself. I listened to music. I thought of making a phone call, but there was no one I wanted to speak to, no one. I just sat there for the rest of the day, and when it grew dark I made supper, watched television and went to bed.

If there had been only one day like that, it might not have been so horrible. But day after day went by, and except for forays for food, or a trip to the psychiatrist, I lived this same empty, lonely, desperate existence. And I saw no way to change it.

On the occasional nights when I had dinner with

friends, I only felt my loneliness reinforced. Dinner over, I returned to the empty apartment and they to a world of people, children, husbands, jobs. Everyone told me again and again how brave I was. But I couldn't accept their praise. I was failing; loneliness was winning, and I hated seeing myself so purposeless, so empty, so unresourceful.

"Barbara, I don't think the lithium is doing you much good," Tom Rosen said. "And since you're not responding, I'm going to have to put you on Thorazine."

I liked Tom. I trusted him. But suddenly I was terrified. I had seen the graffiti on the walls at Longview: FEEL NOTHING, BE NUMB, TAKE THORAZINE. "No," I cried. "I don't want Thorazine. I'm numb as it is."

"O.K. Maybe we'll wait a bit. But we've got to get you in touch with your feelings. What are you thinking about Eric? We must get you in touch with your anger. Here's a pillow. Talk to the pillow. Pretend it's Eric."

I was embarrassed. How could I do that? Tom was holding the pillow. He expected me to hit it, I thought, so I did. "Why did you do this? What for? I thought you loved me. I hate you. I hate you," I said hitting the pillow, but then I looked up at Tom. "I don't hate him," I said. "That's the problem. I don't hate him at all. I don't feel anything."

Tom shook his head sadly. "O.K., Barbara. We'll wait a few days to see if you're feeling better, and if not we can talk again about the Thorazine."

When the session was over, I took a cab back to the apartment. He had been recommended highly. He was a good doctor. Why wasn't it working? What was I doing wrong?

Eric never called to say goodbye. He picked up his things from the doorman, but I was not certain he had left the city until his part-time secretary, Libby, phoned one day. He had let her go and moved out of the little office in East Harlem, but he owed her back salary. It wasn't much, she said, but did I have his new address so she could write? I told her I didn't know where he was.

It was a relief to know that he was gone. Every time I left the apartment, I had been terrified that he was waiting for me in the lobby, or that we would meet on the street. I couldn't walk out of the building without nervous glances to the right and left. And now there was another item of unfinished business I could take care of—the beach house. Every weekend I had thought about going out there, but I couldn't face it—the memories, the possibility that he might be there. I even feared that he might have destroyed the place.

I called the rental agent. She would be happy to show the house. In fact, she had some people who were looking for that very thing. When she called back to announce that they loved it and wanted it for the month of August through Labor Day, there was no mention that anything was out of order. But I knew I had to get things ready, anyway clean, pack up Eric's clothes. I couldn't do it alone. I called Edie and she offered to drive out with me in my car on a weekday morning when the traffic would be light.

That morning I phoned the garage to tell them I was going to pick up the car. "It's not here," the man said, and I knew immediately what had happened. Old Sammy had gone to Boston. "Oh, yes," I said, fumbling for words. "I forgot. It's out at the beach. I guess we won't be needing our space anymore. Please send me a bill for what I owe you."

Edie shook her head. "That bastard! He knows he can't have you. Let him have the goddamn car."

I nodded. "Yes," I said. "Let him have Old Sammy." I took a train out later that morning.

As I walked into the house, I realized I had never been there alone. We had always been there together. But it was no time to think about that now. I had to clean this place and make the six-eleven train back to New York. I started sweeping, washing windows, doing laundry. I had my head inside the refrigerator, scrubbing the shelves with a sponge, when the phone rang.

No one but Edie knows I'm here, I thought, as I ran to answer it.

"I know where you are, Barbara." Eric began talking in that clipped monotone. "I always know where you are."

"Where are you calling from, Eric?" I began nervously. "What do you want?"

"I want you, and I want our life back, and I want some explanations. Why didn't you want to see me? No one would see me, none of your friends, and I want to know the reason why."

"Eric," I began softly, "don't you know why? Don't you know what you've done, to them, to me?"

"What are you talking about, Barbara? Just what have I done? All I've ever done is love you."

It was then I realized that Eric had no idea he had done anything destructive. I couldn't believe he had no guilt, no sense of self-recrimination. And I knew there was no point in arguing with him. "I can't talk now, Eric. I have a train to catch. And please, if you do love me, leave me alone." I hung up the phone.

I sat on the chair by the desk, still holding the wet sponge. I looked out the sparkling glass windows at the ocean, watching the soft rolling breakers splash along the shore. I blinked. I saw Eric and me making love on the deck, protected by the high dunes on each side. I saw him standing in this room on a ladder, measuring the beams in the ceiling. I remembered music, and loving, and laughter, political fights with our friends, cold beers after tennis, and brutally raw April nights when we snuggled together by the fire. "Will I always be haunted by him in this house?" I wondered aloud.

I pulled myself out of my reverie, finished cleaning the house and called a cab. I would make the six-eleven.

"I'll never lie to you," Jimmy Carter was saying. "And that," I muttered, "is your first lie, Mr. Carter." I was sitting on the bed in front of the television, with a chicken sandwich and a beer from the delicatessen. The phone rang. It was Eric, calling from Boston.

"I've found a wonderful doctor up here who special-
izes in schizophrenia." It was that same hollow voice
and I remembered his telling Jonathan over the phone
that I was an acute schizophrenic. "He's better than
Laing. He treats people with love, not pills. Why don't
you come up and see him, babe? I'll meet you, and you
don't have to tell anyone you're seeing me if you're
embarrassed. Remember no one knows you like I do."

I hung up without saying a word and walked into
the dark living room. I lit a cigarette, inhaled deeply
and sat smoking in the darkness, in the cold dark air,
the only sound that of the moaning air conditioner. I
closed my eyes and began to cry. I cried and cried for
the loss of love, the loss of me. Tomorrow it will be
better. I've got to make it better. But in order to have
anything, I must have me. Who am I? Where am I?
Dear Lord, help me find me.

The phone rang again. I thought it was Eric, so I let
it ring, hoping my service would pick it up eventually
and I wouldn't have to listen to that awful voice. But
the service didn't pick up, so I answered, trembling. It
was my mother.

"Is that you, darling?" she said. "Are you all right?
I've been ringing and ringing."

"I just walked in the door," I said.

"Lou, Lou, I've got Barbara on the phone. Pick up
the extension. How are things, darling? How are you?"

"Fine, Mom. Things are terrific. Just had dinner
with Edie and Jonathan, who introduced me to a man
who is divine. I'll be going back to work soon and Dr.
Rosen says I'm doing beautifully."

I don't know if she believed me or not. I didn't
know how to explain that my life was still in pieces,
that the feeling of not having me was ruining everything. She had been brave, supportive and wonderful,
and I didn't want to alarm her.

"Hiya, baby." It was my father. "What do you say
you come to Europe with us, get away from New York
for a while?"

I knew they had postponed their vacation because of
me. I didn't want to go to Europe, but I urged them to

go. "Really, there's nothing you can do for me," I said. "I have to live my own life, Mom. There's no reason why you shouldn't go."

My father sounded relieved. My mother still wasn't sure. "Are you certain you'll be all right?" she asked nervously.

"Yes, and I'll write. Don't worry."

I felt an enormous sense of relief when we hung up. They would go away, vacation in their usual haunts in Capri and the south of France. I will not be responsible for ruining their summer. Not that, too.

"You are a schizophrenic, Barbara, but many people recover and have wonderful lives. You can beat the illness. It isn't hopeless, not anymore."

Tom had said the dreaded word schizophrenic. I had been badgering him for a diagnosis for weeks and now he had made it.

"Introduce me to one person who has been depersonalized and recovered," I said. "Introduce me, Tom, to one person who's beaten this horror and I'll feel better."

"I can't do that ethically, Barbara. But I know people who were more ill than you. They beat it. And Thorazine will help control the psychosis."

"Not yet, Tom, not yet. I don't feel psychotic and I don't want Thorazine. I'm thinking of going back to work in September. I've got to get out of the apartment. I'm living like a recluse."

When I left his office, I ran to a bookshop near my apartment and bought every book I could find on schizophrenia. I read Laing, and Freud, and Perls, everyone. No one said it was hopeless. Everyone agreed it was treatable. But no one agreed on a course of treatment.

I am schizophrenic. Eric was right. How do you become schizophrenic at forty years old? Had the Valium controlled it all those years? Is that why the symptoms occurred only after I stopped taking the pills? I read and reread the pages of the books—looking for proof that it was hopeless, looking for an excuse to die.

The summer was going by. In July I never went back to the beach house. I stayed in the dark cool bedroom of my apartment rather than go anywhere. The symptoms of numbness increased. I began to experience wild thoughts. Animals, people falling, voices screaming and crying. I was afraid to go to sleep because the moment I closed my eyes the horror movies in my head began. I saw pictures, fragments of faces, an eye looking at me, a shrieking mouth, a relative, a friend, a doll I once owned. Stories about people I didn't know spun through my brain and I felt I couldn't control my own mind. I had thoughts about lizards and toads, monkeys and elephants. I didn't know where I was. I wanted to do nothing, wanted to see no one. I lived on Coca-Cola and sandwiches, eating alone in my bedroom. Like a small, furry animal, I stayed crouched in the cool darkness, preferring that to the strain of being with other people. I went out only to see Dr. Rosen. He was still trying to get me to express my rage at Eric. He made me feel guilty because I couldn't experience my own anger. "What's wrong with you, Barbara," he said one afternoon, "that you can't hate him? He was terrible, hateful to you."

"I loved him before he was hateful," I answered. "Don't you understand? Love doesn't die so quickly."

I stopped reading the newspapers, stopped watching television. I could not think. I knew I was giving in to madness, but if I was mad, I was mad. If I was hopeless, I was hopeless. I would live it out. I grew more despondent every day. Edie and many of my other friends called often, urging me to go to the beach, meet them for dinner or play tennis. No, I wanted to see no one.

August came, my house was rented and now I had a perfect excuse to live like a frightened animal, hidden in the darkness of my room. Jonathan and Edie, who had been my lifeline to the world, were off on their trip to Israel. Then Eric's letters started arriving from Boston, letters in which he wrote: "You've always been sick. Everyone's always known that, but I love you. You are a schizophrenic, but if you come see me in

Boston, my love can make you well. Who knows you better than I?" I trembled. How could I muster the strength to fight the sickness in myself as well as whatever was consuming him?

My therapy was definitely not going well. Dr. Rosen told me if I continued to be this depressed, I would have to go to a hospital. "No," I said, "there will be no more hospitals."

"Then, Barbara, I want you to start taking a small dose of the Thorazine. You won't mind it, really, and it *will* help you."

"Are you sure it won't make me more numb?"

"I'm sure."

"But I thought it was an anti-psychotic medication. I'm not psychotic now. I know it."

"It will help you, or else I wouldn't suggest it."

I walked out of his office with a prescription in my hand. I was deeply depressed. Thorazine, the end-of-the-road medication, the when-all-else-fails drug I had read about in the books. And Tom Rosen wanted me to take it.

I walked into a drugstore to have the prescription filled. I was embarrassed as I handed it to the pharmacist. A zillion films on understanding mental illness, on this being the age of enlightenment and generosity of spirit toward mental patients, even a chorus of angels on high telling me there was no shame, couldn't have erased the sense of humiliation I felt about having a prescription for Thorazine. Why didn't you feel that way about Valium? I asked myself. I had to admit I'd often winced when I ran into drugstores to have that prescription filled. I had never liked the idea of *needing* anything. But this was worse.

The pharmacist didn't bat an eye. He didn't even look up at me. Still I darted out of the store and fled back to the apartment. I took the pill, a small, round, white capsule, and within thirty minutes I had fallen into a stupor on the bed. I felt as if I were in a coma. When I woke up my tongue was so thick I couldn't talk, and the sense of unreality was worse than ever. All right, lady, you'll keep taking them anyway. Dr.

Rosen is a good doctor and he says they will help you. Desperate, I promised myself I would give Thorazine a try. A few days and maybe the side effects would disappear.

Labor Day was approaching and I would have to see Alan about making a film. He had assured me his budgets for new films would be coming through soon. My dear old friends Barry and Lisa Travis had invited me to their house in Princeton for the weekend. We would play poker, a twenty-year-old tradition that had withstood abortions, divorces, career changes, and now mental illness. Barry and Lisa were one word—BarryandLisa. They were an advertisement for marriage. They had been the first of my friends to leave the city for the suburban life. And although their politics had grown conservative through the years, we could good-naturedly kid each other about that. I could call them fascists and they called me a commie and it always turned out all right. They had known, and liked, Eric, and they knew what I was going through. Lisa had been calling all summer, urging me to come out for a weekend, any weekend. And so I finally consented.

I drove to New Jersey with my friend Paula Sondheim and her husband, Mark. Paula was sexy, exuberant, filled with whimsy. She was crazy like a fox. Mark had left his wife and family to marry her. Now they had a family of their own. Together they had made a new life, and after ten years, they were still as happy as the day they were married.

The weekend was a disaster. I felt less real than usual, and I attributed it to the Thorazine. I couldn't follow the conversation; it was too fast for me. I felt dumb, slow-witted. I kept pinching myself, telling myself I had eyes and could see, therefore I had to be. Playing poker was impossible. I just sat there frozen, immobile, unable to participate. I couldn't follow the cards, didn't know when to bet. I folded winning hands. I was frightened and embarrassed. I knew everyone could see that I wasn't there, but no one said anything. Finally I went up to the guest room, collapsed on the bed and began to cry. I tried to still my sobs, so no one would hear me. I was sure I was losing my mind.

When I got back to New York, I knew I couldn't handle it anymore. Jonathan and Edie were back from Israel and we were to meet for dinner the following night. Something had to be done. We would decide at dinner.

I walked into the restaurant Edie had selected, a small and cheerful health food place not far from my apartment. I was nervous. I hadn't seen them since their return, but I had spoken to Edie over the phone and I knew she and Jonathan had been talking about the gravity of my situation. I tried to be nonchalant, but the moment I saw them, tears filled my eyes. They were my dear friends. I had had a disastrous summer and had missed them so while they were gone. The month of August was lost to me. I had lived like a mole and seeing Edie and Jonathan reminded me of sunlight and fresh air and health.

After hugs and kisses, Jonathan looked at me for a long time and then as gently as he could he said, "What the hell is going on with you and Dr. Rosen, Barbara? Why aren't you feeling better yet?"

"Oh, Jonathan, he put me on Thorazine, and I feel more numb than I did before."

"That's what you told me over the phone," Edie said. "Why Thorazine?"

I said that I felt split, my thoughts separate from my emotions, my love from my hate, me from me. I felt subhuman. "Tom says I'm schizophrenic and Thorazine can help all that."

"Is it helping, Barbara?"

"No, it isn't. Not at all. Oh, Edie, what a burden I've been to everyone this summer."

"You were never a burden. Stop that, Barbara," Jonathan snapped. And then Edie launched into the subject at hand. "I have a friend, Barbara. His name is Leon Roth. He's one of the best analysts in New York. I called him up after we spoke on the phone. I told him you said Rosen thinks you're schizophrenic. He disagrees and he thinks Thorazine is all wrong for you. He wants you to see a man named Kurt Bernstadt."

"Edie," I said, "I can't bear the thought of another psychiatrist."

"But Barbara, this man is world-famous. Please give him a try. Roth says he's wonderful." Edie was talking fast now, pressing me. "At least go for a consultation. Usually it takes months to see him, but with Leon's help, I know you can get in soon."

I nodded. I would go. They looked at me gratefully, but I knew I was the one who should be grateful. They were trying to help me save my life. When, I wondered, would we be just friends again? When could we meet without thinking or talking about that night, about Eric, about Barbara the Sick? And when could I give to them? I wanted to be well.

They walked me home in the soft September night, sharing my burden, trying to solve the riddle of my existence. I would call Kurt Bernstadt in the morning, I promised. Maybe he had a miracle up his sleeve.

Columbia Presbyterian is a huge, sprawling hospital complex located in the northwestern corner of Manhattan island. The cab sped up the West Side Highway. Looking out at the gray mist caressing the Hudson, I remembered driving up that highway with Eric, crossing the George Washington Bridge, to spend the weekend with friends in New Jersey. I was a walking free-association machine. Everything reminded me of something in my past: the light, the pattern of the clouds, the reflected sunlight, the scent of rain. My brain, as if on cue, transported me to another time, another place, another memory of years long past. Although I had read about that experience in Proust, now I treated it only as pathology. I couldn't function in the present when my mind was so crowded with the shadows of the past.

Dr. Kurt Bernstadt had a tender smile and warm eyes. "Consultations last ninety minutes," he said. "I suggest we meet three times and then I'll give you my recommendation. But I'm afraid I'm too busy to take on any new patients at this time. Now tell me, what can I do for you? What happened to you?"

I was disappointed. As often as I had said I wouldn't know what I'd do with yet another psychiatrist, I liked this kindly man and believed he could help me. How could I begin to tell him the story, my gothic nightmare, and then walk out knowing he wouldn't be my doctor? And shall I tell him the long or short version?

"I took Valium, I went off Valium and then terrible things happened." That's how I began and soon I had told him everything about Eric, about Chatahoochie, about Longview, about Thorazine, and now about how desperate and hopeless I felt.

After we discussed my situation for a while, he said solemnly, "Barbara, you need help. I think you must go to a hospital."

"I can't go to a hospital," I said. "I've been talking to my boss about going back to CBS. I've even picked a subject for my next show." Despite the despair of the last month, I had been thinking about doing a film on a small Long Island town that was, I thought, flirting with fascism. The town leaders were banning certain books in the high schools. Kurt Vonnegut and Philip Roth books had been impounded. "Work will make me better, Dr. Bernstadt. I know it. I want to do this film. It's important."

"Barbara"—and he was speaking firmly now—"I don't think you should be on Thorazine, nor do I think you are schizophrenic. But you are still suffering from the aftereffects of Valium withdrawal. I think we need to find another drug for you, and it must be given to you under the strictest medical supervision, If you go back to work, you will only be embarrassed at your inability to control the illness. Since you have what seems to me are paradoxical reactions to drugs, we can find the right one for you only in a safe place."

"It's safe nowhere, Dr. Bernstadt, when you feel like this. I don't want to go to a hospital."

"I have associates in Greenwood Hospital in Connecticut. I can recommend it highly. It is a fine hospital. Think about it, please."

My heart felt heavy. That's two, I thought. One more and you're out, Barbara. I told Dr. Bernstadt I would think about it.

I walked out of his dimly lit office and found myself in a cab heading south, heading home. I wanted to weigh very carefully everything Dr. Bernstadt had said. My parents were back from Europe and my mother was due to arrive in New York today. I would go home and think and then call her. I had to speak to Alan who was expecting me back at work. Then I'd call Edie and Jonathan. I wasn't sure if I was relieved or not at the idea of a hospital. I had to think it over.

I sat in the darkness of my living room, looking out at the lights of the city. It was a muggy September evening and I realized I hadn't even turned on the air conditioner. I smoked cigarette after cigarette, trying to think about everything all at once. I wanted to die. I didn't want to go to a hospital. If I couldn't be whole, if I couldn't be well, I didn't want to live.

I thought of the bottle of sleeping pills I had saved since Dr. Rosen began giving them to me earlier in the summer. Pills. There was a pill for everything—for tranquillity, for sleep, for death. Maybe there was a miracle pill that would give me back my life? I knew now there was no miracle pill, but I admitted to myself I wanted one. Without it, I wanted to die.

It was a hard choice that night, the choice between living and dying, and it wasn't even really that. To choose to go to a hospital, one opted to survive, not to live. I knew what health had been like, although the memory was getting foggy. How could I settle for being some semifunctioning, hopeless cripple? What would a hospital do? But I knew that if I stayed in that apartment I would die. So I had no choice, because I loved life so very much—my friends, my work, my life. I didn't want to go to another mental hospital. I just wanted to be Barbara.

I went to the phone and dialed my mother's hotel.

She knew I had seen Dr. Bernstadt and she was waiting to hear from me. To live, to die, to survive—I didn't know what I was going to say to her, but the moment I heard her voice, I broke into tears and found myself saying, "I'm going to a hospital. He says I can get help in a hospital. Mama, I have no choice."

7

Gordon—
Six North

I walked down the long, antique-filled corridors on the main floor of Greenwood Hospital, amazed at the elegance—the sheer luxury of the place. A few pills, I thought, and I'll be home. I didn't know that they weren't offering pills and that I would never really want to go home.

I sat with my mother and Edie that afternoon in the admissions office on the main floor while a woman asked me to fill out forms and inquired about medical insurance. "No," I told her, "I have no medical insurance."

"Then you'll have to give us a check for five thousand dollars," she said crisply. "The cost is eighteen hundred dollars a week, and since you have no insurance and you don't qualify for Medicaid, we must have the money in advance."

No, I certainly did not qualify for Medicaid, I told myself proudly, not wanting to think of the dollars it would cost me because I didn't. I wrote out a check to Greenwood Hospital for five thousand dollars. That means I won't be here long, I thought to myself. Only three weeks. I *have* to get well soon. Staying here will be like riding in a superexpensive taxi with the meter running even when I sleep. The woman accepted the check with a smile. I had the feeling they didn't get many cash customers.

"If you'll just sit here for a few minutes, please," the

woman said, "someone will come down to take you up to the hall." She gathered her papers off the desk and left the office.

I saw the frightened look on Edie's face, saw my mother trying to be strong, both of them holding on. "It will be all right," I said, trying to force a smile. "Don't worry. It will be all right."

"Of course it will, Barbara," Edie said.

"Of course," my mother echoed softly.

A short black man walked into the room. "Are you Barbara?" he said, looking at me.

"Yes, I'm Barbara."

"I'm your social worker. We'll go up to the hall now. If your friends would like to accompany you, that'll be all right."

The three of us stood up and I reached for my suitcase and radio—all I had brought with me. "Don't bother with those," he said. "Someone will bring them up to the hall after they've been checked."

"Checked for what?" I asked curtly.

"Everything must be searched," he said firmly.

"I don't have any weapons," I snapped.

"Barbara!" my mother cried. "The man is only doing his job."

This place felt different from Longview. Something very serious was going on here, and I knew I hated it already, knew I was going to loathe every bloody moment of it.

The three of us rode up in a cavernous elevator, which stopped on the fourth floor. A private part of me didn't want my mother or Edie to be with me. Everyone kept calling it a hall, but I knew I was being taken to a ward and I didn't want them to see it. Something told me this wasn't going to be like Longview with eighteen neurotics staring into space. Something told me this was going to be worse. And it would be even more humiliating because Mother and Edie would see it, too, see that I had been reduced to living in an insane asylum. I wanted to spare both of them the pain of such a scene. But it was too late. We were led down what seemed to be an endless corridor. Not knowing where we were headed, saying nothing, the three of us followed my social worker to my new home.

Suddenly the ambience of quiet elegance took a turn for the worse. We had reached the "hall," a large, dark corridor lit by turn-of-the-century grotesqueries for lamps. The air had a foul, thick, sick smell of smoke, of urine. Fighting! Crying! There were people clutching blankets and pillows, someone muttering to himself, men and women walking around in circles going nowhere, a young man sitting with his head between his hands, rocking back and forth, a woman shrieking obscenities. Young people dressed in jeans and skirts walked by. Were they attendants or patients? I couldn't tell. It was mayhem! No antique furniture here, just secondhand Salvation Army couches and chairs worn through as if the pattern of the fabric had been erased by too many hours of pain.

I could not repress my instant hatred of the place, my belief that it was inappropriate for me. I knew intuitively that this place would make me sicker. "I can't stay here, not here. This is an asylum. *Marat/Sade* to the tenth power. I'm not that sick!" I looked over to observe my mother's face. I could see she was disturbed. Edie was biting her lip, and I knew what that meant. I tried to control my terror to protect, to reassure them.

A pretty young woman with short, dark hair walked over to greet us. "I'm Debbie, the head nurse, and your one-to-one," she said, smiling. "Will you follow me into the office, please? Your friends can wait outside."

She led me to a glass-enclosed room and I sat on a folding chair. "May I have your purse, Barbara?" Debbie said quietly. "And if you have any jewelry on, or any medication with you, please give it to me."

"I want my purse," I snapped. "It's my purse and I want it."

"We will hold your money for you," Debbie answered softly. "It's dangerous to keep it in your room. Someone can steal it. When you need money, just ask Frances, who runs the office. She will be in charge of your account, like in a bank."

Reluctantly I handed Debbie my purse, the Louis Vuitton purse my mother had brought me from Paris. It must have looked strange, a woman dressed in old jeans and a baggy sweater, carrying that expensive purse. She began to empty its contents in a large wicker basket. No, I wanted to cry out. That's mine, that's my purse, my things, my life. Don't you know what you're doing? You're stripping me of my identity, you're treating me like a convict.

"I'll take the perfume, the mirror and the tweezers for now, Barbara," Debbie said. "We'll return your things in a few days. But for now I must take all your make-up and your jewelry."

"Why?" I demanded angrily.

"You could hurt yourself with them," she said after a few seconds.

Suicide! She's thinking of suicide. And as I looked through the glass enclosure at the frenetic activity going on outside, I thought to myself, Or homicide.

"And I've taken the credit cards, too," she added, "so they'll be missing from your wallet when you get it back. But don't worry. We'll lock them up safely for you."

"What in God's name is dangerous about a Bonwit's charge card?" I asked.

"It has sharp edges," she said matter-of-factly. Then she turned to lock and label the basket: GORDON—SIX NORTH. "We'll send your clothes up in a few days, after the name tags are sewn into them," she said finally. "Here's your purse and a robe to wear tonight."

This place made Longview look like a luxury hotel.

"Now," Debbie said brightly, "I think your therapist is waiting to meet you. Why don't we join your friends and walk down the hall to meet her? Her name is Julie Addison and I think you'll like her."

Her? Her? My doctor is a her? I had never had a woman doctor. I wonder if she knows anything. Oh, Barbara, what sexist, chauvinist thinking, I chided myself. What a fraud you are.

My mother, Edie and I followed Debbie down the

hall. Strange-looking people sat on couches and chairs and stared at us as we walked by. A dark woman approached us and said, "Christ will cleanse your wounds." She was wearing a turban and had a shawl thrown dramatically over her shoulder. "Christ will save you from yourself," she said. I recoiled.

Debbie was explaining things as we walked along. "Here's the dining room," she said, pointing to a room that adjoined the hall. I was shocked. The dining room was right here, not in a different building. This was a prison! A black boy wearing a hat and a dirty green jacket came up to me and said, "Hi. You must be the new patient. Welcome to Six North." He extended his hand. "My name is Jeff. Got a cigarette?"

I fished among the few things left in my purse and gave Jeff a cigarette. I found a book of matches and offered them to him. Debbie took the matches out of my hand. Then she reached for a lighter in her pocket and lit Jeff's cigarette. Such service! They light your cigarettes! For eighteen hundred dollars a week, they should, I told myself.

"I'm sorry, Barbara," Debbie said. "I must have overlooked these. For the first forty-eight hours you can't have any matches. You will get to know all the aides and nurses, but as your one-to-one, when you have something special or important, just call me."

I wasn't listening to her. So it wasn't elegant service. Matches, fire, death, I thought. Everything on Six North was considered a possible weapon. Would Debbie as my one-to-one protect me against violence? I wondered.

We reached the end of the long, dimly lit hall and Debbie opened the door to a small, bare office. A young woman sat poised on the edge of the desk. As we filed into the room, she stood up and walked over with her hand extended. "I'm Julie Addison, Barbara."

I gave her a limp handshake and stared at her. She was tall and slender. Her long hair was jet black. Her eyes were sea blue behind large tortoise-shell glasses. She was beautiful! She's a goddam beauty queen, I thought. She doesn't even look like a doctor.

"I will be your therapist, Barbara," she said.

"Would you introduce me to your friends?" My mother gave her a forced smile; Edie was staring at her, too, I noticed.

"You are a doctor?" I said with amazement.

"I am a psychologist, Barbara," she said.

"You mean you're not even a medical doctor?" I cried. "Why, you can't even write a prescription for pills!" I heard my voice rising; I felt the color rushing to my cheeks, color filled with rage. "Mother," I practically screamed, "I've got to get out of here! This place doesn't even have doctors!"

"There is a unit doctor who prescribes medication for patients, Barbara," she said calmly. "I work closely with him. But we don't even know if medication is indicated, so we'll wait on that."

I went on railing at her for not being a bona-fide doctor, for being young, for being a woman, forgetting that my experience with men of medicine was one of the reasons I was standing there. She had become the target of all the rage, all the disappointment, all the fear I felt about being incarcerated on Six North.

She didn't say a word. She just watched me until I quieted down. Then she said, "I think it's time for your mother and Edie to leave and for us to talk, Barbara. I want to show you your room. You should meet the other patients. Really, it's time."

I was ashamed of my bratty behavior. I turned to my mother and Edie. "Don't worry," I said. "I'll be all right. I'll be all right, Mama." They nodded, saying nothing.

Dr. Addison and I walked them to the elevator. I heard her say that I would have no visitors for a while, no phone calls, and part of me felt a sense of relief. I wanted to see no one, talk to no one. Edie hugged me and started into the elevator. My mother and I held on to each other, tears squeezing out of my eyes, tears filling hers. "Barbara darling, take care, take care," she said. I saw how strong she wanted to be for me and that made my pain more intense. The elevator door closed and they were gone.

Dr. Addison led me back through the madness and chaos of the hall to the small, glass-enclosed office, where I met some of the rest of the staff—the nurses, the attendants. Everyone was in street clothes—no uniforms, no starched whites. I was introduced to a young nurse named Connie. She had long blond hair and looked like a cheerleader. "You will be on C.O. for forty-eight hours, Barbara," she said. "That means you will be under constant observation until we get to know you, even while you eat and in the bathroom. And someone will be outside your room watching while you sleep. But don't worry, it's something everybody goes through."

"Why is that necessary?" I said angrily, and I turned to Dr. Addison. But I knew the answer just by looking at her: to see if I would hurt someone, to see if I would hurt myself. My anger faded as I reminded myself that this was a mental hospital, not a resort hotel. It's the major leagues, Barbara, and you have to play by the rules. Don't start rebelling and fighting now. If you do, that will make it worse.

"Look at it this way, Barbara," Dr. Addison said. "It's company, someone to talk to." She was smiling. "I'll see you tomorrow. I must run. I'll be by in the morning and we'll talk a little." She left the office and walked down the hall toward the elevator that would take her out of Six North, out to sanity. I wanted to run after her and say, Please, take me with you. I'm not crazy. Get me out of here, please!

It was still midafternoon. I sat in the hall, with Connie standing beside my chair. I smoked cigarette after cigarette. She reached into her pocket for her lighter again and again, watching me as I watched the madness everywhere.

There was so much sheer sound: a television set flashing ancient cartoons, a phonograph blaring out the abrasive noises of the Grateful Dead—for those who would be, I told myself. Sighs, whispers, moans, cries of anguish, the screams and shouts of patients acting out their pain. I saw it all. And all the while that third eye, that monitor I had developed in the past months, was watching too, watching the madness, calculating, keeping track, observing me observing the hall. It ensured my identity, always reminding me of where I was, observant, critical, my sentinel, my savior—my nemesis.

Day became night. I know I ate dinner, but I don't remember being in the dining room. I was still in shock from the noise of the hall, the terrible human sounds mingled with the television, the jangling pay phone, and always, always the phonograph.

And then came the night sounds: twenty-five transistor radios, each spilling out horrid music from the cell-like rooms along the hall, music that drowned out the muffled whispers of the night staff that guarded our sleep. I held on to the bed, still dressed in my jeans, still wearing my scarf, lying on top of the blanket. I was afraid to sleep. I was terrified of being hit. I could feel the thickness of the violence on the hall and so I stayed awake through the night. A large black man sat in the doorway of my room, watching me. He was my protector. I was troubled when sometimes I looked up and found him dozing in his chair.

The cacophony of night noises pouring out of the rooms somehow reminded me of CBS. But then I used to love hearing the sounds of the different films being made, the sounds of work, the sounds of happiness. These were sounds of pain and anguish, accented by the low voices and the laughter of the attendants on the hall—sounds of wretchedness interrupted by anonymous mirth—and I couldn't turn them off. Then in the middle of the night I heard new noises: the voices of screaming women, shrieking like hyenas in the night: "Unlock me! Get me out! Unlock me!" The cries came from the floor below Six North. Who could those women be? Holding on to the bed, I looked out at the black man, who was smiling at me, and thought: A rolling stone gathers no moss. Remember, Barbara? You know what that means. But hard as I tried, I couldn't figure it out.

It was my second day on Six North. I was no longer on C.O. After following me around for a day, the hospital staff had decided that I was not dangerous—not to myself nor to anyone else. I was sitting on the ancient green couch outside the room where I had spent the night, waiting to see Dr. Addison for our first session. How much had Dr. Bernstadt told her? Where would I begin?

I was getting to know my fellow patients on the hall. The dark woman in the turban and the shawl said she was from Ethiopia. A nurse told me she was from Hartford, Connecticut. Lara was a young woman with an anxious, haggard look. She was married, had two children, and one day she started washing everything in her home. Her husband discovered her ironing sheets at four in the morning. She couldn't stop cleaning. "I'm a manic-depressive," she informed me, "but Dr. Addison—she's my doctor, too—is going to help me. She'll give me a pill soon called lithium. I can't talk anymore. I've got to wash my hair." And she was off to the bathroom for the third time that morning.

A young black man, Don Collins, had introduced himself at breakfast. He was twenty-five—a psychology student who worked as an aide on the hall. Aides were different from doctors or nurses; they played backgammon with you, took you for walks, got you towels, talked with you and policed the hall, refereeing the fights that I was beginning to learn were a regular occurrence on Six North. I liked Don instantly. He wore thick, steel-rimmed glasses, turtleneck sweaters, jeans and sneakers. He had a goatee, and a ring of metal keys attached to his belt jingled as he walked. Every door on the hall was locked. To leave, to go anywhere, to do anything, someone had to let you in, someone had to let you out.

While I was sitting there waiting to talk with Dr. Addison, a tall, mannish-looking blond girl of sixteen came stomping down the hall. Her name was Iris and I had already been warned about her. "She hits and bites," Lara had whispered to me. Moments of violence from nowhere. Iris was bellowing at the top of her lungs. "Goddam fucker, goddam shithouse, get me out of this place! The CIA put me in here and I want out. Someone fed me cookies while I was sleeping and made me fat. This goddam fucking shithole! Someone's making me fat with injections while I sleep!" She began to pound on the glass window of the nurses' station. Then she found a coffee mug and lifted her arm, ready to fling it through the glass. Don steppd up behind her quickly and wrested the mug from her hand.

I was horrified, but watching everyone else's reaction, I had the feeling that this was not an uncommon occurrence, that violence was an intrinsic part of life on the hall. No one had told me yet that Six North was being converted into a long-term ward for schizophrenics, that it was notorious as the most violent hall in Greenwood Hospital. That I would learn later.

At last I was summoned to the half-empty office at the end of the hall where Dr. Addison and I had first met. And so my sessions with her began. I felt numb, dead, anesthetized. That third eye still monitored my every thought, and I wanted to talk about that, about my symptoms, about Eric. But no, we had to start at the beginning. Julie Addison wanted my whole history. On that first day she asked me to talk about my parents, my childhood. I resisted, not wanting to go into all that, thinking it was irrelevant. But she persisted.

I was still too angry and frightened to concentrate on much of my external world, to make critical assessments of the people around me. I don't remember all that went on in that first session, but I do remember that Dr. Addison sat with her feet up on the desk, sipping a Diet Pepsi. She didn't smoke or take notes; she would never write one thing down in all the months we talked together. Unlike Dr. Robertson, who recorded everything, she didn't even have a pad in front of her. She just sat there, listening, asking questions every now and then. When she was particularly interested in what I was saying, she would take her feet off the desk, put both elbows on her knees, lean forward close to me, as if she wanted to shut off the world to hear me better, as if she were devouring my words. She was so beautiful. She's younger than I am, I remember thinking. She's only a psychologist. She isn't Jewish. She's from St. Louis. What can she know of my particular brand of urban angst, of Jewish neurosis? What can she know of my pain, this cool WASP beauty?

I began to tell her stories about my life in Miami Beach, where most girls of my generation grew up to be veritable Jewish princesses, safe and spoiled by their parents until they made the "right" marriage. Mindless, nonthinking, shopping, cooking, they then disappeared into the shadowy nonworld of their husbands' careers. I had never, *never* wanted that kind of life, and for years I had been viewed as the aberration in my family, the one who left town to make it on her own—the one who got away.

At first I didn't remember a great deal about my childhood—only some of the things I had mentioned cursorily to Dr. Allen through the years in what I thought was therapy. I had never liked to play house or play with dolls much. I liked *doing* things: reading, swimming, going to the movies. I couldn't remember ever dreaming of a home, a husband, babies—the things young girls were supposed to dream of. And I had always been a rebel, in school and at home. I was indignant when the teacher asked me to bow my head in prayer, furious when filling out elementary school forms that asked my religion. I was not ashamed of being Jewish; I just couldn't imagine why anyone needed to know that. So I had written "none." I was called an atheist at ten. Two years later, filling out an application for junior high school, I listed my race as "human." I was called a Communist at twelve.

I told Julie of my father who during the Depression had moved with his family from Boston to Miami; and of my mother, whose family had made the move from New York's Lower East Side. Both families had come to Florida as the new frontier. In those days Miami was still a swamp; the giant concrete hotels that today block any view of the ocean hadn't been built. It was a young, booming pioneer town, heady with the knowledge that it could become a great resort. With a little luck and a lot of hard work, there was money to be made.

My mother and my father met through mutual

friends and got married. They were both in their mid twenties. My father worked in a drugstore, my mother in a jewelry shop until I was born two years later. Not long after that my father was able to buy his own drugstore on the southern end of Miami Beach. There was a soda fountain, a pharmacy, newspapers and magazines, toys. It was a magic world for a little girl, and I can remember the sights and smells of the store as clearly as if it were yesterday. The war had just begun, existing Miami hotels had been commandeered as barracks, and the store was always crammed with soldiers. I marched with them on the way to school, carrying a toy gun and singing "Around her neck she wore a yellow ribbon." I watched them do calisthenics on the beach. They were a natural part of my life. The store was a twenty-four-hour business for my father. It seemed that he was never home. But my mother and I were seldom alone. There were grandparents, uncles, aunts, cousins, on both sides of the family. Birthdays, anniversaries, religious holidays—there was always something to celebrate, something to bring us together.

What did I remember of the years when I was an only child? Not much. But I had a vivid recollection of the night my brother, Eddie, was born. I was five years old. Sitting in the bathtub, I heard my father enter the house, slam the door and make a phone call. It was unusual for him to be home so early. He was talking to Johnny, the man who worked with him in the store, and his voice was jubilant. "It's a boy, it's a boy, thank God! It's a boy."

Years later I could still feel the twinge of childish pain I had experienced that night, the sense of loss. They were over, my years as queen bee, most darling child, most special little girl. And I must have known it instantly, sitting there in the hot soapy water, hearing my father celebrating, laughing with his friend. A few days later my mother returned from the hospital. She had retained a great deal of water during her pregnancy. It had become impossible for her to wear shoes, or to hold anything in her hand, and I'm not sure I believed she would ever come back herself, much less with a baby—my brother, a son.

"Julie," I said, pausing to light a cigarette, "I have read enough Freud to know about sibling rivalry and the Oedipal thing. I can't be that trite. I can't be that casebook, not me."

She smiled and sipped her Diet Pepsi. "Go on, Barbara," she said.

Did my life really change after Eddie was born? Was I indeed rejected? Not really. Actually, I didn't remember. Besides, what the hell did all that have to do with Eric and me?

Julie urged me to keep talking.

I did remember that my mother's father spent most of his time with my family. After Grandma's death he moved in and lived with us. Grandpa played with me every day for hours. He took me to the park. I remembered one game we used to play, sitting in the late afternoon on the screened porch looking out at the street. We tried to guess the color of the next car that would pass. I loved that game and even now I could hear Grandpa saying, "Barbara, I bet, I bet"—and he would pause to light his pipe—"I bet it will be red."

"No, Grandpa. I bet it will be white."

I remembered Grandpa vividly. Yet I didn't have one memory of my father during those years, not one. Later my mother explained to me that my father worked all day and most of the night at the store. That's why he wasn't there to play with me, talk to me. He had no time. So Grandpa was my surrogate father, friend, protector, adviser.

But soon after Eddie was born, when he was old enough to be wheeled to the park, Grandpa had a new interest—that adorable, blond, bouncing baby boy. No five-year-old girl could compete with that. Not in a family where the male child is a gift, the girl child a curse. I was never treated like a curse, but the family name would be carried on by my brother, not by me. And after all, boys are boys.

Hearing myself say that, I told Julie it was all so classic, it was a cliché.

"That's why clichés exist, Barbara," she said, laughing. "That's why truisms are true, because they happen all the time."

That was a beautiful insight. I was crazy because I was a cliché. How was I supposed to handle that? Would I ever find out what was wrong with me? How could *she* know, no matter how many stories I told her about my past? And if she insisted on hearing everything, this was going to take forever. Still, it was a beginning, and after our first session we sat in that dreary office almost every day and talked. It was not the cocktail party conversation of Dr. Allen's office, nor was Julie like Dr. Robertson, admonishing me like a naughty schoolgirl. These were painful memories. There were tears and anger, and I would leave Julie's office hungry for peace and quiet. But the sounds of the hospital were everywhere. I didn't know how to make internal silence, I was becoming so filled with the litter of the past. My mother's and father's words were infiltrating my brain: "Good girl, that's a good girl, I'll hit you, be good, help the baby, don't fall, don't fall, watch your step." These antiquities, irrelevancies from a long ago time, were transporting me to the past, destroying any experience of the present. They were the loose ends of the childish regression I had experienced in the apartment, part of the epoxy that had held me together for years. Now they fluttered around in my head like bits of confetti with a life of their own. There was no more Steve, Edie or Eric. No more me. My present was the noise of Six North, the clatter, the blare of the phonograph, the whining television, the fights around the pool table. Lonely.

So lonely. A friend once described lonely by saying that if it were a color it would be white. At first I was too busy being sick to be lonely; too wretched to miss anyone; too busy warding off the intrusive thoughts, fighting the feeling of numbness to be lonely. I didn't know that acute symptoms are the psyche's way of saying you are frightened, lonely, loveless, depressed. That's why you feel all this insanity, all this psychotic pain. You would rather make a hurricane in your head than experience one legitimate emotion—loss, fear, anger, sadness, anything.

How can you cry and not feel anything? After each session with Julie, the symptoms always returned—the numbness, the hollowness, the unreality, the terrible thoughts. I sat for hours on the couch outside my room, crying or staring into space. Some of the healthier patients were permitted to leave the hall for occupational therapy or go to the gym for recreational therapy, but I stayed there with those too sick to leave. I refused to paint or play with clay, or make potholders. No, I clung to the worn green couch backed up against the dirty green walls of a hall heavy with the smells of three generations of illness. It might be an exquisite autumn morning, the air outside filled with the smell of burning leaves, those leaves that still clung to the branches of the trees on the hospital ground carrying on a fashion show of colors that I, a city girl, had seldom seen. But I wouldn't even go outside for a walk, preferring the stench of the hall, the thickness of the sick air.

I stayed there helplessly day after day, trying to stifle and then ultimately surrendering to the giant roller-coaster waves of tears that filled my heart. If a nurse or an aide paused to glance at me, I sometimes remembered a fragment of my old self, my old dignity, and burning with shame, I would run to my room to cry alone. I wasn't sobbing about one thing, one loss, one memory, Eric. It was existential crying. I was crying for the lost me. Who was I? How could I be anything if I didn't know who I was?

This was depression, Julie told me. I had thought depression meant simply sadness. I didn't know one felt crazed, insane, dumb, dead, numb, enraged, hysterical, all at once. Depression is a killer.

My films had been about social and political oppression. Still, I was not prepared for being oppressed, for being victimized, for being in a mental hospital. I had made films unearthing scandalous conditions in places like this. What was I doing here alone, crying, acting like an infant, feeling desperate? Where was the camera crew? Steve and I could edit all this craziness into a dynamite film. The problem was I couldn't edit me out of it. I was the patient, the victim—Barbara the Sick.

I had made films on the indignities of old age; I had filmed people talking about the pain that comes with poverty, race hatred, mental illness. I had experienced that pain as much as anyone who is lucky in society can experience it. Yet now I realized that I had never experienced it wholly or even fully understood those people. I had never been one of them. In a sense my work had been a flirtation; I had buzzed around human wretchedness like a gadfly, walking in and out of nursing homes, single-room-occupancy hotels, prisons, Watts, Harlem, people's pain. I had always retreated at the end of the day to my world of good things—a good man, a good home, good food, my good life. Now, imprisoned in sickness with twenty-four other maladapted losers, I couldn't remember the old life, the old Barbara.

Was it only in Jewish families, I wondered, that children feel special, watched over by some benign, omnipotent deity, while clinging firmly to atheism? Did other people think they were protected from cancer, war, illness, even death, by some guardian angel, some all-loving authoritarian being that hovered facelessly in the clouds? And now in the middle of the biggest crisis of my life, where was my guardian angel, where was my protector? Was this happening to the Barbara who used to say, "I love my job so much that if CBS ever knew, they'd make me pay *them* to work there"?

But Julie didn't want me to talk about those things. She wanted the whole picture. She had to be able to feel that she knew Eddie, my mother and my father as well as she knew me. It was important to talk about my childhood; even though it sounded trite, she wanted to know it all. "How did you get on with your brother?" she asked one day.

We had the usual childish rivalries, I told her, and for most of my young years I viewed him with scorn and annoyance. He was in my way, interfering with my world, annoying my friends, always wanting to be included in my plans. I was older than he; I didn't want any part of him. Years later, when he was going to college, we would become friends. When he married and his wife was expecting their first baby, I flew to Miami, wanting to be there for the birth of his child, wanting to be part of his life. We grew up together, that's all. Another cliché.

"How did your brother feel about you?" Julie asked.

"He idealized me," I said. "He was proud of my mind, my accomplishments. I was his big sister."

"Were you ever punished for something you did to your brother?"

I didn't remember. "My mother was always threatening to punish me for something," I said.

"Were you a bad child?" Julie said. "What did you do that made your mother threaten you so often with punishment?"

I didn't know. All I knew was that whenever I did something wrong, even if by accident, I was terrified of being punished. It wasn't being spanked that frightened me. I was afraid that my parents would leave me alone or abandon me in a hospital.

"Did it make you angry, always having to be good, having to smile, having to perform all the time to ward off being abandoned?" Julie said as she reached for the can of Diet Pepsi.

I lit a cigarette. "I must have been furious," I said, "but I really don't remember it."

"Tell me of a bad thing you did," she asked gently, "something that deserved punishment."

"It was Thanksgiving and my mother was making fresh cranberry sauce for the first time. I was playing in the kitchen near the table where the berries were cooling in a big earthenware bowl. Oh, Julie," I interrupted myself, "this is too trite. I can't go on with this."

She urged me to continue and I told her that I remembered my mother asking me to return to a neighbor a bottle of iodine she had borrowed earlier in the day for a cut on my brother's knee. I said no, I wanted to go on playing. "Barbara, do it now!" she screamed. Petulantly, I took the bottle of iodine and stood there insolently, shaking it, playing with it, loosening the cap. Then to my dismay the bottle slipped out of my hand and fell—*plop*—right into the bowl of hot cranberries.

I was petrified. I remembered my mother telling her friends that she was going to make *fresh* cranberry sauce. I remembered how excited and proud she had been when she announced it to my father. She heard my tiny scream and looked to see what had happened. I told her, through my tears. She turned pale, then beet red with anger. Before she could speak, I flew from the house.

I spent the whole day hiding under a big car in a garage a few blocks away. My brother, who was five at the time, discovered me after hours of searching. How he knew where to find me, I never learned. He said I was going to be punished by my father when he came home from work. I told him to leave me alone. I was going to run away forever. But finally I relented and stole back into the apartment as quietly as I could.

Julie, her elbows on her knees, was leaning forward intently to hear the rest of the story. "Well, what happened? Did you get spanked?"

I couldn't remember the end. "I've never known what happened that night," I said.

Julie told me not to force it, it wasn't important.

"I really can't remember that," I said, "but I can remember the smell of the grease under the car, the color of the cranberries, the look on my mother's face, the smell of the iodine as it poured into the bowl of steaming berries."

Julie asked if I remembered other times when I had been bad.

"No," I said. "That was the worst. And it was an accident. I didn't do it on purpose."

"I believe you," she said, smiling, "I believe you. The question is did your mother?"

I didn't want to become involved with the other patients. I spoke to them only if they spoke to me. They were not real. Only my pain was real. But between sessions with Julie, I sat on the couch outside

my room watching them, taking in all the madness.
Lara's head was always wrapped in a towel. She
washed her hair at least ten times a day, and when she
wasn't doing that, she was busy dusting the battered
furniture in the hall. One day I saw her scrubbing
Scrabble tiles and Ping-Pong balls. I learned to ignore
Joe, a long-haired and bearded boy of eighteen who had
been on the hall for two years. He spent the entire day
walking around in circles that were designed to keep
the buildings and the sky in his world from falling
down. Even in the dining room, he got up between
mouthfuls and turned in circles.

Joe was harmless, but Iris was another matter.
Shrieking her obscenities, she threw and broke things
—ashtrays, billiard balls, lamps. Jeff, a fourteen-year-
old black boy, was always bumming cigarettes. The
survivor of a broken home, of the hell of the inner city,
of the gang wars of the South Bronx, he had been
committed to Greenwood. He sat in the hall all day,
strumming "Honky Tonk Women" on a bruised guitar,
or watching cartoons on television, or bothering the
nurses, or picking fights with Joe and Iris and then
retreating to a couch to strum more verses of "Honky
Tonk Women."

Roger was a paranoid schizophrenic. All the other
patients were considered "treatable"; he was the one
truly insane person on the hall. He, too, was violent,
and time and time again, Don and Debbie had to
wrestle him to the floor. What was he doing here? I
wondered. But if he was too crazy for this place,
Claudia and Kathy, two teen-age girls, seemed too
sane. They simply lived on the hall, using it like a
dormitory. They went to the hospital school every
morning carrying their books, and returned every afternoon. I couldn't understand why they were here at
all.

A young woman named Ellen was admitted a few
days after I was. A wife and mother, she weighed
eighty-four pounds and was suffering from malnutri-
tion. Anorexia nervosa. She would stand in front of a
mirror, her hands on her stomach, saying over and
over again, "I must lose weight. I must lose weight."

Her husband had committed her. As far as I could tell, I was the only one on the hall who had not been committed by a parent, a relative. And when the other patients learned that, they were amazed. Why would anyone enter this hall voluntarily?

Julie Addison was one of five therapists who worked with the twenty-five patients on Six North. In addition to them and the doctors who appeared periodically on the hall, there were psychiatric nurses who prepared the morning and nightly medication tray, art therapists, music therapists, aides, attendants. They all wore a cluster of keys attached to their waist—the easiest way, I had decided, to tell the patients from the staff —and they all went about their duties briskly, purposefully. As I watched them, I was always aware that I was doing nothing, that I was mindless, staring, vacant. Julie arrived every day early in the morning, dressed in tailored pants and a beautiful sweater, her make-up perfect, long hair shiny, carrying a Mark Cross attaché case. She would nod hello to me as I sat there on the couch outside my room, dressed in a shabby robe and slippers, holding a coffee mug, smoking a cigarette, or just gazing dully into space. I always felt embarrassed and wanted to say: I used to look good, I used to walk purposefully, I once had a briefcase filled with papers. I wasn't always empty.

But it was such an effort to do anything, even to think coherently. I decided that I had lost the power of deductive and inductive reasoning. I knew I could think associatively and that, I told myself, was childlike. Each morning I grabbed the one copy of *The New York Times* on the hall and tried to read it through. But I couldn't understand all the words and found that I couldn't remember an hour later what I had just finished reading. I dutifully did the daily crossword puzzle. I recited the multiplication tables and the capitals of the states, tested myself on the plots of books I had read, rewrote the scripts of movies I had seen—all this to try to get my brain to work again. But it was useless. I couldn't break through the stultifying fog that covered my head like a shroud.

Even in my sessions with Julie, I was numb and

unresponsive as she continued to make me rummage around in my past. I recited the bare facts. I told her that my father's business kept improving as I was growing up, and eventually he purchased a restaurant-supply company that snowballed into an enormous enterprise. We became more affluent, cars bigger, homes more comfortable, and for Eddie and me, better clothes, piano lessons, tennis lessons, all the accouterments of success—the stuff of Philip Roth novels.

But then Julie wanted to know what kind of people my parents were, how they treated each other. Like most parents treat each other, I answered glibly. I hated the times they quarreled. Not that they quarreled that much; they didn't. But I couldn't stand it when they did. They tried so hard to please each other. She with her cooking, her clothes, her make-up; but sometimes it seemed nothing was enough. And he tried, too—by making more money, being more successful. But like her, he must have sometimes felt that nothing was enough.

"And with you, was it the same way?" Julie asked.

"Yes," I said softly. "I felt pressured by both of them, and when they did quarrel, I wanted to be reassured that everything was really all right. I wanted to ask them, Do you love each other? Do you have a nice life? Do you make each other happy? Tell me of your tendernesses, of things you shared when you were young. But I never said anything. I often think they hid their tender moments from Eddie and me. And because I didn't see enough of them, I surmised there weren't any. I know my father cared for all of us somewhere deep within him, but it may have been hard for him to show it to my brother, to me, to my mother. I know he cared enormously. And, Julie, I turned out to be a sensitive, demonstrative woman. How the hell did that happen? Why didn't I become a frigid, tight-assed, unfeeling woman?"

"Because you were always your own person," she said. "Besides, there were probably tendernesses your parents shared in private that you never knew about. Like many children, you only saw the hurtful times, not enough of the loving times. Some parents are afraid to exhibit much affection to each other in front of their children. That doesn't mean there isn't any." Then she asked me again to tell her about other times, times when I was bad, bad enough to be punished.

I remembered another story. One night all our relatives came to our house to see Eddie, just back from the hospital, and to see movies my father had taken there of the circumcision. I was lying in my room, hearing the laughter and the voices of my aunts and uncles and cousins, talking and congratulating my father. I wanted to look at the movies, I wanted to see why everyone was so happy. Silently I stole out of my bedroom and sat crouched in a little ball on the floor, looking at but not really understanding the movies my father was projecting on the screen. I watched my aunts and uncles kissing my father and mother in the hospital room and saw fleeting glimpses of the new baby. Suddenly my father noticed me there. He was furious. He pulled the cord of the projector from the wall and began to spank me with it in front of my mother, my aunts, my uncles and cousins. I was humiliated. Why did he have to hit me with the cord? In front of everyone! I just wanted to see the pictures of my new brother. The nurse and my mother never let me in his room; they were afraid I would infect him with germs. I wanted to see him. But I must have done something terrible, because my father was hitting me. I cried and cried. But most of all I felt the humiliation of being punished in front of the whole family.

"He must have been embarrassed," Julie said quietly. "He must not have wanted you to see your naked baby brother."

"But, Julie, I can remember it like it happened yesterday. I told Dr. Allen about it a couple of times."

"What did he say?"

"Nothing. Something like it must have been terrible for me. But, Julie, it was worse than terrible. And those are my memories of being bad, of being punished. And I'm afraid you're right—they *are* more clear to me than memories of love, tenderness and sharing. That's terrible, isn't it?"

She wouldn't comment, she wouldn't interpret yet.

She had been urging me to talk about my childhood for so long and now at last all my memories came pouring out, all my childish fears. I told her about Chatahoochie, but I couldn't remember exactly how old I was when all that craziness began. I only remembered the words my mother used: "If you're not good, we're going to take you to Chatahoochie where the crazy people are, and leave you all alone." I would be terribly frightened. I just *had* to please her. I didn't want to be left in that terrible place. I didn't want to be like my grandmother.

My grandmother. Whenever my parents talked about my mother's mother, it was in hushed whispers. I knew something was wrong with her. I knew she was "strange," but no one ever said what was wrong. She never went anywhere, her dresses were always frayed, she never combed her hair, and my mother didn't like me to play with her. Grandpa took care of her until she died, and even then I don't think I ever told Mother how frightened I was of my grandmother. But I was.

"Perhaps your mother was frightened, too," Julie said. Then she began talking about internalizing. She told me that my mother had projected her own fears onto me, and subconsciously I had internalized those fears and her desperate apprehensions about her own life. But she had also projected her aspirations, her dreams of success, of being accomplished, of having learning. I internalized those parts of her personality, too, Julie said, but the child is not selective.

I heard her talking, heard her words. It was hard for me to concentrate on what she was saying, but suddenly I felt I was literally exploding with rage. So I had internalized my mother's dreams and ambitions as well as her neuroses and her fears—the good parts and the bad. We all do. And my young psyche, unable to distinguish, ate it all up and digested it. I had thought that it was all me. Ten years in therapy with Dr. Allen had never helped me understand that.

"What did you two talk about?" Julie asked, frowning as she stood up and gathered her papers.

I didn't remember, I didn't remember.

The session was over and I left her office and

walked back to the hall filled with memories of Eddie, my parents, my grandmother. I could see the color of the light in my bedroom when I was five; I could hear the ticking of an old clock that had been in the living room when I was a child. It was terrifying to have so much of my childhood so accessible, sense memories and all.

I went back to my room and lay down on the bed, trying to stem the rage I felt toward my parents. Why hadn't *they* been healthier, why had they projected *their* neuroses onto me, an unknowing child, trying to grapple with the complexities of the world myself? It wasn't fair, it wasn't damn fair. How could anyone survive such threats, such cruelty? I knew it hadn't been done intentionally; still, it had affected me profoundly. I vowed that I would never see them again. I couldn't risk any more of their craziness being laid at my door. I was up to my waist in neuroses of my own.

Just at that moment Don came to my room with a message that my parents had called. He was aware of what Julie and I were discussing, so when he looked at me knowingly, I crumpled the message in my hand and threw it on the floor. "It's hard to face all this stuff," he said gently. "Want to play some backgammon?"

I shook my head. I wanted to be alone with my anger, alone with my disappointment. For forty years I had carried around this baggage, as Julie called it, and the hollowness I now felt she described as a new self, a self devoid of the excess baggage of the past, a self that needed new experiences to replace all those old fears. She was talking about psychic things, yet the emptiness was physical to me. I felt so light—not carefree light, but frail—that the wind, the slightest will-o'-the-wisp breeze, would blow me down. And rage toward my parents was a burning fire in my head. I decided that night, despite how much they loved me or as much as I had loved them, it was over. If I had to move to Europe or California, it was over; I had to be free of them. Maybe it was too late but it was all their fault. It was because of *them* that I married Stan, fell in love with Bill and Eric, stayed with a therapist like

Dr. Allen, who hadn't helped me. All I had inherited were emotional problems.

With that realization, suddenly I felt better. It wasn't Eric, it wasn't me, it was them, them, them. I looked at the crumpled message on the floor, looked at the pictures of my parents and my brother in my room, and thought that Eddie had escaped a lot of this shit. I, as the first, the eldest, had received the brunt of their apprehensions. By the time Eddie was born, I had already absorbed most of it, and I hated him for that, for having survived, for having a wife and three beautiful children, for being happy. It was his fault, too.

God knows, it wasn't *my* fault. After all, if I was such a hotbed of neurosis, why did I have so many good friends? Why was Edie hanging in there with me, bombarding me with caring and affection? I thought of all the people I had ever known and loved. Their faces flickered ghostlike past me, and surreal, as if I had a Moviola in my head and Steve and I were editing the rushes of my life. Let's see, we'll get rid of Stan and Eric, put Mother closer to Father, Eddie here, Barbara there. See, Steve, it works, it works. I knew we could make it work.

But then I opened my eyes and there was no Steve, no film, no family, no friends. I was in the goddam hospital alone, and I had to be the camera, the splicing machine, the tape, the film. I had to find a way to put the pictures together all by myself. I yearned for Steve's knowledge, his sensitivity and good taste. Together we could do it. We had done it with Jeanie, and the film was a great success. But remember Jeanie died. This time the woman has to live, and you're on your own, Barbara, just the way you always wanted to be. The trouble was I hadn't planned on doing a solo act in my forties. It had always been my fear, but not my plan, never.

So I was in Chatahoochie after all. Maybe it wasn't exactly the place my mother had threatened me with, but metaphorically I was there, a bad little girl being punished. And in the back of my mind there was a part of me that was willing to forget the pills had helped send me here, part of me wanted to take all the blame. And so I thought, How appropriate. You have feared this all your life. You have dreaded hospitals and illnesses for years, and now you've got it all—self-fulfilling prophecy. You're in the big time now, baby, the big time.

8

A Workable Truce

The hospital's reality soon became my only reality. I was at the mercy of my sickness. Turning in and away from the world I had known, not answering letters, not returning phone calls, I was safe in the womb, being taken care of, feeling mad. In a matter of days my new sick friends on the hall seemed more real to me than people I had known intimately for years.

The only part of the day that mattered was talking to Julie. And in my pain and frustration, I saved up all my anger for her. She became the target for the rage I felt about being in the hospital, my rage against my parents, my rage about everything. As days went by and the pain in my head increased, I cried out to her, "There is no end to worst in this illness. Each day is the worst. It's a living death. Please help me." I called her names and attacked her professionalism when she wouldn't give me the medication I demanded. "Dr. Bernstadt said I *need* medication." I railed at her like a spoiled child. "That's the only reason I'm in this loony bin—to find the right medication. I'm not crazy. I'm *not!* For God's sake, give me a pill. Something! Take my money, take my beach house, take anything I've got. If you were a doctor you would end my suffering, please!" But she always refused, telling me again and again that to have a lasting recovery, I had to take nothing. Pills couldn't bring back my life. Only I could do that. It was my best chance.

I told her I'd fake it. If she wouldn't help me, I'd fake being well to get out of this hellhole. Then she said, without batting an eye, that she would take me to court. She meant she would have me committed, and she knew that I knew she could do it. Most voluntary patients, as I was, don't know that mental hospitals can claim the prerogative of committing a patient if he acts "against medical advice." "AMA" means something very special in a mental hospital, and I had seen how it worked when I filmed my documentary on the abuses of the psychiatric profession. You don't decide when you're ready to leave a mental hospital. The doctors do, and if they decide to keep you for "your own good," then being a voluntary patient doesn't mean a thing. While I was in the hospital, I never met one patient who claimed before a judge he was being detained against his will and won. And Julie used that threat of commitment against me. I hated her for it.

"You're a doctor, Julie. You're supposed to be a doctor who helps people," I said to her one day. "Aren't you ashamed that you haven't helped me, that you won't give me something? I hate you. I hate you. You have no humanity. You don't help people. You cause pain."

But she just sat there calmly. Finally she said, "I am trying to help you, Barbara. I'm trying to stop this self-destruction. If you destroy me—and you won't— you will destroy yourself. I represent your world, everyone who ever loved you, everyone you ever loved."

"You represent *no one!*" I cried. "I'm not projecting other people onto you. It's *you* I hate!"

I ran out of her office to my room and slammed the door. There was no lock, but I knew if I slammed it hard, that would keep her out. It was Friday. I wouldn't see her again until Monday. And as the weekend went by and I sat numbly watching all the sickness on the hall, seeing the violence, hearing the clamor of the phonograph and the television, I thought only of Julie. I had wounded her and, worse, I had meant it. She *was* trying to help me save my life and I had attacked her. I was filled with guilt. I asked the nurses on duty that weekend to try to reach Julie at home. I wanted to apologize. I was so ashamed. No, they told me. It wasn't urgent. It had to wait until Monday.

On Monday I sat in her office, unable to look her in the eyes. "Want some Diet Pepsi, Barbara?" she asked as she sat back in her chair and put her legs up on the desk as she always did.

"I'm sorry, Julie, so sorry."

"I believe you, Barbara. But don't you think that your attempt to destroy me is a necessary part of the process? I would have been worried if you hadn't tried."

"Why is it necessary? Why? I hurt you and I meant to, wanted to."

"I know. And if you persist in the battle, it will be a Pyrrhic victory. You will lose everything. I'm not your enemy, Barbara. There is a part of you that tries to destroy your own happiness. That's what you showed me on Friday. It's strong of you to let me, let us both, see that terrible destructive side."

When our time was up, she extended her hand, appraised me coolly and then said softly, "Same time tomorrow, Barbara." Then she was gone and I was sitting in the chair, looking at her desk, staring at the begonia on her window sill. I was entrusting my life to this twenty-eight-year-old woman who looked like a fashion model and said that there was a part of me that wanted to destroy myself. I remembered her words: "You will try again to destroy me, Barbara. You will keep trying to destroy yourself. But I won't let you do it. I'm very strong. I can take it."

So we went back again to my childhood and I began to scrutinize my personal life the way I would research a film. I had never done that before. I had shoved so many things aside, put on blinders to things I didn't want to see. My own innate repressive mechanism, Julie explained, combined with the insidious repressive functioning of Valium had made me worse than Scarlett O'Hara. I'll think about it tomorrow. The trouble was I never did. Removing the Valium had blown the lid off my brain and everything came spilling out like Pandora's box.

"But dammit," I said to Julie, "that's the way Dr. Allen told me to do it. He insisted on it. And that man is *your* colleague."

Julie shook that off with embarrassment, telling me it would be unethical to comment. But finally she said, "I think he was wrong."

Letters from my friends poured in, offering love, hope, laughter. There was always something from Edie: a note, a card, a clipping. Lisa wrote twice a week, every week, about the mundane things that filled her world: Barry's business, her daughter's braces, the League of Women Voters. She had the strength to understand that I needed continuity, even if it was *her* flow of life. I needed to know the world was going on so that I could be part of it when I returned. My zany friend Paula sent me a letter I still cherish. "Don't get too normal, Barbara," she wrote. "We loved you the way you were."

Some friends didn't write, couldn't write, perhaps because my sickness, my being in a mental hospital, threatened their sense of themselves, quickened the fear that if it had happened to me, it could happen to anyone. Too close. I understood. This was not a broken leg or a malignant cyst. It was a malignancy of the spirit, and although they couldn't know that the terror of death in life is worse than dying, they may have thought my disease was terminal. I thought so myself, and you don't send a funny get-well card to a friend who is going to die. There are very few people who know what to say to someone who is "mad." Best advice: send a plant and a hug.

I clutched at the letters and cards I did receive. I read them over and over again, and sometimes they made me sad. They reminded me of a Barbara I wasn't anymore, reminded me of love and happiness and doing. But I also used them as an affirmation of my being. "I must be Barbara," I said to myself. "Mother called, Edie sent a card, Lisa wrote." But I still couldn't speak to anyone on the phone, couldn't write back. To respond would mean that I understood what had happened to my life, and I still didn't have a clue to how to put it back together.

Besides, how could I care about their lives? I was too sick to care about anything. But the guilt I felt about not caring for the first time in my life was enormous. That guilt was one more nail in the coffin of my mind, and to me my apathy was as pathological as Joe walking in circles or Lara washing her hair. I remembered caring intensely about so many things. Now I didn't care about anything and I hated myself for it.

"Tell me more about your father, Barbara," Julie said.

He started to work when he was twelve years old, I told her. He lied about his age and got a job as a truckdriver. He never graduated from high school, never went to college. He was self-educated in the street world of survival, like so many first-generation Americans. He had to scrounge for every penny, probably never dreaming when he was a young man that he would become so comfortable later on. "But what kind of man is he?" Julie said. "How do you remember him when you were growing up?"

"He always was hypercritical of the people close to him, urging them on to greater accomplishments, urging them to be more successful, more attractive. That's probably why I turned out to be Little Miss Marvelous, Julie, always trying to please him, always performing, the best in class, the teacher's pet, the most popular, the most successful. The trouble was that I sometimes felt no matter what I did, it wouldn't be enough."

"Did you feel that he really didn't care about you?"

"Sometimes. But deep inside I knew he did. He always gave me everything he could, Julie, even when he couldn't afford it. Everything. I know he cared. At the risk of sounding like a poor little rich girl, I can tell you he always managed to give me the material things —clothes, college, trips to Europe. I know how hard it was for him to make all the dollars to give me and my brother so many creature comforts. Maybe I got confused, maybe I felt I wasn't loved enough just for being me, that I had to keep performing to get his attention. I guess I felt pushed. I had to keep producing, keep moving, going up and up. He may have pooh-poohed my achievements to me sometimes, but I knew that behind my back he bragged about his daughter's success to his friends. My mother did, too."

I paused to light a cigarette. "Oh, what's the point of all this?" I said. "If you think when I was five I wanted to seduce my father, steal him from my mother, and frustrated by all that, spent the rest of my life looking for father figures, that's bullshit. It's too easy. Too convenient and too trite."

"No, Barbara, I'm not thinking that, not at all. Tell me about your mother. You've said she was ambitious for you, too."

"Yes, but somehow it was different. I remember being little when she told me about her life as a young girl: how rough her brothers had been with her while she was growing up, what it was like to be poor and to have a mother who was always sick. I used to feel sad, wishing my mother had had a better life. God, it even pains me now. And when I was young, she would tell me stories about what my life would be like when I was older, her dreams for me, dreams that included an education, success, happiness. I wanted so to please her. I wanted to have all those things. I loved her and I wanted to be able to give them to her. But sometimes I felt guilty that I might have them someday and she never had. Between her ambitions for me and my father's constant criticism, it was inevitable, wasn't it?"

"What was inevitable?"

"That I would become a compulsive workaholic, holding on to my desk and my job like it was a life raft, my sense of self dependent on outside factors. No wonder there was no Barbara without work. Now I understand why the past summer was so terrible. Without work, without Eric, I was experiencing a twenty-carat identity crisis."

"But don't you understand, Barbara," Julie said, "it was as if you walked into your mother's dreams? You lived out her fantasies of success, a career, things she wanted for herself, and you did it well. You had a great career, you brought home the bacon. And the fears she had for herself, her mother's life—you walked into her nightmares, too. You have lived out her dreams—the best and the worst. You're free now, Barbara."

I struggled to understand, to put things together. "It was fate, Julie. Kismet, predestination," I said. "So much for free will. I never had a chance to be anything but an ambitious, insecure career woman. Terribly neurotic."

Julie laughed. "Terribly common, Barbara," she said. "But neurotic people are seldom boring."

"I'd rather be boring than in a mental hospital," I quipped.

"Did your mother's ambitions for you include marriage and a family?" Julie asked.

"Of course," I said. "They still do. She'll never give up hope."

Julie had met my mother only once, on that day when she and Edie brought me to the hospital. But I'd had a feeling then that she was observing my mother as closely as she was observing me. And now she said, "Have you ever noticed that sometimes when your mother speaks to you, it's not as if she is talking to a grown woman? Sometimes she speaks to you as if you were still a little girl?"

"My mother has always spoken to me like that," I said.

"Don't you find it strange?"

"No. That's my mother. That's the way Sally is. I'll always be her little girl."

All mothers were like mine, I thought. All mothers loved their daughters so much that they wanted them to stay small, stay home, so they can continue the mothering. I told Julie the joke about the Jewish mother pushing her daughter in a wheelchair through Saks Fifth Avenue. A salesgirl, shaking her head sadly, comes up to the mother and says, "Oh, that poor child. She can't walk. How terrible." And the mother responds, "Thank God she doesn't have to."

I waited for Julie to laugh, but she said with a frown. "That's an awful joke, Barbara." Then she started to tell me more about the empty-nest syndrome. She said that my parents probably feared that my adulthood would mean emptiness for them. Subconsciously they wanted me to stay home, stay in the orbit of their world, and they, to use Julie's words, infantilized me.

I pounced, armed with one more black mark against Sally and Lou. But Julie wouldn't let me get away with another wave of anger. "All parents do that to some degree," she said. "But eventually it's up to the child to handle it."

I slumped back in my chair, glaring at her. "How can I explain?" I said. "Children in families like mine are always brought up in a smothering way, especially the girls. Everything was a threat to our survival. Don't touch the toast in the toaster or we'd be electrocuted. Don't swim right after eating or we'd drown. Don't use a public toilet or we'd die of some dread disease. I'm surprised I've lasted this long. It was all done out of love, out of caring. I know that. I wanted to be sturdy and strong, but my mind was filled with a chorus of don'ts: don't do this, don't do that, watch out, don't fall, don't eat, don't live. How can you understand that?"

"I understand it perfectly," Julie said, her composure cool, her eyes gazing at me steadily.

"Thousands of other girls are raised just like that and they don't end up on Six North. So what good is all this?"

"It's good for you to talk about it. For the first time in your life you are looking at yourself. You alone, without pills, looking at your life. It's important to know it all."

"I don't know *anything!*" I cried. "And you won't help me. Why won't you help me? Why do you make me go through all this?" Suddenly I stopped. "Oh, God, you're right. I *am* behaving like a little girl. A spoiled brat."

I remembered my behavior those terrible weeks I spent in the apartment with Eric, the tantrums, the stamping feet. "Is that what this is all about, Julie?" I said. "Some subconscious wish to regress, to be a child again?"

"It's not that simple, Barbara. There is a part of you that has always wanted to be strong, independent, successful on your own. But there is another part that loves being a child, that wants to be treated in an infantile way."

"Schizophrenic," I said. "I *am* schizophrenic if there are two Barbaras."

"Not at all. You are one Barbara. It's two aspects of the same personality. There's a difference, you know."

"And you think my parents are responsible," I said. "That's why all this talk about my childhood. Listen, Julie, no one locked me in a closet or beat me as a child, if that's what you're driving at. Parents, parents, parents! I have wonderful loving parents, for Christ's sake. I come from a nice, normal home. No pathology, I swear. I was a normal kid. Why do you persist in this?"

Julie was smiling. "Well, that's some progress. Last week, if you recall, you were furious at your parents. You blamed them for everything."

"But, Julie, it *was* their fault, wasn't it? My mother filling me with dreams of glory but not really wanting me to grow up. My father supercritical every time I tried to do something different. No wonder there are two Barbaras."

"Don't be harsh on your parents," Julie said. "All parents project their own dreams for themselves, as well as their private terrors, onto their children. It's passed on to us like an inheritance, like a gift. It is real, it is specific, just like the chromosomes we inherit. Both your parents wanted you to be strong, Barbara, but they also wanted you to be safe. I think that's what you want, too."

"Of course that's what I want," I said, my anger rising again. "Who the hell doesn't?"

"You're right. Everyone feels a little dependent, a little needful, wanting to be loved and protected at the same time they want to love, to be strong, to give and be independent. It's the universal neurosis, Barbara.

And most people learn to live with it. But with you it's a battle, a battle with yourself."

"Barbara the child versus Barbara the adult. My mother's love and my father's criticism."

"You've got to stop looking for scapegoats," Julie said. "It's time to start living your own life again."

"But how can I if my parents' personalities are still inside me, if I'm constantly engaged in a war with myself?"

"Give up the fight and make peace."

Our time was up. "Barbara, you've been here for over two weeks," Julie said as I got up to go, "and you haven't left the hall once. Why don't you paint or go to the gym? You know you have my permission to walk outside on the grounds. Why don't you ask Don to take you?"

"Because I'm sick!" I said, standing in the doorway glaring at her.

"All right, Barbara. We'll talk again tomorrow."

So I had the universal neurosis. Terrific. Soul sick is soul sick and Julie didn't have any answers, no ready program, no prescription on hand to make me recover. It seemed we talked, over and over, about the same things day after day. I had to admit to myself that Dr. Allen and I had never talked like this. But Julie wouldn't permit me to dump on him. She was always reminding me that part of me wanted that kind of patchwork therapy, the pills, a part that loved going to a shrink, entertaining him with my life, being bright, attractive, almost perky with him, not doing serious work on myself, not growing. It wasn't that I had consciously shied from the pain of therapy; I had been going to Dr. Allen for so long that I simply thought that's what therapy was. Julie called it show-and-tell time, and she made me realize what a colossal waste those years had been. More than that, they were destructive years. For while I showed and told, he prescribed increasing dosages of Valium for me. He was a treat-the-symptom man, and a part of me that I did not yet understand was happy just to get rid of symptoms. I didn't know that covering the symptoms would turn small problems into giant conflicts, little demons into monsters. I had repressed so much—so much anger, so many tears—for so long.

Julie told me that the primary problem with tranquilizers is that you are unable to articulate your anger. As long as I took the pills I had been incapable of feeling the anger necessary to make changes in my life. I knew she was right, and I was paying a terrible price for it now. "God, how many women are doing the same thing I did?" I asked her. "It isn't healthy to walk around incapable of yelling, feeling, smelling, tasting. It isn't healthy to walk around with half your senses burned out by a chemical you're ingesting, supposedly to help yourself."

Julie agreed with me completely and said that I was still suffering from the aftereffects of withdrawal. But she wouldn't let me blame the drug for everything that had happened. The part of me that had stayed with Dr. Allen, and mindlessly swallowed a potent chemical to function, was a part I still refused to admit existed; Julie was trying to make me confront that infantile, docile, submissive, nonthinking person. I didn't like what I saw, but no matter how I tried to avoid the confrontation, Julie always brought me back, saying, "It was *you* who went to him for ten years, *you* who took the pills, *you* who repressed the fact that Eric was troubled because you were so needful of his love."

I screamed with rage at her. How could she say such things to me, why was she being so cruel? I had already come apart once. Eric had blown my psyche wide open by telling me to feel guilt, express anger, analyzing and reinterpreting my life. Now Julie was doing it all over again. And I was afraid that I couldn't tolerate the pain of being taken apart again. Besides, I told her, I was getting bored with me.

"I'm not, Barbara," she said. So we continued talking. And I could see what she was doing. She was chipping away at my rage—my rage at my parents, Dr. Allen, the pills, Eric, the world, for doing this to me. Pretty soon there would be no one to blame but me, and because I wasn't ready for that, I fought her with all the sarcasm, anger and tears I could muster. Every step of the way.

In that sick environment, the mad part of my psyche thrived, growing stronger despite all my resolve. Part of me was comfortable there, nourished by the sickness, and I decided everyone was lying to me, including Julie. I had to be sick if they had put me with other patients who were so disturbed. Eric was right; I *was* schizophrenic, no matter what Julie said. Madness is the ultimate dependency and I was in the ultimately dependent place, where people watch over your mind; not a kidney, not a pancreas, but your mind.

My mind had always been the best part of me, better than my legs, my face, my hair. My work, my relationships with people, had always required a good head and a good heart. But now I couldn't think straight. And far from experiencing my heart, I felt like the Tin Woodman in *The Wizard of Oz,* who had no heart. I was body and brain. But nothing connected. I experienced rage and random tears, unassociated with thought. The battle I was fighting between dependence and independence, love and hate, health and sickness, was neither emotional nor intellectual. Yet it consumed my whole being, and I decided that mental illness is an exaggeration of the human condition. Julie was right. We all experience the same conflicts. It's only that in mental illness everything is blown completely out of proportion.

On the days when I had no session with her, Julie often dropped by to chat for fifteen minutes or so to see how things were going. She always knew where to find me: on the green couch outside my room. But one day she found me in the cafeteria, and we had a cup of coffee together. I was still grappling with the idea of two Barbaras. Was there really a part of me that was a little monster trying to destroy all the rest? I told Julie that if I wasn't schizophrenic, then I was at least a split personality.

She smiled. "Why do you always think in formulas and psychological slogans, Barbara? You treat life as if it were a rebus with some simple solution. Why do you reduce everything to psychological terms?"

"I reduce it to understand it better," I said. "You psychologists talk of pattern behavior. What was my pattern?"

Julie put down her mug, and when I looked at her, all the racket of the hall was obliterated and we were just two women friends having a talk over coffee. "In many of your relationships you were dependent, the little girl. In others you were strong and independent. There was no pattern except that you often seemed to settle for something—or someone—less than you really wanted. And when you were disappointed, you accepted pain as if you deserved it. You were well prepared for pain."

I was shocked. "I've never thought of myself as a doormat. I hate the image."

"But you aren't a doormat," Julie said. "Sometimes you just had rotten judgment. Idealizing some people, blinding yourself to their flaws, seeing what you wanted to be there."

"Why, Julie? Why did I do that?"

"We're trying to find out."

When she left, I went back to the hall, so heavy with smoke and sound, so thick with craziness. Roger was in a rare moment of calm and he started telling me about his travels to all the planets in the solar system. Iris wanted to know if I would play dirty Scrabble and Jeff tried to bum a cigarette. I walked past them back to my room, wishing I could find a psychic eraser to expunge all the negative programming, all that had contributed to my tolerating—needing—pain. I had never known it was there. But now, suddenly, I saw everything clearly: a brilliant ugly color, a picture of neurosis. And I wanted to scratch it out. But it was me, and I had to be the eraser. How could I rub out one part of me without destroying all the rest?

I had fucked it up, really fucked it up. What's a nice girl like me doing in a script like this? In plays, at least there is a third act, a synthesis. I felt I had lost some vital synthesizing ingredient that would help me mend, help heal the rift in my brain. It felt like a chemical loss, a physical lack, but no, Julie said it was psychological. Damn, that meant I had to do it myself. Why didn't I grow up right the first time? I thought, tossing on the narrow cot. It's so much harder now.

Three weeks had passed and I was still being tossed around minute to minute, hour to hour, by giant swells of emotion. It was like being in the path of a hurricane, and all I could do was hold on. Kind staff members would come into my room and extend their arms to me. "Barbara," Don said, "there are times when you need people. You have to learn when you're being dependent and when you really need. Now you need people, Barbara. Hold on."

And I would hold on to the bed, hold on to the strong arms of Don or one of the other aides or a nurse, as the skyrocketing surges of emotion shoved me about. I felt as if my insides were being torn out, that I was disintegrating. I had no choice but to accept their kindness, the warmth of their arms, the strength of their health and, most of all, the tenderness that was implicit in each gesture they made toward me. Later Don told me that helping people through such crises is like midwifery. He could withstand all the anger, all the pain, only by knowing that the personality of the patient was being regenerated in the midst of the crisis. No physical birth can compare to the anguish of being born again—if that is what it was. But I was lucky. I had strong, tender, wise people helping me. I swallowed my humiliation and clung to them for support.

But I kept spinning around, not knowing where I was, imagining I was being tossed by the giant twenty-foot waves I loved to watch from my house at the beach in the late fall. I tried to capture the fading memory of that other woman, the woman who loved and laughed, the person who gave. She was gone. I had never been her. I spent hours saying to myself, I must be Barbara. I bought these jeans at Different Drummer, Bill gave me this ring, Edie sent me this letter. Dammit, all these people know me. I must exist. It didn't work. In fact, it only confirmed my fear that without external things I simply would not exist. Only in the incessant crying could I feel anything, and deep as the wound was—I felt I was crying for all of humanity's sadness—I preferred the tears to nothingness.

I remembered the silly mind game we played in college. If a tree falls in a forest and there is no one there to hear it, is there any sound? Does sound exist without ears? Does Barbara exist without someone else present to confirm her sense of existence? I felt dead and since I had been brought up in a society that treats doctors as gods, a society that worships a pantheon of drugs, I still begged Julie to give me a pill to bring me back to life. "You're letting me get too far from myself," I screamed. "I don't remember me. You're making me invisible!"

"You're making yourself invisible, Barbara," she said, sitting placidly behind her desk. "And only you can make yourself uninvisible. No pills."

I stormed out of her office, ran back to my room and threw myself on my cot. She followed me. "You'll spend the rest of your life in dark rooms," she said. "You'll lie here forever."

"Get out, Julie," I barked shrilly. "I can't stand you right now. Get out!"

"It's safe here, isn't it, Barbara?"

"Yes. It's like a goddam womb. But at least in here some of the screaming noise in my head stops."

"Let me open a window," she said. "You can't breathe in here."

"Thank you," I said. "I'm sorry I talked to you like that. I'm so tired. Forgive me."

She opened the window and then turned and left my room.

I had been in the hospital about a month when I decided one morning to go to the occupational therapy building. Julie had been urging me to go, but I told her I knew I would never regain my sense of self playing with clay or weaving a basket. Now I wanted to get away, at least for a while, from the sickness and squalor of the hall. Was that progress? I didn't think so. I was just curious to see what the other crazies were doing.

Once I arrived in the large, airy OT building, I found myself strolling from room to room, just looking. People of all ages were deeply involved in working with clay, weaving cloth, making pot holders, doing needlepoint. I forced myself to sit down and try to do something. But I only had to glance at the man on my left or the woman on my right to feel hopelessly inept. As I tried to make something out of the lifeless gray clay I held in my hand, somewhere deep inside me I heard a voice saying, "It's eleven o'clock on a Tuesday morning and you're sitting here modeling clay for your health. Barbara Gordon, *you* are in occupational therapy, next thing you know you'll be weaving baskets." And I gave up in despair and wandered into another room filled with even more people purposefully engaged in the making of something. But in the art therapy room, I saw gobs and gobs of bright acrylic paint, and the brilliance of the colors knocked me out. I took a brush and began literally throwing the paint on a canvas. If I couldn't tell Julie, I could show her the anguish I felt. So I decided to draw the color of the fire blazing in my head—an orange, yellow, red jungle of a fire. Then I painted the gray fog that seemed to surround my brain like a shroud. And that afternoon I brought the childish primitives to her office so she could see what I no longer had the words to describe. Like a five-year-old home from kindergarten with her finger paintings, I rushed in the door saying, "See, Julie, this is how it hurts. This is how I feel. This is how I look. I'm a monster. See my monster."

She looked at the paintings and smiled. "A gentle monster, Barbara."

So the painting began: faces with white, empty eyes, monsters, ogres, coffins, dead men, gray, black, brown, umber. It would be a long time before I would look outside and paint flowers.

If you have ever flirted with the idea that a couple of weeks in a "sanatorium" might not be so terrible —that it could be just the place to recharge your tired psyche, tune up your system and just hang out languidly sipping white wine, reading Keats, and taking long walks with a doctor who looks like Gregory Peck and Robert Redford combined—reconsider. It is not Keats in the afternoon, it is Bugs Bunny in the morning; it is not woodland walks, it is endless pacing around a room acrid with the smell of cigarettes and tired upholstery.

It is up at seven-thirty, bed made by ten of eight, breakfast over by eight twenty-five, cartoons at nine, the morning program of activities at ten, lunch at twelve, afternoon activities at two, dinner at five, "nourishments" at eight, in bed by eleven, lights out by twelve. Sweet dreams. And what the hospital people discouragingly called "nourishments" consisted of peanut butter, jelly, cereal, doughnuts, cookies. Empty calories for empty minds. It is being reminded all day and every day that "they" hold the keys. They determine when you eat, what you eat, when you sleep, when you walk, when you paint, and when—or if—you leave the hospital. And it's being too sick to care.

And so the rigidly scheduled days went by formlessly. Each day was interminable, but the weeks flew. More seconds per minute, more minutes per hour, more hours per day than anywhere else in the world. Time doesn't move in a mental hospital; it hangs there with you. I had to fill in the long hours that stretched before me between my sessions with Julie. I sat smoking outside my room, went to the OT building to paint, started taking occasional walks on the grounds with Don or one of the other aides, had endless conversations with other patients—those who were well enough to talk; I was indifferent to the others. I read everything I could get my hands on, even if I didn't understand what I was reading. I began writing long letters to Edie and Lisa. I watched Joe walk in circles, I listened to Roger tell me about the mountains on Mars, fought off Iris's propositions in the john. Iris, who broke lamps and windows when she didn't get her way, wanted me. Wonderful.

Julie and I were still talking about my parents, but I was no longer a little girl. I was a teen-ager on my way to college. My father wanted me to go to the University of Miami, and tried to bribe me with promises of clothes, a convertible, my own apartment. But I wanted to go away to school, not so much to get away from my parents as to get away from Miami Beach. I hated its false values, its neon and rhinestones, its acquisitiveness, its status-seeking population. I didn't want to end up living in a cultural desert with the mind of an orange. I didn't want to major in jai alai handicapping and water skiing. I wanted to go to Vassar and then live and work in New York. That's what I said, but what I really meant was I didn't want my mother's life. I used to watch her getting ready for my father when he came home from the office, running to put on make-up, often to be ignored when he walked in, exhausted and sullen after a day at work, wanting only to have a drink, to relax and watch television. I had to get away, and when my mother interceded, he relented. I was accepted at Vassar and that was that.

"All right," Julie said. "That's something else you can thank your mother for."

"But I don't think she really wanted me to go away," I said.

"Are you sure? You've said she had great ambitions for you, that she wanted things for you that she never had."

"Then why did I feel so guilty about leaving them?"

It was at Vassar, I told Julie, that my life really changed, changed in a terrible way. I was touring the campus, riding my bicycle on my first day in Poughkeepsie, when suddenly the brakes didn't hold and I found myself careening down a steep hill. I fell and ended up with my head through the spokes of a wheel. A broken collarbone was all the doctor discovered and I had to walk around in a neck brace that gave me the posture of a West Point cadet. But months later I developed two herniated disks, and those disks would cause me pain for the next twelve years. Worse, they introduced me to the world of Valium. Several orthopedic surgeons gave me Valium, which is really a muscle relaxant, for my back, and so when Dr. Allen prescribed the same drug for my anxiety attacks, it was like returning to an old friend. If I hadn't taken Valium all those years for my back, I don't think I would have treated it so cavalierly as a tranquilizer. I made the mistake of thinking of it as medicine, not as a drug which should be handled with care.

"Millions of other women make that same mistake," Julie said.

"Why?" I said. "Why don't their doctors tell them the truth? I have a haunting, almost obsessive picture in my head, Julie: thousands of women all across the country being given pills by male doctors. Men sedating women, tranquilizing them, helping to rob them of themselves. It's obscene."

Julie had to agree with me. These men were her professional colleagues, but she hated the picture as much as I did. She knew I wasn't putting down the whole profession, just the doctors who played fast and loose with people's psyches.

Vassar was all right, I told Julie. I loved being on my own for the first time in my life. But Poughkeepsie was too remote for me, Vassar a little unreal. I wasn't cut out to live with WASP debutantes or the Jewish princesses from New York, who made the Miami variety look like rank amateurs. I had my heart set on New York, so I transferred to Barnard for my junior and senior years. And that caused another family flap: little Barbara all alone in the wicked city. They finally acquiesced, but I'd had to struggle.

"We all have to fight for what we really want," Julie said. "If not our parents, then ourselves."

She always reminded me that my real battle was not with my parents, or with pill-pushers, or even with her. It was with myself. And she had finally succeeded in dissipating my rage. Our sessions were more tranquil now; there were no tantrums, fewer angry cries. My anger had turned inward, toward myself for having botched everything. But Julie warned me about that, too. "Don't be too hard on yourself, Barbara," she said. "It doesn't have to be unconditional surrender. Just a workable truce."

I had been in the hospital about six weeks when Julie said it was all right for me to go on my first pass into town with a staff member. The problem was that the staff was always so busy wrestling Roger to the floor or policing Iris, there was very little time left for the other patients. But Julie wanted to reward me for the progress I was making and Don understood that. So it was he who came in at eleven on his Sunday off and took me to a diner for lunch and then for a long walk to show me the town of Greenwich.

I was so excited. It was like a first date. My first trip off grounds. Don and I talked and talked. By now we were becoming friends and I wanted to know all about his life. After his training, Don told me as we walked through the sleepy Sunday morning town, he wanted to return to the black ghetto in Brooklyn, where kids like Jeff could be reached before it was too late. At the hospital Don was paid to care. But *how* he cared. Someday, I thought, as we headed up the long hill toward the main building, some young kid in Brooklyn will have this marvelous man for a therapist. I remember he told me that morning that things have to get worse, everyone gets worse, before the climb back up. "And you're going to make it, Barbara."

It was Don who warned me about self-pity. One afternoon he found me sitting on the couch outside my room. I had refused to go to lunch and he wanted to know why. "Because I can't stand it anymore," I said, "sitting in that grim dining room with people eating with their hands, belching, farting, stealing food, smacking their lips, jabbering to themselves."

He put his hand on my shoulder.

"You're feeling sorry for yourself, Barbara, and you don't have time for that. You have work to do." He was right. Of all the wasted emotions like guilt and envy, self-pity is the most pernicious and the one most likely to take over just at a time when you can afford it the least. The combination of self-pity and self-hatred was lethal, I discovered, like Valium and alcohol, and I had to fight it daily. But why-me-lordism has a way of cropping up when you're not looking. So I told Don that I thought the only way to beat it was to remember what God is supposed to have said to Job when he cried, "Why me, Lord?" "Because sometimes you just piss me off."

Don laughed and I laughed and he said, "O.K., that's better. Now how about doing something? Why not go over to the kitchen? I heard you baked a cake yesterday."

"On one condition," I said. "Whenever you hear self-pity in me again, scream at me, please. While others may argue about whether the world ends with a bang or a whimper, I just want to make sure mine doesn't end with a whine."

Still I foundered in self-pity, anger, sickness. And there were moments when I relapsed into brattiness. It was wasteful stuff, but I couldn't help it. And Don was always there to pick up the pieces. "Don't give up now, Barbara," he said. "You've worked so hard against injustice. You fought against Nixon, the FBI, the CIA. You've fought for other people's rights. Can't you fight just as hard for yourself?"

I tried to laugh through my wretchedness. "Oh, Don, that melodrama will never play. No one would believe this conversation." Then I burst into angry tears. "No, I can't fight because there's no me, and besides, I'm fighting me and I'm tough. Oh, Don, I never wanted to have me for an enemy. I want so to be well."

He smiled, his brown eyes gazing at me through his steel-rimmed glasses. "You will, Barbara. You will. Soon."

9

Endings and
New Beginnings

It was late October. Seven weeks had gone by. I was taking a walk on the grounds of the hospital with Paul Mangello, one of the aides, who had become my friend. The trees were still covered with brilliant orange and yellow leaves. The air was crisp and sweet. I had always loved autumn, the autumn I had never known in Florida or in New York. You sure picked the hard way to experience a country autumn, Barbara, I said to myself.

Paul was an intense young Italian with thick black hair and enormous blue eyes. He and Don were close friends. I had felt their closeness, and wanted to be part of it. Like Don, Paul was on his way to being a therapist. We had talked about life, love, parents, growing up, night after night when he worked the night shift. I had surprised him with a painting to hang in his office when he became a doctor. I was shocked at how happy he was with it.

When I returned to the hall, I went to Julie's office. She was a few minutes late for our session that day, and I sat there looking at the begonia on the window sill. It had grown a great deal since the day I first saw it. Seven weeks. Barbara, seven weeks.

"I heard you baked a cake for Lillian's birthday, Barbara," Julie said when she arrived. Lillian, an elderly woman, was a new patient who was being treated for depression.

"Yes, I did," I said. "And I think she liked it."

"I know she did. She told me."

I had forgotten that Lillian was Julie's patient, too. Then I wondered, Is she going to tell me I was a narcissistic little girl looking for attention or that what I did was an adult, giving thing?

She read my mind. "Let's talk about it. How did it make you feel baking the cake?"

And so the session began. More scrutiny, endless examination of everything I did. And from baking a birthday cake for Lillian, I learned that day that I had to live with ambiguity.

"We do things for many reasons," Julie said. "Because we want to give, because we want to be loved. Nothing is clear-cut, Barbara. We do everything for a number of psychological motives."

"Damn it, Julie, it was just a birthday cake for a lonely old woman in a hospital. Of course, I wanted her to be pleased and to like me. But truly I felt sorry for her. A birthday. Here, of all the Godforsaken places!"

I admit that I was thinking of my own birthday, which was only a month and a half away. But if Julie was thinking the same thing, she didn't mention it. At the moment, as far as she was concerned, I was twenty-one years old and just graduated from Barnard. "Let's pick up where we left off last time," she said. "How did your parents feel about your staying in New York?"

"You know Sally and Lou well enough by this time," I said. "There was another battle, of course. They wanted me to come home. I think they were proud of me when I got a job at NBC, even though I was just a secretary. But they were so fearful of my living alone in New York that I moved into a hotel for women just to pacify them. It had a fancy name, but that was the only thing fancy about it." I remembered that in spite of a sliver of a view of the East River from my tiny room, it was a sordid and dispiriting kind of place. Many of the women there were waiting for babies to arrive, the fathers long gone. "And I had to fight off the advances of the lesbians," I said. "The gay liberation movement was still a long way off and the only 'coming out' that went on was in the communal bathroom."

Julie was smiling. "And that was your glamorous introduction to New York."

"Me and a lot of other girls I knew. All that and breakfast and dinner, for eighty dollars a week. The food was inedible, the bathroom unbathable, my life unlivable. I was finally able to convince my parents that I would rather brave muggings and robberies in my own apartment than molestation in the shower room."

"Did you like your job?"

"It was a beginning," I remembered. Filing, typing, making coffee—and learning everything I could about broadcasting. There was no women's liberation movement in those days either, and most of the girls I knew didn't talk about careers. But I think I was different even then. I *wanted* a career. I was young, I had potential, I felt full of hope for the future and not at all homesick. If anyone had said to me then that twenty years later a therapist would tell me to give up my dependence on my parents, I wouldn't have believed it. I felt truly liberated. I had cut the cord and was happy to be on my own.

"Tell me about where you lived," Julie said.

"Greenwich Village. Where else? It was all I could afford. But I loved my little studio apartment. I built a bookcase out of boards and bricks and filled the place with plants and books and records and new friends. It all seemed so wonderful and new to me, but I suppose hundreds of other girls were doing the same things, living the same way. Another cliché."

"Try typical, for a change," Julie said. "What did you parents think when they saw your apartment?"

I lit a cigarette, suddenly remembering another hurt. Damn you, Julie, why do you make me remember these things? "My mother was the only one who ever saw it," I said finally. "My father never came to visit."

I knew what she was thinking: I hadn't really cut

the cord at all; what I had was just a long extension. But she didn't say it. She asked me why.

"I don't know. But after I talked to Dr. Allen about it, I concluded that my father never really accepted the fact that I was on my own. Or maybe it was painful for him to visit an apartment where I lived as a woman, not his little girl."

"And your mother?" Julie asked.

"She was just the opposite. She came to visit every chance she got, helped me pick out furniture, sent me recipes. But my father never came, even when they were in New York together. I've never decided whether he didn't care enough or cared too much."

"Probably a little bit of both," Julie said.

I smiled. "Ambiguity?"

"Right. You must learn to live with ambiguity, Barbara. Yours and everyone else's. Life is not a film with good guys and bad guys. It would be easier that way, I know, but it isn't like that."

I left her office that afternoon both exhausted and exhilarated, despairing that I had repressed so much, that I had tried to make things what they weren't, but hopeful that I could develop a new candor with myself, that something good would emerge from all this. I promised myself that I would start dealing with life squarely, and hardest of all, accept uncertainty or ambiguity. I would have to give up black and white. I would have to learn to live in the grays, in the middle.

That night Roger had a violent outburst. Don and Paul were trying to give him his medication and he started slugging them both. He broke Don's glasses. Roger was only a tall, thin skeleton of a person, but he had the strength of some prehistoric beast, and when he began flailing at them, the nurse rang the alarm buzzer, and aides from the other halls came running to help restrain him.

I turned away. I didn't want to remember any of this. I realized again how people like Don and Paul risked their lives daily working in this place. Iris and Jeff giggled and laughed, which fomented another outburst from Roger. They, like many of the patients there, seemed to feast on violent episodes. I ran to my room. But even through the door I could hear the aides running back and forth, struggling to subdue Roger. And I could still hear his wails and shrieks after they dragged him down the hall and locked him in the quiet room.

At last Julie and I began to talk about the men in my life other than my father. It was almost a relief, because I could remember those relationships, or at least I thought I could. I had been over the same ground with Dr. Allen. But somehow Julie made me look at things, look at myself, in a different way. Dr. Allen was interested in my pathology. Julie asked me to share my pain.

I told her about my short-lived marriage. It began during my senior year in college when the phone rang and a man who said his name was Stan Rossman was calling. It seemed he was a college professor from Los Angeles who knew my cousin. He was in New York on vacation and asked to go out with me. We dated on and off for three years. Every time he came to New York, we spent hours poking around the city together. He was a tall, handsome man who smoked a pipe. And I was still young enough to believe that men who took philosophical drags on pipes were deep thinkers, that the long silences and long looks really covered a mind brimming with new ideas and concepts. It didn't occur to me then that people who are that silent, that introspective, might really have nothing to say or share.

"Did you love Stan?" Julie asked.

"I wasn't sure. I was twenty-four years old. And Stan was thirty-five and so sure of everything. He still wore his Phi Beta Kappa key on his tie. He was proud of it. I was deeply embarrassed when people came up to him and asked what it meant, and he would begin to boast about his academic honors of so many years ago to someone who couldn't have cared less."

"That would have worried me, too," Julie said. "Why did you marry him?"

"I don't know. Even Dr. Allen wanted to know

more about that. I suppose I felt trapped. For the first year or so, I had the perfect excuse. I had no intention of giving up my job in New York to become a professor's wife in Los Angeles. But then he got a job at Rutgers and the phone calls from my parents began: 'When, already—when? You're drifting, Barbara. When are you and Stan going to do it?' "

"Oh, Barbara," Julie said with a note of frustration in her voice. "Are you back to scapegoating again? That couldn't have been the main reason, really."

"I'm not blaming them, Julie. It wasn't their fault. But that was the reason. I didn't want to be married at twenty-four. I wanted a career, travel, excitement, new people. But I felt I was a disappointment to my parents in so many ways and I wasn't strong enough to ignore their constant pressure. All my friends knew what was going on. None of them really thought Stan and I would be happy together. But when I finally accepted his proposal, suddenly everyone was ecstatic. Barbara was getting married. Another Jewish girl was getting married. She won't be alone. I felt no joy; only a loss of my innocence, a loss of adventure. Still, if everyone was so pleased, I had to be doing something right."

"Tell me about the wedding," Julie said.

"A Jewish wedding in Miami. Typical," I said. "Hundreds of people laughing, eating, getting drunk. Relatives I didn't even know I had. And I felt like a sacrificial goat."

How had I let it all happen? Julie didn't press me for any more details, but I did tell her one story. At NBC I had worked my way up to a job on a documentary series about women, a job that included researching the subjects—subjects like menopause and frigidity—talking to psychiatrists and then working with the actors who played in the fictionalized dramas that my boss, George, wrote. The series was really very good and I loved my job. Stan and I had agreed that I would keep working after we were married. But this was in August and the wedding wasn't until October.

My mother was handling all the details, loving every

moment of it. I felt my wedding was a present to her. But one day I was sitting at my desk getting ready to go to a studio in Brooklyn to tape the show. I remember the actors were Dane Clark and Carol Lawrence. George was tearing all over the office and everyone was in the usual last-minute panic. The phone rang. It was my mother. Calling from Florida.

She usually didn't call me at the office, and I thought something had to be the matter, something terrible. But she began with small talk, so I felt relieved. Tragedy, which always lurks just around the corner as far as I'm concerned, had been eluded once more. "What is your favorite song?" my mother asked nonchalantly.

George was looking at me from the hall, pointing to his watch. It was time to go. I didn't know what my favorite song was, but Mother insisted she had to know *now*. So I told her my favorite was "But Not for Me," by George Gershwin.

"How does it go?" she asked.

By now George was frantic. "Time to move out, Barb," he called loudly.

Caught between my mother and my boss, I chose Mother and found myself speaking the words: " 'They're writing songs of love, but not for me; a starry sky's above but not for me.' "

"Wrong," my mother interrupted. "That will never do."

"What do you mean, it will never do?"

"We can't play such a sad song at your wedding."

"At the wedding? Mom, that's two months away. Why in God's name do you have to know now?"

"The band has to rehearse," she replied calmly. "It's for your first dance with Stan."

By now George was hysterical. "For Christ's sake, Barbara!" he shouted.

"What's your next favorite song?" my mother said.

I hung the phone over my shoulder and started gathering up things on my desk. " 'It's All Right with Me,' by Cole Porter," I said.

"Tell me the words," my mother said.

With George and the two actors watching me with

astonishment, I began singing softly into the phone: " 'It's the wrong time, it's the wrong place, though your face is charming, it's the wrong face.' "

"Oh, Barbara, that's even more sadness," my mother said with despair.

"Can I help it if I like loser songs?" I said.

"Well, we certainly can't play that," she said. "What's Stan's favorite song?"

" 'A Foggy Day,' by Gershwin," I answered, proud that I knew my future husband's favorite song.

"How does it go?" she said.

" 'A foggy day in London town had me low, had made me down.' "

"More sadness," my mother said in an exasperated tone.

"Wait, Mother," I said excitedly. "I think it ends happily. Listen. 'Suddenly I saw you there, and in foggy London town the sun was shining everywhere.' "

She was satisfied. It would work. I hung up and fled out of the office, down the elevator and into the waiting limousine. All the way to Brooklyn, George looked at me as if I was a lunatic.

"But that's the song they played," I told Julie, "two months later."

Julie was laughing so hard that I began to laugh with her. "Oh, Barbara," she said, wiping her eyes.

"I wish the rest of the story was that funny," I said. "But our marriage was a disaster, Julie. A disaster from the very beginning. Because of his job at Rutgers, I had to move out of the city I loved to a dreadful New Jersey suburb. If I wanted to keep working, I was the one who had to commute. Up early, then the train to New York and the train back to New Jersey, shopping, cooking, doing the dishes. No time to be with people in either place. I hated it. And I soon discovered that Stan and I had nothing to say to one another. I'd thought maybe after we were married I could get him to take off the Phi Beta Kappa key, but no, his new state of matrimony didn't alter the fact that he wore it daily as a badge."

"I'm sure that wasn't the only thing that bothered you," Julie said.

"Just one of thousands," I said. "Somehow he seemed to turn into a different person, or maybe he was the same person and I'd never really seen him. After a day at NBC, I would rush home and cook dinner, only to hear him say, 'There isn't enough color to this meal, Barbara, and the vegetables are the same consistency as the meat. You should have taken more trouble. You should have spent as much time preparing this meal as you do on your job.' Oh, Julie, he was jealous of me. And I was only a researcher on a documentary series."

"A lot of men react that way," she said. "How did you feel?"

"I was furious. But I never said anything. We never talked about it. And I found myself taking out my resentment in mean, petty ways. Stan just adored Western omelets. My form of protest was to go to the supermarket and buy the eggs, the tomatoes, the onions, but not the green pepper. The next morning when Stan asked for his Western omelet, I cheerfully chopped up all the ingredients and then announced at the last moment with dismay, 'Oh damn, I forgot to buy a green pepper.' I should have left for Reno or screamed or yelled, but no, I didn't buy the green pepper. Was there a pattern there, Julie?"

"Still looking for a formula?" she said. "Everything black or white?"

"Dr. Allen said I married a man just like my father."

"That may be part of it, Barbara. But just because we're going over some things in your past, that doesn't mean everything is pathology. Of course you wanted to please your parents by getting married. Of course you wanted them to love you and approve of you, and that affected your judgment. But it sounds to me as if you married a sexist bore, and someone who couldn't have been more wrong for you. Oedipal, perhaps. Masochistic, a little. But it was a neurotic choice, not a psychotic one. You deserve a spot on *Name That Tune* and a Purple Heart for staying with Stan as long as you did. But you weren't crazy. Not then, not now. You're healthier than you think."

"Then what happened to me, Julie? What about Bill? What about Eric? Have I done the same thing over and over again?"

"That's for another day," she said. "And thanks for making me laugh. You laughed, too. You really laughed, Barbara. I keep telling you you're all there, if you'd only trust yourself. You're really more intact than you know."

We walked back down the hall together, she heading for the glass-enclosed office to make notes for the nurses about medication for her other patients and me to my room to get my sketch pad. I was working on some stuff at OT—a still life with a bottle and a bowl of fruit—and I was eager to get back to it. I found myself skipping, literally skipping, down the hall. It had felt good to laugh. I missed so much of my old life—love, friendship, work. And now I realized that I missed laughing, too—the wonderful, joyous, liberating, warm, marvelous feeling of laughing. Today was the first day I had laughed in months.

I tried to hold on to that good feeling, and that night, as I fell asleep, I could almost hear the combo at my wedding playing "A Foggy Day," could still see the look on my parents' faces as I danced with my new husband. How could they be so proud and happy, I had wondered. I didn't love him at all, and I thought everyone knew.

Every Friday morning on the hall there was a meeting of the entire "community," a term used by the members of the staff in their unending, but futile, attempt to foster a sense of mutual concern for that space we all inhabited. Most of the patients on Six North were too sick to participate in this democratic exercise. Nevertheless, it was the one time a week when all the nurses, the day shift and the night shift staff, the attendants and the therapists were present. We sat in an enormous circle in the day room. Dr. Michael Wald, who was the one "medical" doctor on the hall, conducted the meeting and patients were asked to voice their complaints. It was like a huge group therapy session.

For the first several weeks that I was on Six North, I

just sat sullenly there in the circle without saying a word. What was I doing at this Mad Hatter's tea party? But before long I began to speak up, usually to complain about something. Julie said it was another sign that I wasn't really crazy.

We talked about the same things week after week. But the one thing that really bothered me and some of the other patients was the constant noise of the phonograph. We felt that the heavy, pulsating rock music was provocative and incited the violent patients toward destructive behavior. Besides, I heard myself saying during one meeting, it was a pain in the ass: the incessant noise, the same record playing over and over again. We kept asking the staff to restrict the hours that the phonograph could be played, and eventually we won. There could be no music for two hours after dinner. At last there was a chance for peace on the hall, a few moments without music hammering away inside your brain.

We complained about the bad food, the rudeness of the kitchen staff. And during one meeting, a patient suddenly asked why she wasn't given passes for the weekend. I blinked. Passes. Passes home. I'd be doing that soon. Julie said that in three or four weeks I could start having overnight passes. It was early November. Maybe I'd be home for my birthday after all.

During the meetings I always watched Julie. Some of the therapists took the occasion to show off for the other staff members present. Julie sat there quietly, observing it all, but she never said a word. Whatever she thought, she kept to herself. I had the feeling that she wasn't perfectly at home on the Six North team, that she didn't like to ask bullshit questions. Joyce Roberts, a woman therapist from Texas, was just the opposite. On a morning after Jeff had stolen something, Roger had been put in the quiet room and Iris had broken a window, Joyce Roberts could always be counted on to ask with a smile, "And how is the mood of the community this morning?" I hated her patronizing drawl, her interfering, her assumption that she knew all about a world she left every evening. Julie always respected the patients and sat like an observer, not a pseudo resident, at the meetings.

One Friday Dr. Wald obviously had something important to talk about. "Won't you please come join us. This is about you." Roger kept on rocking and then arms over his eyes, rocking in the corner of the room. Joe, who was walking around in the center of the circle and cackling, was the next target of Dr. Wald's attention. "Please, Joe, come sit and join us. We have to talk about something of great interest to the hall." Joe ignored him.

Dr. Wald looked perturbed, but was determined to continue. "You all know we are seriously concerned about Roger's outbreaks of violence. Roger, come join us. This is about you." Roger kept on rocking and then got up and began pacing back and forth at the other end of the hall. He didn't want to be any part of this. Still, Dr. Wald and the other staff members tried to inveigle him into the meeting. I had heard that in the acute form of schizophrenia, it was best to try to talk to the patient as if he could hear, as if he cared, as if he were normal. Roger heard nothing.

Finally Dr. Wald gave up and started the meeting without him.

"Roger's outbreaks are a serious concern to us all," he began. "He almost hurt Don and Paul the other night and we on the staff feel that he is a danger."

I breathed in deeply. I had felt for a long time that Roger was too ill for the hall, too violent, too unpredictable, and I had voiced my concern despite how cold or cruel it seemed. We are in peril every moment he is on the hall, I had said at the meeting just the week before.

"So we have decided," Dr. Wald continued, "that he is to be given EST. Electric shock treatments. Now that may be frightening to a lot of you, but we think it will help Roger very much. What are your feelings about that?"

Jeff jumped up out of his chair. "Shock treatments —wow, man! Far out! I've heard of that. Gonna juice him up good, huh, and he won't fight no more? Right, Dr. Wald, right?"

"Sit down, Jeff. Now I know some of you have experienced shock treatments, and we think it's best if you talk about your fears and your memories. But first of all I want to assure you, it won't be painful to Roger. He will be asleep. Shock treatment is not the barbaric and painful procedure it used to be. And we have explained all this to Roger's parents."

I was surprised by the number of patients who spoke up and said they had had shock treatments, either here or in other hospitals. When I was researching my film on the psychiatric profession, one of the doctors told me that with the discovery and use of the powerful tranquilizers and other chemical agents, shock treatments were seldom prescribed anymore. Here I had evidence to the contrary.

"I had shock treatments once," Lara said, massaging her hands nervously.

"Oh, who the fuck cares?" Iris interrupted.

"Please, Iris, let Lara continue," Dr. Wald said.

"It doesn't really hurt," Lara said. "Now please may I go wash my hair?"

And it doesn't really help, I thought. But that morning I felt there was greater concern shown for the fears of the patients, and for the repercussions that Roger's shock treatments might have, than I had noticed before. I wanted to congratulate Dr. Wald for taking the time to talk to us about it.

In the weeks to come, we would see Roger heavily sedated and strapped to a long white table like a stretcher, and then Paul and Don would wheel him out of the hall. We were prepared, we had been warned, and we all waited eagerly for some improvement in his condition. He had been on the hall for three years. Three years! And he was still violent and unapproachable, and spoke to practically no one. He ate, he walked, he slept a deep Thorazine sleep. Maybe the EST would help him. God, why was I still hoping for miracles?

"Barbara, you've referred to Bill a number of times. I know he must have been very important to you. Tell me about him."

I knew Bill was next on our agenda. But how could I tell Julie about the man I had loved so deeply? There was so much happiness and then so much pain. How would I begin? I looked up to see Julie waiting for me to speak.

"I was working as a writer on a television show, still married to Stan, when I met a man, Julie—a funny, bright, talented man who was also on the show. I fell in love with him instantly, instantly! He was married, I was married, but we weren't able to stop ourselves. He was almost ten years older than I was, but with him I felt more alive, more real, more in love than I ever had before."

I watched Julie's face to see if I could detect a hint of disapproval, a judgment against the two of us for breaking the rules. But as usual she seemed sympathetic, interested and nonjudgmental.

"With him, Julie, it was easier to endure Stan's resentment of me. And Bill, unlike Stan, wanted me to achieve more, to be a better writer, to grow. Since the show traveled all around the world, Bill and I often had two weeks together in marvelous places—the pyramids in Egypt, Mardi Gras in New Orleans, Carnival in Rio, San Francisco, the Bahamas. I felt like Cinderella with him. He was a friend, a lover and the best damn storyteller I had ever met. When we returned to New York—Bill to Scarsdale and his family and me to Stan and New Jersey—we would lunch, talk, dream, and plan for the next trip. If it hadn't been for Bill, I would probably have left Stan much earlier. But because I was so happy, felt so loved, I could stay in that terrible marriage, keeping my special secret. Do you know, Julie, that many people blamed Bill for my divorce, but in truth he kept me in the marriage longer."

"Did Bill promise to marry you?"

"Oh, yes, many times, and I believed him. But I knew it was a long shot. He was devoted to his two children, his suburban way of life. Finally I took the initiative. After Stan and I agreed that we were both too miserable to continue, I went to Mexico and got a divorce. I lived through it somehow with the help of

Margaritas, and returned to New York. Inside, I suppose, a secret part of me was hoping that if I was divorced, Bill would leave his wife."

"But nothing changed?" Julie asked.

"Nothing. It turned out he preferred the security of his family life to testing the unknown with me. It had lasted six years, and I knew he really loved me. But I also knew I had to leave the show to save myself. Maybe, just maybe, he would follow me. But he didn't."

"Was that the end of it?"

"No; he called me for months after I left. I'll do it, Barbara, after this birthday, that anniversary, this holiday, that trip. But I refused to see him. I knew it was over. Years later we would be friends again, able to have lunch and talk. But I never stopped caring about his life, his career, his happiness, just as I know he continued to care about mine."

"Did your parents know about him?"

"I told my mother, so I assume my father knew, too. She disapproved, of course, but we never really talked about it. The funny thing was that when it was all over, I was afraid to tell my parents the real reason I had left the show. Eventually I told my mother the truth. And she and I conspired to make believe I had left because I didn't like the hours. But our plan backfired, so ultimately I had to tell my father the truth, too. His reaction was peculiar. He was relieved. It was only a man. He thought I had been fired because I had failed at my job. It was worse, I tried to tell him. I had failed at love."

"And that brings us full circle to your arrival at Dr. Allen's office."

"Yes. I had started seeing him at the time of the divorce. But that summer, the summer after I left Bill, I had my first bona-fide, certifiable anxiety attack."

"Tell me about it," Julie said.

"I was riding in a cab with a man I was working for when suddenly the air felt thick and I thought I was choking. At first I believed it was the smell of his cigar. But it was more intense than that. I jumped out of the cab into the street and rushed to Dr. Allen's office. 'It is called anxiety,' he pronounced flatly. Out came the prescription pad and he recommended Valium, my old friend from my back-injury days."

"Why do you think you felt anxious?" Julie said.

I laughed. "Jesus, Julie. I was divorced, the man I loved refused to marry me, the job I had wasn't nearly as interesting as the one I'd had to leave. I was lonely —lonely and terribly sad. Aren't those reasons enough, for God's sake?"

"I didn't mean to make you angry," she replied. "I was just trying to make a point. When there are real reasons for anxiety, Barbara, that's not psychopathic. Did the Valium help?"

"Yes. The attacks came and went, but I knew the pills would help me and I went on living. I was only taking two milligrams a day. Eventually I found interesting work again, writing and producing documentaries. It was a challenge and I turned out to be good at it. The anxiety seemed to subside when I got involved again—involved with people, engaged in my work."

"Then why do you think they became more frequent and intense after you met Eric?"

"You're the doctor," I said. "You tell me." I didn't mean to be sarcastic, but I knew we were thinking the same thing. That first summer when I was faced with the loss of love, the loss of work, the need to make a new beginning, was a precursor of last summer, when my life fell apart again. "Was that the reason, Julie?" I asked. "All the years I was with Eric I was terrified that the whole thing was going to happen all over again?"

"Don't you think that was part of it?"

"Yes," I said softly. "I've always wanted my life to be a steady flow, a continuity. But it seems it's been nothing but stops and starts, endings and new beginnings." I tried to smile. "So what's the pathology level on the story of Bill—on a scale of one to ten? Father figure again? Masochism? Clutching at something I knew I couldn't have? The dependent little girl who knows she is being bad and deserves to be punished?"

"I've got no easy answer for that one. But there was no pathology. Just pain, some of which you caused yourself, and I'm sorry you had to go through that. But it was part of growing up."

"Oh, Julie, I love you. No pathology—that's your favorite phrase. If there's no pathology, what am I doing in a place like this?"

"I sometimes wonder myself."

"Well," I said, "just wait until I tell you about Eric."

I was becoming friendly with Kathy and Claudia, the two teen-age girls who lived on the hall and attended the high school run by the hospital. We took walks to town together, painted together, listened to music together. They seemed to be completely normal teen-agers, and one day I asked them why they were here. Why were two young girls living like coeds in a place with sick people like Roger and Joe and Jeff and Iris? Why did their parents permit it.

I knew that each of them had behavioral problems and some bouts with depression; each had messed with street drugs; but neither of them was sick, not mental-hospital kind of sick. Claudia was fourteen and looked twelve, with a round face and an impish smile. Kathy was fifteen and beautiful, with short-cropped hair and large brown soulful eyes. She could have been the ingénue in a Broadway play. They were troubled, but what teen-ager isn't? I wanted to know the truth. Why were they here?

The truth. They didn't get along with their parents, so why not put them in a mental hospital? It had good doctors, a good school—and they had psychiatric insurance. I couldn't believe that any parents would put their children in an institution because they had insurance. I looked at Claudia, deep in her eyes. Was there any other reason, a reason she hadn't told me? No, it was as simple as that. It was cheaper than boarding school.

One morning, Claudia and I were having coffee in

the crowded hospital cafeteria. At this point my status in the hospital had been raised to that of "Open Hall," which meant I could come and go as I pleased as long as I met Julie for our sessions and was back on the hall by curfew at four-thirty. Claudia and I sat there watching the other patients, the doctors and nurses, as they filed by carrying their cups and trays. Claudia was terribly upset. She had to spend a weekend with her mother, whom she hated, or else with her father, whom she hated even more, and we were talking things over.

"You've got to make plans for next fall, Claudia," I said. "You must."

"But don't you understand, Barb?" she said, pouting. "They want me to live with one of them and go to a private school next year. That's what all these visits are about."

"But wouldn't you rather do that than live in this horrid place?"

"No, I'd rather stay here. I really would."

"With Roger and Joe and Jeff and Iris and all the noise on the hall? You can't mean that, Claudia. You can't."

"Well, it's true. And it won't cost my parents any money. I still have two more years of psych insurance. So what's the difference?"

"I can't believe that either of your parents is so hateful that you'd rather stay here. That's the difference."

It was a conversation we'd had many times. But all my reasoning proved futile. She went on and on about how it wasn't so terrible here, she had freedom, the kids in school were great, she could bake and paint at OT, bowl at RT, she had her own room. What a life, I thought, what parents, what demons they must be, to make Six North seem like a good alternative. But whenever that subject came up, Claudia became close-mouthed, tight-lipped, and the little furrows on her young brow deepened. She didn't look like an imp anymore. She looked like a troubled young woman, and I felt helpless.

I complained to Julie. "I can't believe the hospital

would permit Claudia to stay. It can't be that hungry for patients, for dollars. What kind of place is this that keeps patients because they have insurance, that mixes troubled teen-agers with schizophrenics and hard-core psychotics like Joe and Roger?"

"You're putting me in a terrible position, Barbara. I don't know all about Claudia's background and neither do you. I'm sure her parents aren't totally the ogres she describes them as being. You can't believe everything the other patients tell you. Dr. Wald is her doctor and I'm confident he wouldn't keep her here if he didn't think it was necessary."

"You can defend this place; you have to," I argued. "But I know it's more scarring for her to live here than at home or in a boarding school. The only reason she's here is because it's free."

"Not for everybody, Barbara. I hate to bring this up, but the deposit you gave the hospital is gone and there's quite a bit due on your account. You really should see Mr. Thomas in the finance office."

Money! With all the talk about Claudia and insurance, I had forgotten. The meter was ticking. Eighteen hundred a week. My five thousand dollars was gone and I owed at least three thousand more. I promised Julie I would take care of it. We were both embarrassed by the discussion.

"Now we only have a few minutes left, Barbara. We've spent practically the whole time talking about Claudia. I want you to get your money's worth."

"I'm sorry."

"I'm not, at least not in one way. Have you noticed, Barbara, that you're spending a lot of time talking to the other patients these days, caring about them? Lara told me that you lent her some perfume when her husband came to see her. And you bake cookies and cakes and pass them around the hall."

"You make me sound like a Girl Scout," I said. "Or a therapist."

"No, but it's a sign that you're getting involved again. The old Barbara." She began to gather up the papers on her desk. "But it can also be a way of avoiding yourself. When you first came here, all you wanted to talk about was Eric. Now that we're ready to talk about him, you seem to be putting it off. Why?"

"I'm scared, Julie. It's as simple as that. I'm scared of what I might find out about myself."

That night a new patient arrived. He was young, but I couldn't be sure of his age because of his dark beard and unkempt hair. His clothes were ragged and torn. He walked like a robot, stiff, unfeeling. One of the other patients whispered to me that he had been transferred from Bellevue and he was heavily sedated. Jeff went up to him. "Hi. You the new patient? I'm Jeff. Got a cigarette?" Don shoved Jeff out of the way as he guided the young man to the glass-enclosed office.

Lillian, the old woman, had been discharged the day before. She had been given a powerful anti-depressant and some make-shift therapy and had recovered quickly. The young man would sleep in her room. Would he hear Lillian's demons or his own? I wondered. Did these tiny rooms absorb sickness? Did they tell secrets? Did the walls have to be painted more often because of the humidity of the thousands of tears that were shed inside them?

There was a commotion on the hall. "It's my fucking pool stick," Iris shrieked, "and I won't share it with that mother-fucking Joe, that creep!" She started to hit Joe with the pool cue, and Don rushed out of the office to pull her away. "Stay away from me, Don," she screamed at him. "Stay away from me or I'll bash in your mother-fucking head!" Don may have been intimidated by this female hulk, but he moved swiftly and wrested the pool cue from her hand.

The young man, the new patient, watched all this from the doorway of the glass office. Jeff, loving the violence, walked up to him. "Welcome," he said with a broad smile and barely a trace of irony. "Welcome to Six North."

10
Jim

His name was Jim and at first we exchanged stories in the traditional mental-patient manner: You tell me your fuck-up and I'll tell you mine. He asked smart questions of me, gentle but probing questions. I didn't know that Jim, as a seasoned inmate, knew all the shortcuts for getting a story from a fellow patient. But I found him, unlike my other colleagues on the hall, intelligent and sensitive. I told him a brief version of my nightmare, and when I had finished, he looked up at me, frowning, and said, "Eric was a Nazi, a bloody storm trooper. How could you have loved someone like that?" It was difficult to convince Jim that Eric had never shown me the dark side of his personality before.

Then I wanted to know about Jim. What was this bright, psychologically aware young man doing in a mental hospital? He told me of his life—not without humor. He had rejected his parents' world of Glen Cove, Long Island, an upper-class, Jewish enclave where Gucci and Pucci were the bywords, whereas Jim was interested in Marcuse and Zen. He described college in Ann Arbor, Michigan, political activism, then drugs, lots of drugs—grass, acid, speed, more acid. Although he made no connection between his illness and the drugs, I decided there had to be one. He had his first schizophrenic episode at the age of twenty-two.

After he dropped out of college, he led a vagabond existence, living in truck stops, listening to Dylan, fleeing the agenda his parents had planned for him, an agenda that included going into the family business and the life of a stifling, insular suburb. He loathed that life, all it stood for; he became animated as he described the capitalist exploitation of workers that *had* to happen in his father's factory, in *any* factory. So as part of his rebellion he had worked as a ranch hand, in steel mills, in orange groves (better to become one of the exploited than an exploiter, I thought), criss-crossing the country, traveling alone. Lonely.

Then he told me of the accident. He had been driving a cab on Third Avenue when suddenly, from nowhere, he sensed that an old girl friend was in terrible trouble, that she needed him desperately. He could almost see her face, he said, almost hear her voice calling to him. He quickly turned his cab around and began to drive the wrong way on a one-way street. He collided with another car, a young woman was killed, and Jim was convicted of manslaughter and sentenced to six months on Rikers Island, in one of the roughest prisons in New York City. He should have been sent to a hospital. It would be weeks before Jim could tell me of the terrible isolation of that prison, of the violence and what it was like to live with hardened criminals who taunted him. Of fighting off the men who tried to rape him.

The first night we met, Jim and I talked for more than five hours after dinner, sitting side by side on the couch outside my room, wearing robes and slippers. We found out about each other's lives, while Joe walked around in circles cackling to himself, Roger and Iris fought over a pool cue, and Jeff strummed a guitar and sang his inimitable version of "Honky Tonk Women." Over all that groaned the phonograph and the television set, but we were oblivious to the noise, to the people. Jim made me laugh when he said living on Six North was like living in a park, everything public, nothing private. Only when the night nurse, Mae, a large black woman who performed her chores like a martinet, bellowed, "Jim! Barbara! I don't want to tell you again. It's after eleven. Go to bed this minute. I mean it, do you hear?"—only then did we reluctantly say good night, and I heard myself adding, "Sleep well," something I hadn't said to anyone for longer than I could remember.

After that first night we spent hours together, just talking. I felt good with Jim. He seemed healthy to me, not sick like the other patients. He was smart, someone with brains to talk with, and what's more, though I was fifteen years older than he, I had to admit that once he had changed out of his hobo clothes and shaved, he was an attractive, almost handsome man. But his eyes were so fierce. Only when we laughed at each other's propensity for self-destruction did I see a glint of tenderness through the dark anger that covered his eyes.

I used to make films about people like Jim—the social rebellion, the political idealism, the rioting, the drugs. And soon I began to tease him that his life was a loose end from the sixties. I told him that when he talked about his hatred for his father's business, he reminded me of Dustin Hoffman in *The Graduate*. "You should be done with all that sixties rebellion stuff," I said. "Don't you know the seventies is the time of consolidation and making peace with the system?" But he wasn't through rebelling at all. He had resolved nothing toward his parents. And he told me he had been in this hospital the year before for ten months. Ten months! I didn't want to believe it.

So we would talk and talk, laugh and tease each other's craziness. The staff wondered what we talked about for so many hours. I don't really remember. Poetry, politics, our own lives, everything. I blinded myself to the fact that he was a patient, that he was seriously ill. I saw only a tender, hurting young man who at the age of twenty-five had spent too many months of his life in mental hospitals. Much later I had only to hear Timothy Leary's name to feel a terrible rage, recalling the tragic advice he had given to a generation of young people. Jim was probably one of thousands of kids who had followed that advice, who had experimented with mind-altering drugs and who hadn't made it back to reality. In my months in the hospital, I met other young people, all of whom had

bouts of serious mental illness after experimenting
with drugs in Vietnam or here at home. And I had to
include myself in the category of drug abuser. I remembered doing a show in Boston with young kids on
drugs, worrying about their lives, hating the drugs, as I
popped my pills. LSD, speed, heroin, Valium—every
one of the patients on Six North had used and abused
a drug, generally with the complicity or at least the
approbation of their doctors.

The hours that had stretched before me now had a
purpose. Jim was someone to talk with, to get coffee
for, to buy cigarettes for, someone to care about. When
I came from art therapy, I always showed Jim my
pictures, and he hung some of the childish dabblings in
his room. He wrote me poems. Sitting in a locked ward
together, we spent hours reading to each other, trying
to fill the emptiness we both suffered with the warmth
and intensity of friendship.

He was enthusiastic about a poet I had never heard
of: Pablo Neruda.

"How can a woman like you not have heard of
Pablo Neruda?" he said. "I don't believe it. I just don't
believe it, Barb."

"I was busy making the world safe for democracy,
so sue me," I said. "I'm sorry, but I love him now, so
what's the difference? Read me the one about solitude
again."

It was cocoa time and we were sitting on the
wretched couch outside my room. Jim began to read.

> I asked the others after,
> the women and the men,
> what they were doing with such confidence
> and how they had learned their living;
> they did not actually answer,
> they went on dancing and living.

That night Jim was still reading aloud when the
buzzer rang and the aides came running to help subdue
Roger. I was frightened, but Jim said, "Ignore it,
Barbara, ignore it. Just listen to the poetry. Tune it out

so your mind won't retain the ugliness years from now." So I told myself I wanted to hear only the poetry of Neruda, and I tried to block out all the ugliness of the hall with the beauty of his words, with the warmth of our growing friendship. Jim and I were carefully creating our own world in which we could survive this dungeon. It took time, but that's the one thing we could both afford.

The next morning I told Julie about what had happened the previous evening. "Would you believe it? We sat there reading poetry while Don and the other aides tackled Roger, and I was able to block it out. I heard only the poetry, only Jim's voice."

"I believe it" Julie said. "Why do you think I wouldn't?"

"Because I thought I was too sick to make a friend, too sick to care. But he *is* my friend and I want him to get well. I'm so worried about him. And I'm worried that you don't approve of our friendship."

"You are good for each other," Julie said. "You really are. I've told you therapy happens all the time, not just in here." And she smiled one of her "I know you're older and lived more, but I'm younger and your doctor" smiles, an embarrassed smile, which reminded me that we were not equal, that I depended on her for everything—insight, wisdom, advice, passes, discharge. She was a litmus-paper test of my identity and I was shocked that she approved of our friendship. I had expected her to remind me of Jim's illness, tell me of the difference in our ages. But no, she actually seemed happy for me.

Jim's therapist was Joyce Roberts, the tall, angular, talkative woman from Texas, who spoke with a thick Southwestern accent and had a constant silly grin on her face. She was a psychiatrist and like some of the other therapists, always wore a white coat and a stethoscope around her neck as if the accouterments of a medical doctor would authenticate them in their patients' minds. She bustled about like a mother hen and spent hours giggling and gossiping with the nurses who sat in the glass-enclosed office where they could monitor all the doings on the hall.

I had never liked Joyce. I thought she was meddle-some, condescending and stupid. But now I began to realize that she could be dangerous. It was as if all that had happened in this country during the sixties had passed her by; she had been oblivious, she had experienced nothing, seen nothing. She had no understanding of Jim, or his world, or the world he aspired to. She treated him like a little boy, coddling and fawning, and he couldn't stand it. At first I thought I was wrong. How could I be right? But sadly I was. And I discovered that she resented me. When she walked by and saw Jim and me deeply engrossed in talk, I could see her anger. But why? I was a patient. Julie approved of our friendship. How could Joyce be jealous of me? Sometimes when I saw that Jim was backing away from life, not wanting to talk of his terrible pain, I would get him to tell me about Rikers Island or the accident or the peace movement. Then he would connect, feel. He'd be all there. He must have told Joyce that he liked talking with me, and that's why she was jealous. She couldn't relate to his world. She understood nothing of neon-lit truck stops, Marcuse, Dylan—or Jewish middle-class life on Long Island. How could she possibly help Jim?

While I was angry at the childlike, insensitive way Joyce treated him and her other patients, only later would it occur to me that I could have been unfortunate enough to have been assigned her instead of Julie. In a mental hospital, getting a good therapist is like a crapshoot for your soul. I wasn't assigned to Julie because she specialized in needful neurotic ladies from New York. Only because her caseload was lower than anyone else's at that particular moment, only because it was her turn at bat, was she made my therapist. And in the same way Joyce became Jim's therapist. It was all terribly frightening. You cannot choose a doctor in a mental hospital or get rid of an inept one. You must remain with the therapist to whom you are assigned. In a hospital, any attempt by the patient to change doctors is viewed by the staff as a wish to avoid working hard in therapy. It's always the patient's fault; the inept doctor is always protected. How unfair, I thought. It's all timing, chance. We would never treat our bodies the way we permit doctors to treat our minds. Never!

Thanksgiving in a mental hospital. The nurses brought in guitars and we all sat around in the day room singing folk songs and Christmas carols. The staff went out of their way to make the day warm and caring. Even Roger and Iris discerned this was not to be a day of violence. They sat aside from the rest of us, quietly watching us try to make a Thanksgiving happen in that terrible environment.

Julie had left the day before for a five-day holiday, and during our last session she had tried to get me to talk about how it felt, how I felt, about spending Thanksgiving, the holiday of families and friends, of togetherness, in an institution. I couldn't answer her. My sense of loss was ineffable. There were no words, but still I assured her that I would be with Don and Paul and Jim, my new friends, and it wouldn't really be so terrible. We had begun to talk about Eric at last, about the dark side of him which had appealed to the ominously dark side of me. I was still feeling like a Martian, still disconnected, still trying to convince Julie I was a hopeless schizophrenic. But I knew I was more in control, more out of myself and in touch with my environment, ready now to try to solve the riddle of Eric and what had happened between us. Why did Julie have to leave me now? When we said goodbye we embraced, and I wished her a good holiday. But I found myself missing her the moment she walked off the hall.

The day after Thanksgiving was a warm, almost soft prewinter day, and Jim and I decided to play tennis. So, dressed in jeans and sweaters, we borrowed two rackets and three dead balls and played tennis under the big spruce tree that caressed the court on the hospital grounds. We played well, considering we were both fighting inertia and apathy, both battling the rigidity of our bodies, which matched the deadening of our spirits. I had to struggle with the lack of coordination that comes from weeks of sitting. But Jim played beautifully. I didn't know yet that he had taught tennis as one of his many jobs. I was fascinated by the way he moved. I, graceless, angular, darting for the ball; he, effortless, smooth, easy.

We didn't play a set. We just hit the ball. But it was marvelous. Looking at Jim I thought, God, he's a man. And for the first time in months I was aware of sexual stirrings all over me, my body, my breasts. It was like being aroused for the first time, when pubescence has begun, when the world is young. I felt all new and shaky, and when we were through playing, I could walk only with difficulty. I was dizzy with new, new-old, delicious feelings.

I was embarrassed. I hadn't been aware of Jim's body before. I had become familiar with his mind, his heart, his impetuousness, his immaturity, his gentleness. I had not been in touch with his maleness. But I didn't say a word as we stomped through the dead, crunchy leaves that covered the grounds. Happy. I could feel! Questions of right-wrong, young-old, or if he shared my feelings, didn't enter my mind. I wouldn't let them.

He probably felt nothing for this neurotic, anxiety-ridden, aging lady, I told myself. So when these thoughts popped into my head, I dismissed them. But walking next to him, I could smell his maleness, his smell heightened by the activity of the game, and I got dizzy again. For Christ's sake, Barbara, he's a twenty-five-year-old mental patient, a boy with a head burned out from acid. Knock it off or you'll ruin a good friendship. I tried, but the delicious feelings cut through the deadness of my spirit, the hollowness I had felt for months. I knew they were inappropriate, but still I couldn't stop them.

Jim was talking of fresh air, tennis and life. He teased me, "For a forty-year-old lady, you move all right. But your backhand looks like a chicken."

I was smiling, thinking my secret thoughts as we entered the gray-green hall and the thick, sick air, which for once couldn't block out the lightness I was beginning to feel in my heart.

That night after dinner, Jim and I resumed our basic sitting position on the couch outside my room. We were talking and watching the nightly parade: Roger rapping about life on Venus, Iris threatening Joe, the other patients ever moving but going nowhere, marching up and down the hall, pacing, strutting, jabbering. Mickey, a young depressed patient, and Cora, a schizophrenic black girl, were sitting opposite us, staring and listening to our talk, trying to pick up on our energy, our humanity, the normalcy we must have represented to them.

Jim was right. All business in a mental hospital is public, like living your life on stage. If you pee, cry, see your doctor, go out on a pass, miss a meal, all the other patients know about it, and what's more, feel they have the right to comment, just as they believe you care about their bowel habits, medication and weekend passes. I called it the assumption of caring. We watched the evening staff report to the late-night staff. We saw the people-watchers arrive—the men who sat in chairs outside the patients' rooms, watching their sleep. Mae turned off the TV and the phonograph; the patients lined up for their medication. The beginnings of peace came at eleven o'clock.

"Jim! Barbara! It's after eleven. I don't want to tell you again," Mae cried down the hall. We ignored her. I was reading a poem by Cummings: "... who pays any attention to the syntax of things will never wholly kiss you."

And when I finished, Jim said softly, "Come here, baby, I want to hold you."

I was shocked and not shocked. So it hadn't been only me, and I heard myself say that I wanted to hold him, too. But personal contact (PC) was forbidden, and besides, public displays were not our style. So instead we just said good night, sleep well.

"Tonight I'll be sleeping with you," Jim said as he got up.

"And me, you."

I went into my room feeling as I hadn't felt in months. I felt my heart, my soul, my womanness. Nothing had really happened, except everything had happened. The nasty, ugly thoughts that usually circled my brain were quiet that night. My mistake was in thinking they were gone forever. But the grayness that had shrouded me for months was lightened. I was a woman. I could feel. I could give. For I had to have given Jim something for him to want to hold me. And he had said hold, not fuck. He said sleep, not screw. And for me, in the bleakness of illness and in that terrible place, it was as if holding and sleeping and touching were the most important things in the world.

A few days later on a Sunday we were walking on the grounds of the hospital. Late November cold had arrived suddenly, although it was still warm enough to sit under the graceful spruce. His arm around me, my head on his chest, feeling him breathe, we sat together silently, watching the sun disappear into the gray-blue twilight sky.

He kissed me. It was the softest kiss I had ever known. Then we were touching, feeling, groping, our bodies side by side. Primordial animal feelings mixed with affection for the first time. When we paused to look up, the sun was gone and an enormous orange harvest moon was staring down at us. "Let's go," Jim said suddenly. "Christ, we're late again." We drew apart. The satisfaction with childlike exploring was gone. Adult reality had come roaring in. There was no way to sublimate the man-woman thing. So we walked back, unfulfilled, like sad and frustrated adolescents. Still, I was happy. My smile belied the other truth. We had shared something together, something private. It was after that evening that we began using the line "Hold on to your dignity." We would say it often to save ourselves from the constant humiliation that came from just being on the hall.

Joyce continued to play her role as earth mother. Her giggly style, her silliness, her cultural and political experience, isolated her completely from the backgrounds and the values that were part of her patient's problems. She had no real psychological insight, and covered up for that lack by acting like a doting parent. Jim told me, laughing, that a session with her had all the intensity of talking on the phone. When he told her about his past, about tepees in Arizona, about being on the road in America in the sixties, she just looked at him blankly and called him a bad, irresponsible boy. She had no idea what he was about.

"To know me is to know the sixties," Jim told me. And with me he could be self-mocking about his political experience. "I was there," I reminded him. "I filmed you. I was there with cameras and my own political indignation." We laughed about the difference in our ages, but we both understood that I knew the place he was coming from. Joyce didn't and I hated her for that. I complained about her to Julie. I begged her to intervene, to use her influence to get another therapist for Jim. But there was nothing she could do. That's not the way the system worked. There was nothing I could do either, except counter Joyce's jealousy of me with resentful and angry looks. A war was developing between us.

One evening I sat on the couch outside my room, watching the other patients in the nightly medication line. Jim was standing there in his robe and slippers with his hand extended, waiting to be given his pills. He looked so small, so frail, so vulnerable, and we both hated all signs of dependence in each other. It was ironic, I thought, that I who had pleaded for pills got nothing, while in the beginning he practically had to be forced to take medication.

I was still thinking about drugs when he came to join me on the couch and I said to him, "Jimmy, what happened to us? All I did was stop taking Valium."

"No," he said, "all you did was *start* taking Valium."

"Yes," I said. "Just as you had no business taking that goddamned acid."

Immediately his eyes darkened, the furrows in his brow became deeper. I had trespassed on forbidden territory. "That had nothing to do with it," he said fiercely, "and you know it. Now knock it off with the acid."

I had broken the cardinal rule. I was not to dump on LSD, ever. He refused to see any connection between his drug experimentation and his illness. That was because his parents did, his doctors did, everyone did. But he was adamant. LSD had nothing to do with anything. Nothing.

Jim's illness had no external craziness, no displays of madness. His was a quiet melancholy, inertia, passivity, apathy, but never a craziness that I could see. I was different. I still felt lost, terrified, lonely. And that evening after we had changed the subject from drugs to something neutral, something less capable of producing rage, I suddenly had the feeling that I was disappearing into the atmosphere, that I was fragmenting, and all I could do was hold on. I was flooded with tears.

"Jim, it's so scary. I feel like I'm made up of a million billion molecules, and all of them are disintegrating into space. If I don't hold on to the couch, hold on to you, I'll disappear." And then I began sobbing uncontrollably. But through my sobs I heard myself saying, "I can't perpetrate this insanity on you, Jimmy, I can't.

"You can perpetrate anything, Barb," he said. "We're friends. But I feel so helpless when you get like this. I can't help you. I can't do anything." And then he got up and walked quickly to his room.

So I learned to stay away from him during those terrible moments, those moments that were like seizures, when all I felt was sickness. But when I finally stopped crying that evening, he came back and handed me a cup of hot cocoa.

"I didn't mean to leave you, Barb," he said, "but I couldn't stand it. I hope you're not angry."

I looked up at him, my eyes filled with tears, new tears—tears for him, not for myself. "How can I be angry? You're helping me save my life. I won't ever do that again, Jim, ever!"

When I think of Jim now, I have to think of the laughter we shared. But if I ever wanted to forget our age difference, the experiences that came from our being together would jolt me back to reality.

We were painting side by side one day in art therapy. I went to the phonograph to change the record. Jim listened with interest as we both continued painting.

"That's nice, Barbara. Who is that?" he asked me.

"Vivaldi."

"Vivaldi? Is he new?"

"Jim, you're kidding." I laughed.

Vivaldi could have been the new Bruce Springsteen. It would have mattered to the old Barbara Gordon. This one laughed.

And other times we fought. Once he was rough on a fellow patient who had been a soldier in Vietnam. He attacked Earl for finding manhood in fighting, in patriotism. But I knew that was all Earl had for his identity. He hadn't had the money or the status or the education to stay out of the war. And I suspected Jim had. So I attacked him with a ferocity I had never displayed before. And for several days we didn't speak.

One early December weekend, Jim was able to wangle an afternoon pass and so was I. We had lunch in Greenwich and I felt very much like Simone Signoret in *Room at the Top* when I caught the disapproving glare of the headwaiter, who seemed to be computing ages. Jim and I sat close together in a back booth, laughing and touching like adolescents. My heart jumped when he kissed me lightly on the lips. It felt like my first date and my first kiss.

Then the strangest thing happened. I had to go to the bathroom, and there in the restaurant's brightly lighted, tiled and scented toilet, I realized I could lock the door. I could pee in private without worrying if Iris was going to stomp in or one of the nurses, checking to see if I was still alive. Back at the table, I told Jim what a thrill a private bathroom was. It takes so little to make you happy when you're feeling desperate.

That bathroom reminded me of my other life and I said to him, "They just don't know, they don't know I wasn't always terrible, weak and wretched. Oh, Jim, I had a life, and they don't know how much I miss it, how much I want to be well. But whole, not a piece of myself, not a fraction. Oh, they don't know the kind of woman I was."

After a few seconds he looked at me and said, "I

know how much you've lost being here. Much more than I have. For me this isn't much of a step down from prisons or coal mines, but for you . . . As part of your therapy, maybe the hospital ought to see four of your friends." He said this so innocently, so seriously. "And your friends could tell Julie what kind of a person you were before, tell everybody you weren't always sick."

I almost gasped. I loved him so in that moment. He understood me. He understood my loss—my loss of myself, of my life. And he had offered a naïve but beautiful solution. Forget the fights, the jealousy, striking out or avoiding each other when we were hurt or angry. In the crunch, and there were many, we were there for each other. And there is no way to measure the value of the sweetness of someone caring about your life in the midst of sickness. The warmth, the sharing and laughter, and primarily the tenderness, are what ultimately saved us.

But Jim didn't understand all of me. I have always been fairly uncoordinated, a dropping kind of person to whom friends say, "Please don't help with the dishes." I just drop and spill things—coffee, cigarette ashes—all the time. Not in touch with my environment, I suppose. And Jim watched this side of me with baffled amazement. It didn't square with his picture of my New York self. That morning I had vowed that when we went to lunch I wouldn't make a mess, and when it was time to leave, very proud of myself, I said, "Jim, do you realize I didn't spill, drop, smear or break anything?"

"No," he said, smiling a broad smile, "but the straw from your Coke is stuck in the middle of Pablo Neruda."

He laughed and laughed. Julie could work on me for thirty years, he said, and she'd never touch that part of me. "You're crazy," he said, putting his arm around me, and we talked and giggled all the way back to the hospital. We were late again, after curfew, but so what? It wasn't our fault that the sun went down at four-thirty.

That evening I was in my room, replaying our day

together in my head, when outside my door, to my amazement, I heard Jim talking with Kathy, the fifteen-year-old student, about spending a night with her in the dead of winter in a sleeping bag near the ocean. I couldn't stand it. I was livid. How could he? Only this afternoon . . . I refused to speak to him for the rest of the evening.

"If you don't talk to me now," he called to me as I marched to the day room, ignoring him, "we'll never talk again, Barbara."

"I don't care," I said. "Leave me alone. How could you, Jim? How could you? Couldn't you have fantasized with her somewhere else?"

"It was just a fantasy. I didn't know you were in your room."

"It's a question of style, Jim. Obviously, the day meant more to me that it did to you."

Finally he said softly, "She's fifteen years old, Barbara. And besides, I *would* like to sleep on the beach with someone, and you're not the type. You like room service."

No answer sufficed. I was crushed. I went to my room and had a tantrum. It would be days before Jim and I would be friends again.

I had become a pro at institutional bartering in that world where cigarettes are the coin of the realm and different brands have different values. One night I found myself out of cigarettes and told Lara that if she gave me one I would cancel the ten cents she owed me for a phone call. Jim overheard me and said, "You know, Barbara, there's something kind of beautiful and something kind of horrible watching a woman like you survive in this place."

If I could no longer relate to the world of functioning people, I was still clawing to hold on to life. And if I had to narrow my perimeters, and desperately cling to surviving in the hospital in order to get back my sense of self, I would. Maybe someday I would function "outside" again. I wasn't sure.

One day I received a letter from CBS saying that I had been nominated for two Emmy awards for a film I had done the year before. Jim was thrilled for me. A few days later beautiful flowers arrived for me. I didn't understand. It wasn't my birthday yet. Why would someone send me flowers? Debbie, the head nurse, who presented them to me, with Jim hovering close by, told me, "It's for the Emmy, Barbara. We're so proud of you. Thank Jim. It was his idea. But they're from all of us." I blushed with embarrassment and pleasure, thanking everyone.

After dinner that evening, Jim told me that he knew if I had been in New York, it would have been a big thing, two Emmy nominations, with a party to celebrate and champagne. He could only give me flowers. I told him you rarely get champagne even if you win. "This is nicer than anything anyone in New York would have done," I said. "Thank you so much."

I ran to my room and cried and cried. Later that night, my small, dark room smelled sweet and fresh, and pink mums and yellow daisies smiled at me as if to say, "We know we make happiness." As I fell asleep I murmured, "Thank you, Debbie, thank you, Roger, thank you, Jeff. But most of all, thank you, Jim."

Barry and Lisa Travis, Mark and Paula Sondheim, were driving up from the city to take me to dinner, my first pass with friends from the outside world. That afternoon in my session with Julie, I was terribly excited, and she asked, "How will you be tonight?"

"Fine," I said. "I'll be fine. My friends deserve the best Barbara I can produce. After all, they're schlepping here all the way from New Jersey."

"I'm not familiar with New York expressions," she said. "What does schlepp mean?"

"Oh, Julie," I said, "it's not a New York expression. It's Jewish. Don't you know *anything?*" For a moment I pretended to be angry, but then I began to laugh. She smiled and then she was laughing, too. It was a moment of warmth and understanding between us. I had called her medieval and barbaric; she had told me I would die in dark rooms. But now we were both laughing together, reading each other's thoughts, knowing that somehow we had been able to bridge the vast chasm between our worlds.

I had a wonderful time that evening. Paula brought me a plant, Lisa a silver heart. I had told Lisa over the phone a few days before that I felt like the Tin Woodman. "Until you get your own," she said. It felt good and natural to be with them. But somehow after seeing them, filling my void with their love, hearing about their lives, I felt emptier. They were the aberration. Sickness was the norm. And part of me hated them for having each other, for being well, succeeding at life. I had botched it so. I couldn't believe, sitting with them at dinner, that earlier in the day I had eaten with Iris and Roger. Jim, in the sick world, represented health to me.

And sickness as the norm is a real part of hospital living. Letters and visits from my friends always reminded me that there was a world I had once been a part of—and it was still going on. But with sickness all around me, I had lost touch with that world. I could relate only to life in the hospital. It was better than nothingness, which is the way I thought my life would be when I left. I knew that I would have to start all over again from nothing, and I was afraid that the terrible needful part of me would not be able to do it alone.

When I was not talking with Julie or Jim, I was still not really functioning. But I was trying to fill the empty hours with painting, cooking, reading—anything. I complained to Julie, aired my opinions at the Friday meetings of the hall, tried to change things. If the hospital was my world, at least I wanted to have some say in it. Jim didn't care. Every day he slept for hours on a couch outside his room. I hated the institutional mold I saw growing on his back, his caving in to the hospital world. He had spent so many months in jails and hospitals. "Do something—read, write," I urged him over and over again.

"Leave me alone, Barbara. I can't fight it anymore, or fight Joyce anymore. Don't nag. It doesn't become you. Don't be a mother."

"Am I being a mother?" I asked Julie. I was worried that my friendship with Jim was becoming too important to me, that my recovery had too much to do with him.

Julie reassured me that if I were as sick as I thought I was, I couldn't even respond to Jim. But as much as I wanted to talk about him during our sessions, she was in charge of the therapy and Eric was our chief topic of discussion now. It was a slow and painful business, and I was saddened to realize that there wouldn't be a magic moment of illumination, a eureka factor, when I would suddenly sit up and cry, "I've got it, I've got it! When I was six my father said this, my mother did that, and that's why I listened to Eric. That's why a part of me thinks sickness and dependence are more natural to me than health." But no, Julie told me, there won't be one magical day, or one dramatic moment like in the movies, when the hysterical woman gets out of a wheelchair and says to Sigmund, "I can walk, I can walk!" It won't be as easy as that, she said. But I continued to yearn for an epiphany.

It was a cold December day. The sleet was bouncing off the window in Julie's office and it reminded me that I had arrived in this hospital in September. "The seasons are changing faster than I am," I despaired.

Julie propped her feet up on the desk. "Why do you think you didn't want to marry Eric?" she began. She wanted to know when and how he had been transformed from lover to villain, and why I hadn't perceived the change in him sooner.

"I know you're thinking it's because somewhere, deep in the recesses of my subconscious or unconscious or whatever, I suspected something dark and ominous about him. But I don't think that was true, Julie. I think I just didn't want to be married. Children are always, it seems to me, the best reason for marriage, and since we were really too old for kids, I was happy, divinely happy, the way we were."

"Except you couldn't go into department stores or restaurants or cross the street, you were so paralyzed with anxiety."

I grew impatient with her and interrupted. "But that wasn't because of Eric, was it? All that started long before I met him. I agree it got worse after we began living together, but I never thought Eric was the cause of my anxiety. I always had lots of things on my mind—my job, my parents, life. As a matter of fact, I've always had a theory about anxiety. I've decided that my anxiety always increases in direct proportion to the absence of Richard Nixon in my life."

Julie began to smile. She knew where I was headed.

"When he was around, lying, cheating, trying to destroy the Constitution, I was furious, but I had no anxiety. Then he resigned in '74, and I swear that's when my anxiety really got bad. What's more, I bet I'm not the only person who is walking around psychologically crippled by the absence of Richard Nixon in their lives. What do you think?"

"I think he was a perfectly acceptable target for free-floating anger for lots of people," Julie said. "But I hope you're not suggesting that he make a political comeback just so you can feel better."

"Oh Julie, I'm kidding. I've made my parents the scapegoats, the Valium, Dr. Allen, Eric. Why not a disgraced President? But it's true. I really do miss him."

"So do I," Julie said, smiling. "But back to Eric."

"I miss him, too. Not the diabolical sadistic, destructive Eric, but the man who was my lover, my friend. He was the smartest man I ever met. And the tenderest. I still don't know what happened."

"Well, you've given me some clues," Julie began slowly. "He was dependent on you for everything, Barbara. Money, clients, friends, the apartment, the house at the beach, love, friendship, sex. You were his whole world."

"So why in God's name did he try to destroy me? Why didn't he help me when I was sick?"

"He did at first," she said coolly, and then she reminded me of the vitamins, the brown rice, all the errands. "I think he even believed he was helping you when he started to play analyst, encouraging you to remember painful things, to act out, to regress. That's a very dangerous game, Barbara, and that's when things began to get out of control."

"But why did he tell me I was hopeless and schizophrenic, that I'd be lobotomized, that everyone hated me? I begged him to take me to a hospital. Why didn't he do it? Why did he keep me locked up in that apartment? Why did he try to destroy me?"

"I've thought about that a great deal, Barbara. I think he must have gotten so terribly frightened that he panicked. If you were sick, he feared he would lose everything, so he kept you there. And I think he really began to believe that you were destroying him. That made him so angry that he struck out at you. He resorted to violence to try to control you."

"But why did I let him do it? Did I want to be controlled? Was it the part of me that wants to be dependent, the bad little girl who wants to be punished?"

"Really, Barbara, you shouldn't call yourself dependent, just because Eric said you were. He was much more dependent on you than you were on him, even though he fixed the house, grew the plants, drove the car. He was dependent on you for his whole world —your world, Barbara. But subconsciously I don't think he could live with that kind of dependence. He tried to disguise it from himself, from you, by doing all the things he did, by casting you in the dependent role. And you were willing to accept that role. In a sense, you were both playing false parts, but his self-deception was much deeper than yours, much more necessary. And when he thought your illness threatened his security, his emotional and financial security, it evoked a dark and terrible part of him, a part, I might add, that was always there under the surface. And I submit, Barbara, part of you knew it. That's one of the reasons your anxiety increased."

I listened to her, shaking my head. No, she didn't understand. He had changed, seemingly overnight. I couldn't remember ever thinking he had a dark side until he tried to hurt me. "But, Julie," I said, "what about all my friends? They liked him. It wasn't as if they sat around saying to me, You ought to break up with that terrible sick man. I know they liked him. He fooled them, too."

"I have a feeling you force-fed Eric to your friends, Barbara. They liked him because they loved you, wanted you to be happy, and they suspended judgment for your sake. I think you may even have suspected that, just as I think you sometimes suspected that something was not quite right about Eric and about your relationship. You've told me about the ex-wives, the child he never saw, the fact that he had no friends."

"No," I said. "It's not that I'm resisting therapy or being stubborn, Julie. I just didn't see it that way. I loved him. I was happy. The Valium couldn't have hidden that much about him from me. Could it?"

"Barbara," Julie said softly, "we know how much the Valium hid from you about yourself."

The world of Six North, of Joe and Roger and Iris, was far away as we sat there together. Sleet was pounding on the window now and I realized we had been talking for over an hour. But Julie showed no indication of wanting to end the session.

"I must settle this, Julie," I said. "Help me. I can't live with this confusion. How could I have lived for five years with a man who was so troubled and not known it?"

She sat back in her chair and brought her legs down from the desk. Then she took a long sip of her soda. I could see that she was trying to find a way to tell me something important, something gravely important.

"I think a part of you did know it," she began. "But Eric sounds as if he has difficulties that even trained clinicians would find hard to diagnose. And it was further complicated by the fact he was terribly smooth and seemed so normal. There were no signs of anxiety and apparently no guilt. That's why he could tell you, and really believe it himself, that he had done nothing to harm you."

"But how could I love a man like that?" I said.

"You mustn't be too hard on yourself. You must stop thinking in black and white. If you think he was all good, then you blame yourself for driving him crazy. But his troubles were always there. Had you had a fight or separated for any reason, they probably would have surfaced in some kind of violence. And if you believe he was all bad, you blame yourself for having loved him. Either way you can't win. But he was both, Barbara. The world is what it is, imperfect, a world of people—no heroes, no villains, just people. And you've got to learn to accept that, in yourself and in the people you love. Only children idealize their parents and their friends. You are strong enough to see people as they are, not as you want them to be."

"And I saw Eric as I wanted him to be?"

"Yes," Julie said. "Do you know where he is now? Is he still in Boston?"

"I think so. What difference does it make?"

"Because your birthday is coming up, and I think it might be a good idea if I gave you a pass to go to New York to celebrate. It's time, Barbara. Think about it. Now you'd better go. It's getting late and you'll miss dinner."

That night in the darkness of my room, I thought about what Julie had said. If I went to New York, I wouldn't spend my birthday in this place after all. When I was with Julie, she made me feel strong, she made me feel that I could do it. But could I do it alone? Could I ever leave this place for good, make all the changes she asked me to make, learn to live with ambiguity, accepting my own flaws and conflicting emotions about people I loved? Could I ever learn to become a whole person again?

I had loved a man like Eric. Now the only man in the world who meant anything to me was a twenty-five-year-old mental patient. And Julie thought I was well enough to go home for my birthday.

11
Birthday

It was my birthday. I was forty-one years old and living in a mental institution. Jim never let me get away with calling Six North a psychiatric hospital. "Barbara," he would tell me, laughing, "you're in an institution no matter how you say it. It is an *institution.*" And I remembered hearing Fran say, "Be realistic, Barbara. Jeanie has pancreatic cancer. Why can't you face reality?"

Forty-one. I had read Gail Sheehy's *Passages,* but I knew that whatever had happened to me couldn't be passed off as going through Gail Sheehy time. This was no average mid-life crisis. I was still in trouble, bigger trouble than I had realized when I arrived at the hospital months before. It was December, December nineteenth. Forty-bloody-one years old. And where was I going on my birthday? Home. By myself. My first pass. My first solo flight. I was going home for a twelve-hour pass, home from the loony bin. Terrific!

I hadn't called any of my friends, not even Edie. I had decided to spend this birthday alone in my apartment. I had the visits from my old friends and my new relationships in the hospital as proof that I could connect when I was with people. The numbness, the sense of disconnection, was worse when I was alone. I would test it.

The night before my birthday trip, Jim handed me a poem he had written for me as a present. Now it was two in the morning and I was lying on my bed,

breaking the rules, reading the poem with the light on.
I put a towel over the lamp so Mae wouldn't catch me.

> In sanity's sweetness—lies burdens to unrest; to make
>   me see
> The otherside where I too once had lain
> In undenying denial of what I knew to be sane.
> Yet to carry a friend is the burdenless burden,
> For my love has its roots in your heart.
> Your whisper of unapproachable dilemmas
> Is but
> A riddle to my mind; for your essence lies in
> Earthly time.
> And health shall not only enter into sweet solitude's
> Rhyme, but to dance with me, as an old childhood
>   friend,
> Mary, Alice.

My heart felt light. Jim, in the midst of all the pain
of his third hospitalization, had reached into his heart
and written this for me. I put the poem in my drawer,
where I kept all his poems. I would take them with me
and read them on the train. If I got lost from myself, I
would read his sweet words, thinking of his love,
thinking of his talent and hoping he would get well and
out of this place. I fell into a dreamless sleep, eager for
the morning to arrive.

When I woke early that Sunday morning, my brain
was racing. The train, the station, the cab, the apartment—how could I do it *alone?* The apartment would
be so quiet, so empty. It would also be filthy. Great, I
would clean it, scour the demons out, wash the violence away, Mr. Clean the scars, Ajax the memories,
make it fresh and bright and new. I would also have
to expunge the happiness and love that had filled that
apartment in the good times, but I didn't think of
that.

Don knocked on my door and poked his head in,
urging me to get up and greet the day. It was seven-
thirty, breakfast in twenty minutes, and by the way,
happy birthday. It was a new beginning, he reminded
me. Today was the big day.

In my bright-red tote bag I had packed Jim's poems, his copy of Pablo Neruda and a bunch of my paintings. In case of an identity crisis, they would remind me who I was. The Tin Woodman, the Monster, portraits of Jim, a drawing of Don—into the bag that once held tennis rackets, scripts, papers and contracts, I crammed my poetry and my paintings, bringing evidence of what Julie called "my new self" for company. I can do it, I told myself. Twelve hours wasn't such a long time. I'd clean the apartment, go to a movie, or maybe see the Picasso show at the Modern. No one would be there to help. No pills either. Just me.

Broad smiles at breakfast, everybody wishing me a happy birthday. Although it was a tradition for patients to bake cakes in cooking therapy for other patients who celebrated birthdays and anniversaries in the hospital, I had told everyone I didn't want a cake. I wanted no part of an institutional birthday. Their good wishes would be enough. And besides, I wouldn't be there to eat it.

I returned my coffee mug to the kitchen window promptly at eight twenty-five, when the waitress hollered, *"Deeeeeshes, everyone."* Forgoing my usual defiant gesture of waiting until eight-thirty—at $260 a day, I'd drink my coffee when I wanted—I went to my room and started to dress. I had no time to play Jack Nicholson that morning. I would put on "well" clothes, not sick clothes. I wanted to look as if I belonged in New York. Even if I didn't know who I was, I'd play the part.

As I dressed that morning, I realized that three months had passed since I had been home. The thought crossed my mind as if for the very first time. You've been in an institution for almost three months. How's that for a sock of reality? How would I feel in the apartment? I pushed all those thoughts to the back of my head. I would take it step by step. Besides, Julie wouldn't let me go to the city if she didn't think I could handle it.

I signed out at the nurses' station, and all the members of my institutional family came out from behind the glassed enclosure that protected them from the assaults of the hospital world. They hugged and kissed me, wished me luck and happy birthday and have a super day. I said goodbye to Jim, urging him to get off the hall while I was gone. He gave me a kiss on the cheek for my birthday, and asked me to bring him a Care package of pistachio nuts and apricots.

Don walked me down the long corridor to the main door. I was holding my identity bag in one arm; Don was holding the other arm. He took out the huge cluster of keys attached to his waist and opened the door. He kissed me and gave me a happy smile. "You can do it, Barb," he said. "Have fun. Have a good birthday and take care of you. Call if you need any of us. Don't forget, it's not a sign of weakness. Call if you want help."

With strength from somewhere, some part of me I had never been in touch with, I said, "Don't worry, Don, but thanks." And suddenly I heard the door lock from the inside and I was standing in front of the elevator. I decided to adopt a brisk, businesslike attitude. I was going to work. I was on my way somewhere important. I was going home.

The cab was waiting outside the main entrance of the hospital. I passed the admissions office and my head started to buzz with memories, memories of the night that Edie and Jonathan had found me tied up in the apartment. I slid quickly into the back seat of the cab, holding on to my identity bag, and slammed the door, I hoped, with authority.

The driver, a nicely dressed woman, started talking to me from the front seat. "Isn't that place something? I've been working here fifteen years and I never get over it. I'll tell you something, lady, just count your lucky stars you're not one of them. Mental sickness is like no sickness. These people are helpless. I get home each night and thank God it isn't me locked up in one of those halls. They're the most wretched people in the world. You should thank God you're not a patient. It's something I tell you. It's something." I nodded knowingly, unzipped my bag and began to read Neruda before she started asking me questions about where I worked. It doesn't show, I thought. I look normal.

I sat in the almost empty station, waiting for the train. Not many suburban people were traveling to the city on Sunday. I thought of picking up the Sunday *Times* but decided against it. I wanted to see everything, experience the day, the train, the seats, the people, look out the window, smell the air. So I sat stiffly, taking everything in.

Then the terror began. I was disappearing. I reached into my identity bag and looked at drawings of Jim and Julie. I took out my sketch pad and started to draw the faces of the people in the station. Concentrate, Barbara. Drawing always brings you back. Just keep drawing. I know what you're doing to me, I told myself, as my heart began to pound. You're afraid. No Jim, no Julie, no Eric. If you win, I'll have to spend the rest of my life in hospitals. I've flown to Europe alone, walked alone, worked alone. I'll beat you yet, dammit. I'll beat you yet.

The train was more crowded than I had imagined. I was happy to be in a crowd, listening to other people's conversations. What did people talk about out here anyway? I turned to look out the window. Where had I been for months? Where the hell was I going? The train was an express, and as it cut through the suburban towns, I remembered the first time I had come to New York alone, from Vassar so many years ago. The city had always been a magnet, pulling me from wherever I was to come there to live, work, love. From home, from college, from vacations, from more beautiful places, always back to New York. That magnet had to work today. I hoped I wouldn't want to go back to Greenwich tonight, that one look at my city and I'd be hooked again. I'd call Julie and Don. Pack my stuff, I'd say. Send it to me in New York, I'm staying home. No more hospitals. It wouldn't happen.

When the train got to New York, I walked up the ramp clutching the red bag, Neruda's words echoing in my mind: "I have no idea what happened/but now I am not the same." My legs moved me through Grand Central Station. Had it always been this immense? The few people there seemed to be college kids on their way into the city for some holiday fun. The loudspeaker was sending out rays of "Deck the Halls" and "Silent Night." Where *have* I been? I thought. Does it show on my face? Does everyone know? Only colossal narcissism, I told myself, makes you think people care where you've been, where you're going, or even who you are. Just keep moving.

The cab. Central Park West, please. I hadn't spoken that address for months, and now I was shocked to hear it spill out of me reflexively. I looked at the people walking along Forty-second Street. We turned up Eighth Avenue, passed through Columbus Circle, and then the cab stopped. We were there, I felt frozen. Pay the man, Barbara. Get out. Three months. Who would be on duty? I've been in Europe, writing; that's what I would tell him. Just let anyone say, "Long time no see," and I had the answer. It turned out to be dim-witted Dennis, smiling as if he had seen me yesterday. Although a neighbor had been forwarding my mail, I went to the mailbox anyway and grabbed a fistful of bills and cards. I made pleasant talk with Dennis as we glided up to my floor.

I unlocked the door and walked into my apartment. I expected it to be a wreck, remembering the shape I was in that night three months ago when I left. But no, it was shining. How clean and fresh everything looked. The plants had grown, too. Of course; I had asked my neighbor to water them while I was away. I ran from the living room to the bedroom to the bathroom and then back to the living room, touched the plants, looked at the paintings. I went to the windows and gazed out at the sunny December morning. Someone had decided to surprise me and clean the place. Mother!

Now what will I do? I had planned to celebrate my birthday purging demons. I wasn't prepared for so drastic a change in my itinerary. It was only twelve o'clock and I had eight hours in New York to play, to do whatever I wanted. I took my paintings out of the tote bag and placed them all around, the Tin Woodman next to the Picasso lithograph, the Monster next to Braque. The apartment looked familiar yet different, new and old, like mine and like someone else's. The hospital paintings would have to provide continuity.

I sat on the couch with the phone in my hand. No, this was alone day. I wouldn't call anyone. A bath. I wanted to bathe in my own tub, without having to ask Don to unlock the door to the tub room. And I could lie naked on my bed. No one would come in unannounced, glaring a flashlight in my face for "bed check." I turned on the faucets and watched the hot, steamy water rise. In the tub, I shut my eyes tightly trying to let go, trying to end the burning, trying to find peace. No, no, don't go back, Barbara.

After my bath I lay down on my wonderfully firm, king-size bed with just a towel covering me, the luxury heightened by the grim memory of the narrow, bumpy cot I had slept on for months. Then it dawned on me. I'm here. I can lock the door. No one will barge in. I began to cry very softly. They were tears of happiness and relief, but tinged with sadness for all that had happened. I was home, in my apartment, out of that sick place. I was in *my* world.

I thought I had broken the back of my demon that morning. I didn't know then that it would continue to torment me for months. I didn't know that the feeling of disconnection would persist even in my most familiar, in my most safe environment. All I knew that morning was that I was forty-one, engaged in a battle with myself tougher than any fight I had ever had. Melodramatic or not, Don had been right when he said I would have to fight as hard for me, and against me, as I did against the bad guys. If only I knew how to do it.

I lay there for an hour. Then I sat up. O.K. New York is waiting. Let's go celebrate. I was about to dress in the clothes I had just taken off when I realized, This is my house. I have a closet. I can wear something else. I forgot. This is me. I live here. The freedom lost to me in the hospital I can have back. But don't let me be like some enslaved primitive who goes berserk with a taste of freedom. Sip. Barbara. Don't gulp.

My good mood was spoiled by anger at my mother. I did not appreciate her gesture. She had ruined my day by having someone clean the apartment. Even at forty-one, I thought, she's in my life, still treating me like a little girl. Was it her fault or mine? I would ask Julie. But I could already hear her voice saying, "It's nobody's *fault*, Barbara. It's just the way it is. Learn to live with it."

I walked out onto the street, looking at the people strolling along the park that warmish Sunday afternoon. Again the thought crossed my mind: I hope it doesn't show, the fear, the terror, the truth about where I've been. I was carrying my sketch pad and Neruda with me like two good friends. They would escort me wherever I went for months. Like Julie and Jim and Don, they were part of my "New self." I had teased Julie about the way they talked about selves on Six North. It was as if I could buy one at Bergdorf Goodman's. How in God's name do you find a new self at forty-one? And what if the old self is still hanging around, ready to fight to protect its territory?

No complaining, lady. The self-pity level was perilously close to the top, so I decided to have lunch. I walked into the big delicatessen on Fifty-seventh Street, again trying to look normal. No one had to know this was my first meal alone in months outside an institution. I saw people in twos and threes, and mercifully I saw others eating alone. They do it, I told myself, they sit and read and eat all by themselves. What do they think about? I wondered. Do they say, I'm me, I'm me, I'm me? I eat, therefore I am.

I ordered bagels and lox and cream cheese, with a slice of red onion and a draft beer. And when I sat down, I realized I could dawdle. The waitress wouldn't be bellowing, *"Deeeeeshes, everyone,"* in twenty minutes. I sketched as I ate, forcing myself to concentrate on now, not letting myself slip into that numb place in the back of my head which protected me from the terror. I drew that man's face, that woman's hat. The beer was fine and the bagel toasted perfectly. Still, it was not even two o'clock. What would I do now?

I walked past the Museum of Modern Art. Jim and

I had talked about it so often that I decided I would save that for when he got a pass and we could go together. I could call Edie and Jonathan. No, that would be dependent. But it's my birthday. I'd like to have a drink and see my friends. No, you've got to do this right, Barbara. There would be time for friends.

I didn't want to give up and go back to the apartment or the hospital. I wanted to do something, see someone. Everyone on the street looked purposeful, engaged, involved. And I felt empty-headed, isolated, impotent, purposeless. I had to do something. Anything. I wanted to be able to tell Julie how terrific it had been, to describe all the marvelous things I had done with my freedom.

As I made my way down Fifth Avenue, looking at the festive windows, the past suddenly began to intrude. A man, a child, a fleeting glimpse of a woman, and suddenly my brain was filled with memories of another time. I could literally hear, feel, see the images. When I smelled the strong, fresh scent of Christmas trees, I was transported to another Christmas long ago; not always a specific one, but one in the past, not of this time. There will never be any reality for me, I thought, with this brain which functions only as memory, taking me away from now. I wasn't consciously willing this memory game. I was on automatic pilot and I felt helpless to stop it. Throughout that day in New York I had to fight off the past with a stick.

It was uncanny. No man-made computer could be so precise or so relentless. Perhaps when people are healthy, all this replaying of experience, this computation of memories, goes on silently in the subconscious, where it belongs. Maybe that's what dreams are— psychic housecleaning, filtering the then from the now, making connections, deciding what to discard, what to keep. Only I was wide awake and it was my conscious mind that was busy cleaning house.

It was a problem that would endure for months. The loose ends of my life were now free-floating, fluttering in my psyche like the shreds of ticker tape that New York showers on its returning heroes. I was a returning hero to me, and functioning despite the Greek chorus in my head. But how could I let go of the past, hang on to the present? I fantasized Julie's face, imagined what she would say. I tried to find solace in the knowledge that others had done it. Eventually reality would become natural, I told myself. I wouldn't have to fight for it every minute.

At Rockefeller Center I saw the giant tree that towered above the outdoor skating rink. It looked elegant, almost majestic. I was dwarfed by the size of the tree, felt diminished by the throngs of people that were milling about, enjoying a New York Christmas. I thought of the years I had worked in the RCA Building, of the happy, wonderful times, and of the man I loved so very much who had refused to marry me. There, it was happening again. I couldn't receive a single image without my brain transforming it into a memory. Free association unlimited. It was stonger that day than when I was in the hospital, I realized, because I had no diversion from myself.

Again I watched the people walking, talking, laughing. How did they walk and talk so naturally? Was everyone fighting this whirlpool, this lure of the past? Then it struck me that they weren't, that I hadn't before either, that this was my unique problem and only I could solve it; not Julie, not Don, just me. I told myself that all psychosis means is that my psyche believes the now is so unlivable, so unbearable, so contrary to my plans, so different from my dreams for myself, that it will cling to the past as a drowning person grasps a life raft. But I knew the past was not a life raft. It would destroy me. I headed back to the apartment.

I spent the rest of the afternoon just sitting on the couch. But it was *my* couch, not the tattered couch outside my room on the hall. I closed my eyes and practiced the deep breathing Jim had taught me, and although I was trying to make my brain quiet, I was still infused with memories—happy memories of Eric the Good, not Eric the Evil. The laughing, the loving, the building of the beach house, the touching, the caring, the walks we took on cool autumn nights, Sunday mornings lolling in bed. But then sadness cut

me in two, filling me with ineffable feelings of loss. The
hows and whys of love turning to destruction still
plagued me. So much happiness and then so much
wretchedness had gone on in this room. I couldn't
think of the loving times without remembering the
horror. Who was that person, who was that woman who
went crazy here? I began my litany. I am Barbara,
daughter of Sally and Lou. I am, I am, I am. The
catechism didn't really help. But someday, I thought,
I'll walk and talk like everyone else, spontaneous and
unmeasured. Until then I'll do my Hail Barbaras.
Eventually it had to work.

I was savoring the fantasy of being human again,
when I looked at the clock. It was six, and I had to
make the seven-thirty train back to the hospital. The
day was gone, and I hadn't called anybody for help. I
was proud of myself, but disappointed that I wasn't
sad about going back. I heard myself say aloud, "Time
to go home." *Home.* I had called that bloody hospital
home! Dangerous sign; only institutional personalities
talk like that. Watch it, Barbara. You can spend the
rest of your life in places where ladies in white wipe
your fevered brow. Now that you've fucked up with
men in tweeds, do you want to go for ladies in white?

I packed a few skirts and sweaters, watered the
plants, gathered some of my paintings for the trip
back. I stopped for a *Times,* picked up apricots and
pistachios for Jim, and then took a cab to the station.
My first pass, I thought. I've survived the first day of
my new forty-one-year-old self. It was monotonous
and lonely, but I had done it. All the way back on the
train, I tried to think about mundane things: buying
Christmas presents for my friends, seeing people,
working again. But for me, every minute seemed like a
life-or-death issue. How could I think about the future
when I couldn't even hang on to the present? I told the
computer in my brain to please be silent so I could
read the newspaper.

Paul unlocked the door and let me back on the hall.
How was it? Happy birthday. Don had to leave, but
he'll see you tomorrow. Had it gone all right? I nodded
yes quickly and started to walk with him down the

hall. The air was thick with stale smoke. The familiar sick smell of the place almost made me reel. Joe was walking in circles, cackling; Roger sat as if frozen, his arms around his knees in his schizophrenic crouch; Iris was pacing like an animal; Jeff was strumming "Honky Tonk Women" on his guitar.

Then I saw Julie. She had waited for me to come back. And there was Jim. How was it? Did you have a good day? What did you do? I was filled with a heady sense of accomplishment. It wasn't the most glamorous birthday of my life and it was unshared with anyone who cared. But perhaps it was the most important. I had tamed the demon and now I was back with friends.

That night before I fell asleep I said to myself, You did it, Barbara. But my exhilaration was interrupted by a crack from my smart-ass self, that mocking negative part of me that wouldn't let me alone. Terrific, she said. Next week you can go to sleep-away camp. I tried to silence her and remember the day. The struggle between the two of me must stop, or I won't be able to live.

12
Christmas

Christmas was coming. The terrible tinsel, a plastic tree, the angel falling apart from too many exhausting appearances on top of that tired tree. Sad-looking wreaths and ribbons hung in the steamy dining room. The accouterments of an institutional Christmas, which only made everything grimmer and dampened our spirits. But the hospital staff, having done the Christmas thing before, was bent on doing it again. And some of the patients seemed to enjoy it. I hated it for reminding me of Christmases when everything was loving and healthy and warm.

For weeks Jim and I had been planning to spend Christmas together. Julie had decided to reward me for my day alone in New York with a pass for the Christmas weekend. But Joyce was being evasive. Julie knew that he and I wanted to go to New York, and I asked her if she thought Joyce would give him a pass. "In a hospital we never know what helps the patient most, the friends or the therapy," she said. "I think that Jim has helped you become yourself more than I have, Barbara, more than anyone. But I can't tell you what Joyce will do. I just don't know."

"We have to do something about Joyce," I said. "We must." And then I launched into my familiar complaints: her bad judgment, the infantilizing that she had displayed with Jim over and over again.

"We've been over all this before, Barbara," she said. There was nothing to be done. She shouldn't even comment.

"But it's not fair. He's only twenty-five," I said, growing angry. "Please, he must get another doctor. I was lucky to get you. But Jim is getting short shrift— short shrift that could destroy him. Why can't you admit that Joyce is fucking up? You know it's true!"

I was shrieking and couldn't stop. She let me finish, and when I finally quieted down I brought up something that had troubled me ever since she told me about Eric's illness—at least, his suspected illness. "Is there something wrong with me, Julie, something that draws me to troubled men?"

"No," she assured me, "not at all. Not all the men in your life were sick. And Jim is a friend, a new friend you've made in the hospital."

I wasn't sure I believed her, but I forced myself not to think about it.

The next few days Joyce became impossibly coy whenever Jim asked her about the Christmas pass. "Maybe yes, maybe no. If you're good, Jimmy boy." Then a giggle, a nod of the head; when she wasn't mothering, she was flirting. "Wouldn't you rather stay here on the hall and have Christmas dinner with me, Jimmy boy," she would say, "rather than go to New York with *that woman?*"

Jim and I concocted a lie. He told Joyce of a family party on Long Island. And I told Julie I had made other plans, thinking she might feel duty bound to tell Joyce that Jim and I wanted to be together, which would influence her decision about Jim's pass. Not wanting to test Julie's loyalty and trying to protect our Christmas, I said that I definitely planned to be with Barry and Lisa. It was my first and only lie to her, but I would fix that later. And I prayed that both Joyce and Julie would believe us. Jim and I had spent hours together talking about what we would do, where we would go, hours of fantasizing about Christmas. We had to make that fantasy come true.

It was two days before Christmas. I had my pass, but Joyce's last words that day had been, "Jimmy boy, are you sure you don't want to stay? *I'll* be here for

Christmas. It will be a lonely Christmas without you."
She had to work on the hall as the doctor for the
holidays and she wanted Jim for company. Then she
flitted down the hall, stethoscope swinging, the tails of
her white coat flapping like the wings of a decapitated
swan, to gossip with the nurses in the glass office. But
we learned that the staff had out-voted her. Jim was
given an eight-hour pass. He had to be back by ten
o'clock on Christmas Eve.

We had anticipated the worst. We hadn't been prepared for a partial victory. Who could imagine such
craziness? He had spent days pleading and cajoling.
And now he had eight hours and would have to spend
Christmas Day with Joyce after all.

"Fuck it," he whispered to me. "I won't come back.
What can they do to me?"

I didn't know what to say. I felt guilty. I wanted to
spend Christmas Day with him, but I didn't want him
to get into trouble.

It was Christmas Eve morning. Debbie had brought
in a guitar and everyone was sitting around the day
room singing carols. Patients with their bags already
packed were waiting to be picked up by their families.
Fourteen of the twenty-five would not have passes.
They were too sick.

Knowing that I would be seeing Jim late that afternoon, whenever his eight hours began ticking, I faked a
goodbye to him. I kissed the other patients goodbye so
I would have an excuse for a quick hug with him.
Then I grabbed my red identity bag, chock-full of
Neruda, Cummings and oil paintings, and tore into
town. The cab, the train from Greenwich to Grand
Central. There wouldn't be any problem, I thought. I
had done it for my birthday, but now I had something
else to look forward to, someone else to share the
happiness with. I was like a schoolgirl!

Grand Central was strangely empty. Everyone must
have made their getaways earlier. I ran through the
station and jumped into a cab. I shopped for wine and
cheese and coffee beans for my grinder. We would
have good coffee, sleep on a big bed, listen to good
music. We would be human together. I was so happy

when I got to the apartment. But I had hours to kill before Jim would arrive. I cleaned the already sparkling apartment, watered the plants, bathed, then showered. And when I lay down on the bed, I fell asleep. The anticipation had exhausted me. When I woke up, I realized he would be there any minute. I dressed quickly. Oh, I thought, we will make something out of all this.

He knocked on the door and when I opened it there was Jim, dressed in his best clothes, as if he were really going to a party. I stared. He had a rope tied around the waist of a slightly wrinkled pair of gray flannel pants. And a sports jacket! A bona-fide checked sports jacket. No tie; a baggy sweater under the jacket. He had shaved. He looked clean. I almost melted inside when I thought of all the pains he had taken to "dress up" for our rendezvous. I was wearing a long at-home thing that revealed at least the outlines of my figure. My shoulders were bare, and I was barefoot. How frightened we were!

He walked in and immediately began a tour of the apartment. "It isn't at all the way you sketched it, Barb. I told you you'll never make a living as an artist." He smiled one of his tender Jimmy smiles. And at that moment I forgot about the anger in his eyes, which was rarely erased even by his warmest smile.

"Did you expect something more grand?" I asked nervously.

"Well, to tell you the truth," he began, "I thought it was bigger. And the view—well, I thought there would be a gorgeous view. I mean, I can see the lights of the buildings, but it's not a drop-dead view, Barbara. Don't get me wrong, though. It's nice."

After weeks of snacking on pineapple juice and peanut butter and Hawaiian Punch, I ran eagerly to the kitchen to open the bottle of Chablis that was chilling in the refrigerator. The Brie I had bought was running beautifully and I carried everything into the living room, where Jim was sitting looking at my books, my paintings, my furniture, my plants. He was taking it all in, trying to imagine Barbara the Sick in this bright, cheerful environment. He looked puzzled.

The two images didn't fit; and although he didn't say it, I knew he felt it. I hoped he wasn't trying to imagine what had happened here between Eric and me, trying to picture the horror of it now that he was at the scene of the crime.

"How was the train?" I found myself, for the first time in all my days and nights of incessant talking with him, almost incapable of thinking of anything to say. It was preposterous, but I couldn't think of anything.

"It was a train. How was yours?"

We stared at each other and then broke out laughing. We were Jim and Barbara again, able to laugh at our failings, at our nervousness, at the implausibility of our situation. But we had shed the mental-patient image the moment we left the hospital. So we would play it out, always knowing it was lurking there in each of us. We knew everything, almost too much, about each other. But we knew nothing of each other's bodies, of secret smells and private places, and so we were frightened for the first time in our relationship.

And then he leaned over and kissed me very softly on the lips. Maybe sometime in my life I had experienced a sweeter, softer or more tender kiss. I know I had experienced more passionate ones. But now the weeks of groping and adolescent experimentation were almost over. He stood up and we both knew we were going to the bedroom. We kissed and held each other. We looked, explored, touched, and tasted. And then we made love.

"Your body's softer, your skin is softer than I thought," he said, leaning on his elbow looking down at me.

"Not too soft, I hope."

"No, it was just right. Especially for a forty-year-old." And he began to laugh.

"Forty-one," I reminded him. And I laughed, too, a false laugh. No matter how I tried to handle it, the age thing always mattered. But I wouldn't let it intrude. So we made love again. It was real, not a dream, not a fantasy. After months of loneliness, of nothingness, of flirtation and then fantasizing, we were making love—a man and a woman, together, not locked in sickness in that desperate hospital world, but in the health of my apartment, in the warmth of each other's arms. I got lost in sleep where I thought I had been dreaming, waking only to touch him, to watch him sleep. Then I fell back to sleep myself.

When we awoke, it was decision time. He was well into the seventh hour of his precious eight-hour pass. Should he follow Joyce's dictates and go back? If he broke the rules, what story would he give? Finally he called the hospital and told Debbie that he wasn't feeling well and was staying with his family on Long Island for the night. Debbie, not really believing him, urged him to be not well back at the hospital. But he allowed as how he'd rather be not well on Long Island. We both felt like conspirators, and that done, we convinced ourselves we needed and wanted a good dinner.

We went to a lovely little French restaurant I knew. My nasty thoughts, my Martian-like state of nonbeing, were gone for the evening. I still felt like Simone Signoret. Sure I was older, but it didn't matter. Nothing could ruin it or hurt us, at least not on this night.

Back in the apartment, we had more wine, more music, more kisses. Jim wanted to read Neruda and we read to each other, with Mozart, Segovia and Sondheim as the background instead of the Grateful Dead. I lay back on the couch, looking out the windows at the lights of the city, and heard Jim read the lines that had become our nightly prayer: "I asked the others after,/the women and the men,/what they were doing with such confidence/and how they had learned their living;/they did not actually answer,/they went on dancing and living."

Tonight, I thought, though it was borrowed, stolen, lied about, manipulated, we were dancing and living a little at last. There could be more, I thought. It doesn't have to be nothingness. I forgot my sickness and Jim's sickness. I forgot the deadness, the nightmare of Eric, the stench of the hall, heard Mozart and Neruda and Jim's voice, and I wondered to myself: Have I ever been more at peace, have I ever felt so happy?

In the morning I was in the kitchen making breakfast. Jim would only know of instant coffee, I thought, from all those truck stops, all those steel mills, all those institutions. So I ground my French roast beans while he sat in the living room, looking out at the extraordinary sunlight that marked the arrival of Christmas Day. Proud of my coffee, I brought him a cup. Seeking approval, I waited for his comment. He sipped it thoughtfully and then said slowly, smiling, "It's really too high-frequency a roast for morning coffee, Barbara. You should serve a Jamaican blue in the morning, not a French roast."

Jim always surprised me.

Then we put on our coats and walked down Fifth Avenue, looking at the happy, normal people looking at the decorations. A Christmas mass had just ended at Saint Patrick's and we watched the children leave the church, serious and thoughtful at first, then squealing with Christmas delight. Together we realized how much we had missed the sound of children in that abnormal world we were living in—just one of the million elements of humanity absent from the hospital world.

We had decided it was flirting with disaster for him to stay another day. We returned to the apartment and then it was time to say our goodbyes.

"Have a good weekend," he said. We were standing in the foyer, the door remained closed in front of us. I had two more days of the holiday pass to spend alone. He was going back to face the music. I felt I would disappear again from myself the moment he left, but I couldn't tell him that.

"Take care of yourself and don't be sad," I said, trying to make my voice sound light.

"No, I won't get sad."

"What will you do?" I asked, hearing the edge in my voice.

"I'll eat at the diner, then go back to the hospital and write poems. I'll remember, Barbara."

"I'll remember, too, Jimmy, and we'll do it again soon." What could they do to him? I thought.

Reading my mind, he said, "What can they do to me—imprison me for another month?"

We smiled.

"Barbara, don't stay here alone in this apartment talking to the ghost of Eric and playing that shit all over again in your head. See your friends. Don't be alone. I'll have all the people on the hall to talk to. I don't like the idea of your being here alone."

"I will, I will," I promised, thinking to myself how good he is with me, how caring. If he could only care as well for himself.

"Well, I've got to make that train."

We kissed lightly and I opened the door and watched him walk down the hall. He waited a moment in front of the elevator which had just arrived to let out a merry band of holiday guests to another apartment on my floor. Then he was gone.

I walked back to the bedroom and lay down on the bed, smelling the sheets, which still held the scent of our bodies. I wanted to savor it all. I hope he doesn't get in trouble, I thought, as I drifted into a sleep that came over me like two gentle caressing hands. I tried to fight it. I wanted to replay the touching, the feeling, the humaneness of our time together. We *had* had a Christmas after all. Dammit, we had made it ourselves out of whole cloth, out of nothingness. And as Christmases went, it was not the worst I had ever spent. Not by a long shot.

Sunday morning I was invited to a post-Christmas brunch with Jonathan and Edie. I would leave from their apartment for the train. I packed my red identity bag and then bathed and dressed carefully, undecided about what to wear. City-well clothes or suburban-sick. I compromised: a dash of the old style, but a wool hat to keep my head warm. I locked the door, wondering when I'd be back, and then whizzed down the half-empty streets of the Sunday after Christmas to Jonathan and Edie's apartment. Was my skin glowing like neon, or did it only feel that way? I was sure that they would see all the tenderness, the sensuality, that they would sense all the sexual things in me that had been stirred by the night I spent with Jim.

We embraced. I hadn't seen them since our dinner

in Greenwich. Jonathan had bought a bottle of Moët & Chandon. This was a celebration. Barbara was back. I didn't have the heart to tell them that I felt far from a celebration. I had been so lonely after Jim left. I had felt more disconnected than ever. What was the good of celebrating? I wasn't well yet. I looked into their bright, caring faces. If love could make you well, their love should do it. So I repressed all the doubt, all the stories of loneliness and terror. We toasted each other with champagne and kisses and then sat down at the dining table, filled with an array of marvelous food.

We talked and laughed and then Jonathan wanted to see the paintings in my identity bag. We sat on the floor and I described what stage I had been at when I painted each one—the fires and the monsters giving way to flowers and friendly faces. Then suddenly that third eye, that monitor, clicked on in my mind. Who was I, sitting here on the floor with my dear friends on a Sunday? Where were Don and Jim and Julie, where were Roger and Joe and Iris? The apartment was so quiet. I was accustomed to the din of the hall. This isn't real, this ordinary, this lovely day with my friends. What's real is noise and ugliness and the clamor and the stench of that place.

"Are you all right, Barbara?" Jonathan had asked me a question, I hadn't answered, and he sensed that I had drifted away.

My eyes filled with tears. "Not yet, Jonathan. Not yet. I'm still invisible."

Edie looked up at Jonathan with a worried expression.

"What does invisible mean, Barbara?" he asked.

"There are no words to describe what it's like to feel dead and alive at the same time."

"What does Julie say about that?" Edie asked.

"Only that I make myself invisible, that it serves some awful function we're not sure of. It protects me from something, and only I can make myself visible again. But I want to tell you about good things, not sad things. I have a new friend. His name is Jim and we spent Christmas together. We walked, we talked, and..." I stopped myself. I knew I shouldn't say anything more, but part of me wanted to shout about the joy I had felt being close to a person again, sleeping in a bed with someone again. Maybe it wasn't discreet, but I told them about Jim.

They listened intently, and I'm sure they didn't know how to react. So they played it safe by asking me if Julie knew about it. I assured them I wasn't irrevocably in love with Jim. But we had made a Christmas out of all that sickness and it had been so sweet. Their faces relaxed when they saw I had a sense of proportion about the whole thing and then they continued asking questions.

"How long have you known him? Will he be getting out soon?" And I found myself telling them about Neruda and walks and tennis, about kissing and making love. Just talking about it made me connect and I saw that they were happy that I could feel joy again, or if not joy, just a relief from the deadness, from the weight of the illness I had carried as a burden for so long.

Then I was sitting on the train plowing its way through the depressing streets of Harlem. I was trying to hold on to all the memories of the weekend. But I thought mostly of Jim and I tried to remember every moment of our time together to make it last. But it was over. It was already a memory. How had so many hours of planning and anticipation been relegated so quickly to history? I began to feel hollow, to feel more unreal, the brief fragment of connection I had experienced with him was gone. I was invisible.

I realized I was eager to get back to the hospital, to Julie and Jim and Don. They represented the only reality I knew. Edie and Jonathan were part of the old me I wasn't anymore. They were the aberration. I wasn't sad to be on the train with my red identity bag on the rack overhead, holding in my lap the pistachio nuts and dried apricots I had bought for Jim. I was going home.

Julie was sitting as usual, with her feet on the desk, dressed in a sweater and beautifully tailored pants, her eyes covered by large tinted glasses, her long hair loose, make-up perfect. How was I going to tell her the truth? How could I tell her I had lied? Our relationship was based on honesty. I had to tell her.

"Well, how was it?" she said. "How was Christmas? Tell me. I feel like a mother. I want to know everything you did. Everything. I hope it was good."

I stalled for time, reaching into my purse, fumbling for cigarettes. "Julie," I began softly, "there are times when as an institutional doctor you have conflicts. I want to tell you something, but before I can, your loyalty in this instance must be only to me, not the hospital, because it involves someone else, could hurt someone else. In this case you can only be answerable to me." Then I stopped. Hearing myself, I was astounded. "Do you realize I used to make films about conflicts like this?" I said. "Now I'm living it." Forget the irony of the situation, I told myself. What the hell will you do if she says no?

She nodded, assuring me that whatever it was, she would tell no one. And so I told her about the weekend.

Instead of frowning, she smiled. Then, realizing her position, remembering her role as a hospital therapist and caretaker of people's lives, she said firmly, "You know he's already in trouble for staying longer than eight hours."

"Yes, I know. So you mustn't tell, Julie. It would only hurt him. He's got enough grief, without Joyce knowing he was with me." I was begging her, I knew. "I don't care about me. If you punish me, I won't mind."

"I don't want to punish you, Barbara. I want you to be happy. I know what your friendship with Jim means to you. But, Barbara, you're getting well. You'll be going home soon. But Jim will be here for many more months. You have to understand that."

I began to cry softly. "Oh, Julie. It's happening to me all over again."

"What's happening?"

"I'm going to lose the only person I really care about in the whole world."

"In *this* world, Barbara," she said.

Hell broke loose for Jim. He was restricted to the hall. No passes, no walks to town, no coffee in the diner. Any hope we had nurtured of a New Year's together was gone. I felt guilty and responsible. Joyce alternately coddled and admonished him. She guessed we had been together Christmas, although Julie hadn't said a word. "Rules are rules, Jimmy boy." She giggled. "Now be a good boy and go to gym or you won't be one of my favorite patients anymore."

She taunted, cajoled and needled him. She was affectionate to other patients to punish him. She was working out her own problems on the two of us. This was his therapist!

I realized I had to try to contact Jim's parents, tell them what was going on. He had to get away from her, get another doctor. What would happen to him after I left? She would smother him. "Remember, Jimmy boy," she said, "if you're not good, I'll keep you here three more months." And she could. He was facing a parole hearing. He needed her protection and she used that as a wedge. She stopped talking to me completely. What a fool she was, but a dangerous fool. She was messing with someone else's life.

"Punishment is the name of the game, Barbara," Jim said my first night back on the hall after the holiday. We were sitting together on the couch outside my room. I was dressed in my sick clothes again—the old jeans and sweater, a scarf around my head, no make-up—and Jim was wearing his old clothes, too. Had we been attractive, naked and loving together? We were back on that tired couch with space between us, not touching, living in that sick place.

Jim started to read me a poem he had written about our weekend.

I met a friend who wanted me to open my front door.
It jammed like a zipper.
She told me to cry or not to cry
Laugh or not to laugh

But to touch her to make her real for myself and for her
    to know I cared.
We carried on, over and across time, sipping our vodka and

Courvoisier, she compelling me to be real
And feel the skin of her hand in mine.

I wanted to speak of my dislocated self and how it got to
    be so cowardly.
I could only tell of her goodness and the pleasure she gave
    me.
It was quite enough.

But ever more I've had the need to touch and I find my
    environment insincere.
I grew a lot on that day
Became less suspect and felt the mind doesn't have to grow
    old.
She softened my heart, though I didn't cry.
She blew the fog across my chest, though it didn't vanish.
The breeze was dear.

I was terribly touched by his feeling and amazed at
how well he wrote. I tried to tell him how good his
poetry was, but more important, that I felt the same
way.

"Don't you remember on that first walk we took
together, Barbara, when we went to the diner and you
told me it was all right to cry, to feel, to break through
the horror of my days in the prison? I felt more that
day and in the weeks after than I had for years. You
really helped me. Do you know that? And do you
know how much Christmas meant to me?"

Mae was glaring at us. "Jim, Barbara," she barked.
"I'm tired of this. It's after eleven. Now get in your
rooms—I mean it. That's my job, so move!"

Jim looked at me sadly. "I can't stand it," he said.
"I can't stand it, not after the weekend we just
shared."

I tried to be mature. "Hold on to your dignity,
Jim."

"Sleep well, Barbara." He got up and I watched him
walk toward his room. I remembered the day before,
the night in my apartment. Julie had said I would be
leaving this place soon. Why couldn't I do as Jim
suggested so often: run toward health and happiness,
not just flee from sickness and death? But now he was

all my happiness. And Joyce was punishing him. We would have no time together, not as long as he was in the hospital. He would have to be discharged soon, too, I told myself. That's the only way we could be together. I wanted to be with him, wanted him to hold me. It wasn't fair.

13

Going Home

"Barbara," Julie said, looking very serious. "It is the beginning of January. We should start making plans for discharge." She sat there and waited for me to respond.

Discharge! I had watched other patients arrive and be discharged. Now she was talking about me. Was I ready? Would it be like last summer when I left Longview—loneliness, desperation, thoughts of suicide?

She must have known what I was thinking. "I'm talking about a gentle reentry back into the world," she said.

"What world? Julie, what world am I going back to? You and Jim are my world. I've lost everything else."

"That's not true," she replied. "The world you had is still waiting for you, Barbara. And it's time to go back. But it must be gentle. You should start going to the city on weekends and think about finding a therapist."

"You know how I feel about that. I just don't understand why you can't be my therapist. You live in New York, you know me better than anyone. It makes me furious."

"It's part of my contract with the hospital, Barbara. I've told you that before."

"And I've told you about the incompetents and certifiable loons I met last summer when I was hunting for a doctor. I can't stand going through that again."

"We'll help you find someone. Just start thinking about it. I want you to be prepared. You're not going to leave here the way you left Longview. This time you'll be ready."

"But I'm *not* ready," I protested. "I still don't understand what happened. I still don't understand me. Do I *want* to be sick? Am I going to spend the rest of my life falling in love with men I can't have, or someone like Eric? Will I always feel like a naughty little girl who deserves to be unhappy? Tell me what's the matter with me."

"You've never really learned to trust yourself, Barbara, to trust your own strength. And the answer to all of your questions is yes, until you do. Often you've depended on others to tell you who you are—your parents, Bill, Eric, and now even me. And because you've never really believed in yourself, you've always believed what they told you. It's not a unique problem, Barbara. It's a human problem. But I think it's particularly difficult for women. We are torn between our new freedoms and the old patterns of dependence, of being defined by other people. You achieved enormous success in your professional life. You worked hard and earned the respect of your colleagues. Your friends love and admire you for who you are. But I know what you're thinking: that's not enough. It never is, and it shouldn't be. There is another kind of love, a sharing we all need. But we can never find it unless we bring all of ourselves to the relationship, the good and the bad, the strong and the weak. You're Barbara Gordon. Don't be afraid to be yourself."

"I am, I am, I am," I said. "I say that to myself sometimes in my room just to prove I really exist."

"You already have that proof, Barbara. In yourself. The real danger is in making your relationships with other people into something they are not—making yourself into something that you are not, because you think no one could love you as you really are. I think you're beginning to trust your own strength again, Barbara. And when you do trust yourself again, you'll have licked that part of you that thinks it's easier to be weak. And you'll be attracted to the strengths, not the weaknesses, of others."

"But I don't want to leave the hospital still plagued with the same symptoms I had when I arrived."

"I've told you, Barbara, you have the tools to fight them. You're still afraid, and those symptoms serve the terrible function of preventing you from reaching out for life, love, for happiness."

"Goddammit, Julie, I'm not afraid to love again. I won't live as a frightened woman terrified that every man I meet will be an Eric. I won't."

"If you really mean that, then you've got the battle won."

The phone rang. I looked out the window of her office at the cold January day, waiting for her to finish talking with the parents of another patient. How involved therapists are in your life when you're hospitalized, I thought, talking with your family and friends, setting the ground rules for passes, visitors, weekends. Julie held a frightening kind of power over me, but I didn't want it to end.

"I don't want to leave here still sick, still dead," I said when she put the phone down. "I want to be well."

"Hospitals are not to get well in. They're for crises. You'll lose the deadness only by living, Barbara. Every time you took a Valium you opted for deadness, and now you must allow yourself to feel, retrain yourself to feel. Feel everything—anger, love, sadness. Only by living outside, by functioning through the symptoms, can you recover. It will take time. But you'll be seeing a good therapist in the city who will help you."

I began to cry. "Don't you understand?" I said through my tears. "I want *you* for my doctor. It isn't fair."

"This is not a rejection, Barbara. Discharge means it's time to leave, time to live."

"I'm not ready, Julie. I'm not ready."

"I think you are," she said. "Four months is a long time."

That afternoon Jim and I were in art therapy together. I was sketching, he was working with clay. I was thinking about what Julie had said. How could I tell Jim? Finally I just blurted it out. "Listen, Jim. Julie's talking about discharge, finding a new doctor. She's actually talking about my leaving."

He looked up from his pile of clay, and I said to myself, He's known this was coming. He knew before me. "You're too well to be here, Barbara," he said. "I've never known what you're doing in this place."

"But don't you remember how hysterical I was when we first met? Don't you remember?"

"That was months ago. Julie's right. You should get out of here and go back to work."

Neither of us said anything about our closeness, about missing each other. We were talking business, mental-patient business, and we were both seasoned enough with sickness to know we couldn't color it, at least not at this moment, with our emotions.

"Jim, tomorrow's the inauguration," I said to change the subject.

"Where are they holding it?" he asked rather diffidently.

"You're putting me on," I said. "You know where Carter is being inaugurated."

"Didn't they hold it last year in the Rose Bowl?" The mount of clay he was working began to take the shape of a bird.

"Swear you're kidding. Swear it."

"I'm serious," he said, not looking at me.

"But, Jim, it's in Washington, the capital of the United States, where it always is. You know that."

"Well, I've only been around for a few inaugurations," he answered wryly, and I realized he was hurt and angry at me. Angry at my exasperated tone, angry that I knew something he didn't, and I think he was beginning to feel anger because I would soon be leaving. "How many have *you* been around for?"

How many? I thought. We often joked about the difference in our ages. But now he was taunting me.

"Well, how many?"

"Too many, Jim. Too many. Go make your bird."

I told Julie about Jim's reaction. "Nobody seems happy about my getting out of here. Not Jim, not me.

Nobody except maybe Joyce. It's times like these when you find out who your real friends are," I said to tease her.

"I'm happy about it, Barbara," Julie said. And then she exploded her bombshell. "I'm giving you passes every weekend from now on. I want you to go to New York, see your friends, start living your life again. What do you say we set a discharge date at the beginning of February? By then you will have found a good therapist. Dr. Wald has given you some recommendations."

She handed me a typewritten list of names. I stared at it numbly. I seldom saw Dr. Wald except at our Friday "community" therapy sessions, or whenever he checked up on his charges on Six North. But I didn't like him. He strutted around like a peacock and I thought he was abrupt and officious. I wondered if the doctors he recommended would be as cold as he was. "Who do *you* recommend?" I asked Julie.

"Dr. Wald is familiar with your case, Barbara. And he's more qualified to make recommendations than I am."

How could I find a way to tell her how frightened I was, how unready I was, how much I needed to keep working with her?

Once again it almost seemed as if Julie could read my thoughts. "Nobody said you'd go skipping out of here like a kid at recess," she remarked. "Nobody said it would be easy."

It was a terrible time. While I was getting stronger, I was still plagued by the old symptoms of deadness, or lack of identity, as Julie chose to call it. But I knew now I had to go into the city on weekends. So I would leave on Friday and come back on Sunday night, sometimes sitting by myself in the apartment for the whole weekend, other times trying to pick up the threads of my life, seeing friends, making dinner dates. But the trips were no longer charged with the same excitement I had felt on my birthday and when I spent Christmas with Jim. And sometimes in the apartment I found myself holding on to the bed, crying. For in crying, the feeling of nothingness would diminish, and the pain, the sadness, was preferable to nothingness.

Other times I would walk along the streets and past the buildings that were so familiar to me, hoping each time that on this walk, this block, this day, I would connect. It didn't happen and I would return to the apartment disconsolate, eager to get to Grand Central, to take the late Sunday-night train back to Greenwich, back to Don and Paul, Debbie and Jim. We would talk about their weekend, my weekend, and I would connect again, for a little while.

I began calling the names on Dr. Wald's list to arrange weekend appointments. One, Dr. Mildred Stanton, asked me straightforwardly over the phone, "Are you depressed or schizophrenic?" And I answered, "My sickness is I want to be schizophrenic." She laughed, as I hoped she would, and I had consultations with her on two successive weekends. She was a middle-aged woman who wore elegant dresses and drank cup after cup of hot tea throughout our sessions. She was dramatic but she had a kind face. I chose her to be my therapist when I left the hospital.

Things moved rapidly after that, too rapidly. Both Julie and Dr. Wald spoke with Dr. Stanton, and early in the week after my second consultation with her, Julie announced that my discharge date was definitely set for the first week in February.

I just stared at her. "You can't be serious," I said. "You and I have so much more to work on. Dr. Stanton isn't like you. And besides, she can wait. She'll always be there."

"I *am* serious, Barbara," she said. "The first week in February."

There was a note of impatience in her voice, and I didn't like that cool tone coming from her. That wasn't Julie's style.

I began counting the days. Wednesday, Thursday. I didn't tell my parents I was being discharged. I told none of my friends, not even Edie. I hadn't begun to pack, no one was coming to get me. My luggage was still downstairs in the checkroom. Then it was Friday and I was going home for a final weekend pass. Lisa and Barry had invited me to their house in New Jersey.

"Why don't you get out of here?" Jim said. He was stretched out on the couch outside my room and I was sitting on the edge, trying to decide what to do, what train to catch.

"Jim, I'm leaving next Wednesday."

"I know," he said curtly. "I heard from Don."

Just then Debbie walked by. "Congratulations, Barbara. Six more days. That's super!"

All the staff members had come up to congratulate me as soon as they heard. Discharges are like New Year's Eve in a mental ward. Only I didn't feel like New Year's Eve, and I couldn't believe that all these people, supposedly trained in psychology, didn't know why.

Jim interrupted my thoughts. "Why the hell are you still sitting here when you could be in New York?"

"Right. I'll make the three-fifteen," I said impulsively, and stood up. "I've got to go pack."

"Pack what? You never take anything but the identity bag. Now get out of here, Barbara." And he turned away, angry at me for not enjoying my new freedom, angry because he was stuck on the hall for the weekend, angry because I was leaving in six days, angry at everything.

It was Saturday night and I was sitting with Barry and Lisa in front of the fireplace in their living room, drinking brandy. We had just finished a marvelous dinner of steamed lobster, fresh asparagus. I had finally confessed that I was being discharged and they were making the weekend a celebratory one, festive and gay. I don't remember what we were talking about, but as I sat there gazing into the fire, their voices seemed to recede into the distance and I suddenly realized I didn't know where I was. Was I in Miami with my parents? Was I in my apartment with Eric? Was I in the hospital? Thoughts from the past collided with the reality of the present. I became frightened.

Lisa must have seen the look of terror on my face. "What is it, Barbara? What's the matter?"

"I don't know where I am," I said. My heart was pounding and I was breathing in short little gasps. "Oh, God, it's worse than it ever was. I don't know where I am."

"You're here with us, Barbara," Lisa said, trying to conceal her alarm. She put her arms protectively around my shoulders. "You're with me and Barry."

"I can't sit here now, Lisa," I said. "I must try to sleep. I feel more unreal than ever, and all the therapy in the world doesn't stop it."

They helped me upstairs and I didn't even take my clothes off. I fell on the bed, holding on, telling myself, "I'm in Princeton, New Jersey, with Barry and Lisa, my oldest friends. I'm Barbara Gordon. I am. I am. I am."

All day Sunday they tried to distract me from my symptoms filling me with good food, wine, talk, laughter. But I had to fight every moment to be there with them and I was too exhausted and ill to take the train back to the hospital. I decided to spend the night in Princeton and return on the morning train. I phoned the hospital so they wouldn't worry and the nurse on duty insisted I leave the Travises' number.

A few minutes later Julie phoned. "What's going on, Barbara? Why aren't you coming back?" She sounded worried.

"I'm beat from fighting the symptoms. All of them came back with a vengeance this weekend, Julie. All of them." I was furious at her. What good was she? What fucking kind of therapist was she if my symptoms could come back with such a ferocity? All our talk was for nothing.

I was still shaky when I arrived at the hospital the next morning. Julie was on the prowl, looking for me. "Barbara, what happened?" she said. "Tell me what happened."

"I don't know. Everything got worse. I was really so dislocated. I had no idea where I was. It was a nightmare."

"Oh, Barbara, I miscalculated. I'm sorry. I didn't

realize the effect discharge would have on you. I was wrong. I didn't know this would happen. The pain of separation. I should have known. I'm so sorry."

I was confused. What separation, what pain? What was she talking about? "You mean there's a reason for this?" I asked.

"You were experiencing separation anxiety, Barbara," she explained. "Many patients before discharge suffer a regression and experience a return of all the symptoms. But in your case we are also responsible. We were trying to do it too fast. You should have been prepared more slowly. You have had a history of painful separations. You had a depression, drug withdrawal and a death all at once. And I know how hard it will be for you to adjust to life alone."

Later that day we went to see Dr. Wald. Julie felt she needed his help with preparations for my discharge.

"But it's not easy for me to be happy about going home," I exclaimed. "I have nothing to return to, no one waiting for me. I don't know how to live alone. I know I did before Eric, but I don't remember."

Dr. Wald was growing impatient with me. "Why do you want to say goodbye like this, Barbara, with destructive thoughts, by getting sicker? Why do you prefer to undergo all this pain? I'll tell you why. So you don't have to feel the loss of saying goodbye to Julie."

I interrupted him. I found his arrogant, brusque manner deplorable. What the hell did *he* know about pain? "I *have* been saying goodbye to Julie," I said.

"Not the right way," he said with great certainty.

"What's the right way?" I said, turning to Julie. "I'll miss you so very much. Why can't I see you after I get out? If you were the patient, I'd break the contract. I'd break the rules for you."

"You've got to learn how to say goodbye," Dr. Wald said, "without cutting people off, without destruction, without anger—with love."

"Should I keep saying goodbye until I get it right?" I asked peevishly.

"Something like that," he answered. And from the way he began collecting the papers on his desk, I knew the hastily called meeting was over.

The two of them left and I sat in the room by myself for a long time. So they were telling me that the child in me was asking Julie to take care of me, that I would even get sick so I wouldn't have to face the loss of Julie. I was having a tantrum in my head because the child-woman wanted to stay in this place. I walked back to my room on the hall, ignoring Jim on the couch outside my room, ignoring Don, who came up to see what was going on. Angry, livid thoughts filled my head, thoughts directed at Julie, Don, Jim. Nobody cared about me, nobody loved me. I lay down on my bed and began to cry uncontrollably. Now I was having a real tantrum, not just one in my head.

The tantrum persisted for seventeen days. I walked around the hall in a rage. I couldn't say hello or good morning or how are you to anyone without thinking: What do I care? Drop dead! Ha ha, I hate you all! One day I felt so wretched I went into the quiet room. I had always wondered what mysteries transpired there, and I decided that for $260 a day I wanted to use all the facilities. Sitting in the dark, airless room, I began to pound the gray mat on the floor, not looking at Don, who had been assigned to watch me. "Give me a pill, Don. Help me!" I shrieked. "Help me! Somebody help me!"

In therapy Julie and I discussed how unready I had been for discharge. I had told no one, had made no arrangements for Edie to pick me up, hadn't paid the bill, hadn't called down for my luggage. Didn't I understand I had been telling them all I wasn't ready. When would I be ready? I wanted to know. When?

Finally the tantrum began to subside and an adult began to emerge from the cocoon of sickness. A new date, at the end of February, was set for my discharge, and I found myself saying goodbye to Roger, to Claudia, to Debbie, to Jeff and Joe. But how could I say goodbye to Don, to Jim, to Julie? I wanted to believe that Dr. Wald was right, that if I could say goodbye to the people I really cared about without hating them, with love, it would help me. I would grow. But it was so painful.

I resumed my weekend trips to the city to see Dr. Stanton, and one evening I returned to the hall to find Jim deeply engrossed in conversation with a new patient, Linda, a long-haired, blond, sixteen-year-old flower child, who played the guitar and sang folk songs in a high, clear voice. He was already carving out a new friendship, anticipating my departure. Too selfish to think of his needs, of his loss, I thought to myself, too soon, Jim, too soon. The body isn't even cold. Was I that replaceable?

I went back to my dark room and lay down. Julie found me there. "So, Barbara," she said, standing in the doorway, "back to the beginning, retreating to dark rooms." I tried to tell her about Jim and Linda. "I know," she said. "What did you expect?" And during our session the next day she wanted to talk about my anger at Jim for taking up with Linda.

"He's just a boy," I said indifferently, "and a bloody mental patient at that. So what do I care?"

"So now he's a boy." She smiled.

"So now I hurt. Tell me what to do."

"Have you ever thought of how much he will miss you? Tell him how you feel."

"But, Julie, I have my pride. How can I be jealous of that idiotic young girl and her damn guitar?"

"Apparently you are," Julie said.

"Yes, damn it," I finally admitted. "I am."

"Barbara," she said after a few moments, "you've talked about Jim and resuming your friendship when he gets discharged. Shouldn't we talk about that, too? You should be prepared for changes in yourself, changes in your needs. You will want someone stronger than Jim. You've always ignored his problems."

"Another person," I said, "that I'm making into some kind of god because I need him. But don't you see, Julie, he's not sick with me? With me, he's strong and tender and not angry."

"I'm sure that's true, Barbara, but in time you'll see

that your relationship with Jim was appropriate at this time in your life and that you'll outgrow him."

I wanted to scream at her, "Never, never! How can you be so calculating, so cruel?" But part of me knew she might be right.

The days ticked by, closer and closer to discharge. And this time I was trying to do it right. I wrote my parents and called my friends. More and more messages arrived daily; people who heard I was coming home were reestablishing contact. Edie agreed to come and pick me up. She called me every day and I stood there at the hall phone listening to her excited voice. "You're reborn, God damn it, Barbara. You've got insight. You've got your mind. You've got to take care of your body now. Join my health club, then go make films." She rattled away, helping me prepare for reentry. I pictured her at Houston Space Control, guiding her friend in the lunar module back to earth.

I knew I wouldn't be strong enough to go back to work for a while. I was still too spacy. But I would be with people again. I thought of all the hellos I would be saying in the next few weeks. They would be hard, but not as hard as my goodbyes to Julie, Jim and Don.

One day I was sitting with Julie, trying to thank her for her love, her wisdom, her gentleness, her strength, her professionalism. "I'll miss you, Julie, miss you more than you'll ever know."

"Barbara, I'm your whole world right now, everyone who ever loved you, everyone who ever scorned you. In the past you've cut off forever the people who have hurt you. But I'm not trying to hurt you. I'm urging you to go to love, go to life, and enjoy it with all the wonderful intensity you used to have. You can lick that self-destructive part of you, and when you do, it's all there for you. All of it."

"But this is different," I said. "I still need you. You're my best friend. We've been so very close for the last five months. And I don't know how to feel intensely or passionately about life alone. I've forgotten how to be a person by myself. I do love you, Julie, but I think I'm going to be angry when I leave."

"No anger, Barbara. That's inappropriate anger. I would only hold you back now. You're strong enough to do it by yourself. Saying goodbye with love is part of growing up. Try to love me when you get home. Try."

That night, sitting on the hall, Jim and I were talking. It was only ten-thirty, but quiet had come for once before eleven o'clock. The pool table was empty, the TV off, the Grateful Dead put to bed for the night. Roger and Jeff and Iris had gone to sleep early, exhausted from the day's noise and violence, resting up to make more havoc in the morning.

Jim was smiling and trying to be happy for me, but we were both sad that he would have to stay here. Somehow I felt that I was sicker, more neurotic, more needful than he. Maybe he saw little green men, had delusions, but his sickness was cleaner than mine. He was Jim. He seemed whole to me, while I was still having an identity crisis that didn't want to end. I still needed him, too.

"I didn't know how rough it would be for you to leave," Jim said. "But remember, Barbara, health is the norm. Take care of yourself when you get home. Get into meditation, do yoga, eat good food, paint, bake bread, stay in the middle, feel your center. Then go back to work. But be Barbara first. Stay with Barbara."

We smiled at each other. "What about you?" I said. "I don't want you to lie around sleeping away your days. Read, write, walk, use your precious brain." Then, with an enormous lump in my throat, I thanked him. "How can I tell you what you've meant to me?"

"You don't have to thank me. I haven't been much help to you. And we don't have to say goodbye. I'll see you when I'm out of here. We'll fly kites together." He was back to being the spiritual, elfin Jim I had first met, opting for a new career every morning. I remembered how he had said, "I'll be a weatherman or an English professor and wear patches on my sleeves. I'll travel and live in a tree house." Anything but work in his father's business. "I'll teach you Zen archery," he continued. "We'll walk in the park that is your front yard and feed the squirrels. Sleep well, Barbara."

He got up off the couch and turned toward his room. "Oh, God," he said. "Only three more days. I can't believe it. What will I do here without you?"

"You'll have Linda." I tried to say it to be reassuring but there was an edge of bitchiness in my voice.

"She's just a friend, a young kid. Not like us, Barbara." He kissed me good night on the cheek. "I'm going to sleep now." He walked away.

I sat there alone after Jim had gone, looking at the tired old furniture, the smudgy green of the walls. God. I had spent five months of my life in this place. And now I was going home.

Don walked by, his coat over his shoulder. He stopped to speak to me. "It was a quiet night, Barbara, thank God."

"Yes, Don. Thank God."

We both knew I had been avoiding talking with him. Somehow his was the hardest goodbye of all. He was not my doctor, there was nothing sexual between us, but this tall black man with his sparkling eyes had touched my soul as much as anyone I had ever met.

"Do you want to talk for a while?" he said, sitting down next to me.

I looked up at his face, looked at his kindness, remembering everything he had said to me for five months, remembering his first words to me: "Just think what you feel. Feel what you say. It'll be all right." The tears started running down my cheeks.

In the past when I cried, he had wiped my tears away. Tonight he just watched me. He was smiling. "I love you, Don Collins," I said through my tears. "Do you know how much I wish for you? Be a great therapist. I know you will, and I'll never forget that first walk to town, that lunch in the diner. I'll never forget how much you gave me."

"Then that's wonderful," he said, still smiling. "That's my reward, that you'll never forget me. You've meant a lot to me, too, Barbara."

How many hours had we spent talking together,

discussing the presidential election, books, movies, backgammon strategy, sex? I was sobbing now, and I couldn't stop. He put his arms around me and held me.

"Can't you come and visit my house at the beach?" I said. "You'd love the view of the sea. I'll cook good food, we'll laugh, I'll finally beat you at backgammon."

"No, Barbara," he said. "You know you've got to break with the hospital, with me, with Julie, with all of us. You've got to go back to your life."

"But you're part of my life. You're the best part. You're my friend."

We sat there together for several minutes until I finally stopped crying. "And you say you don't feel," he said. "What a liar you are, Barbara. You feel. You're not dead. You feel everything. And you made me laugh. I'll miss your humor and your laughter and your tears when you're gone. We'll all miss you: Claudia, Julie, even Roger. I saw you yesterday talking with him about Uranus."

"The shock treatments helped for a while, but they really didn't work, did they? He's still crazy."

"I'm afraid they haven't worked yet, Barb. But I know Roger will miss you. Sometimes with you he was able to connect."

"It's true. In the middle of his craziness about Uranus and Venus, he talks about John F. Kennedy and how much he misses him. He has unbelievable moments of lucidity, unbelievable."

Now we were Don and Barbara, man and woman, friend and friend. He had stayed to talk with me although his workday was long completed.

Finally he got up to go. "Sleep well, Barbara," he said. "I'll see you tomorrow. I'll give you one last chance to beat me at backgammon."

"Good night, Don." I watched him leave, heading toward the door, reaching for the keys on his waist. How would I ever live without him?

I sat on the couch, looking inside the tiny room I had lived in for five months. Three more nights, I thought. Oh, God, I've been living in a mental institution. But there are people here. When I leave I'll be alone. Who will I talk to at night? I can't work yet. Edie has her own life, Lisa has Barry. The world is made for people in twos. Oh, Jim, Julie, Don, somebody—tell me how to do this alone. I want to be happy about going home. I want to rejoice in my new freedom and dip into health with an enormous ladle. I want to be. There's only one problem. I don't know how to live.

It was my last night on the hall and Jim and I began talking right after dinner. He indulged my sentimentality as I reminisced about our walks, our first pass to town, our Christmas together. His room was filled with my paintings, mine with his poems. I remembered the experience gaps we had shared: "Vivaldi? Is he new?" "Didn't they hold it last year in the Rose Bowl." What had we meant to each other? I thought. Everything. We were wrapping up, but certainly we would see each other again.

"You may not want me as a friend after you get home," he said. "I may not have enough smarts for your friends."

"My friends know all about you and like you already," I said. "You have nothing to worry about. Just get well and get out of here. That's all you have to worry about."

"But you may forget me, Barbara."

"How can I forget half my heart?" I said.

We sat there in silence for a moment. Joe was walking in circles, Roger was rambling on about his interplanetary travels. We looked at each other and laughed. We marveled that our friendship was a product of this terrible place. We had kept each other alive.

"Remember, Barbara," he said. "All neurosis is is lies. All you have to do is give up the lies and you're there."

How smart he is, I thought. "But is survival enough?" I said. "I want to be whole."

"You *are* whole, goddammit. Look, we all have a devil in us, Barbara. Yours was just ruling you for a while. Now it isn't and it's time to get out of here. Besides," he said with an elfin smile, "I've written you a goodbye poem."

Jim began to read from a crumpled piece of paper he had taken from the pocket of his robe.

Thinking of you thinking of me
makes me wonder if springtime feels summer
and autumn winter.

Thinking of you thinking of me makes me feel
thunderclaps of lightning bolting across the sky
and dancing in the face of earth's vestigious organs;
trees and bush, people and anthills.
I wonder if someone once said that "a man can go
crazy for another's thoughts" or something like that?

For if it's so, you must be making me crazy to think
such silly thoughts.
You thinking of me in so clearly a professional
way and yet so endearing I can never forget you
and of
you thinking of me. . . .

"Oh, Jim," I said. "It's our last night. Goodbye to green couches, goodbye to this hall—I can say all that, but I don't know how to say goodbye to you. Who will nudge you when I'm gone?"

"Don't worry," he said, and his dark angry eyes turned soft and warm. "Don't worry, I'll be okay."

"You must ignore Joyce Roberts. Hold on to you. Ignore everything she tells you about yourself. Promise! Don't let her get to you."

"Promise."

Then he looked up. "Mae's coming. Oh, God."

"Barbara, Jim, I mean it!" Mae bellowed from the nurses' station. "Just look at the time."

Jim and I were silent, each of us knowing what the other was thinking. It was better unspoken. Mae was right; just look at the time. And I said to myself, Now she won't have the old Barbara Gordon to kick around anymore.

"Hold on to your dignity," Jim said. "At all times." He got up, tucking the poem back in the pocket of his robe. "Sleep well, Barbara."

"Sleep well, Jim."

He kissed me on the cheek. "Who will say 'Sleep well' when you're gone?"

My tiny room was now barren. My paintings were off the wall, the closets and drawers were empty. I had been packing my suitcase for days. All my credit cards, the mirror, the cigarette lighter, had been returned to me. And they all said to me, You are a person; go live. Only the morning's clothes were left out. I would wear well clothes, not sick clothes, when Edie arrived tomorrow. Only one session left with Julie. What would I say to her? What would I do when I got home?

I went to sleep, but I woke again in the middle of the night, filled with crushing anxiety. I walked up and down the empty hall, hating it, hating that I needed it, hating its smell, its sickness, its inhumanity. It was quiet now, the silence of death. Was that my choice: life or this living death? And why was such a choice so difficult to make?

In the dim light of the hall, I saw the people-watchers dozing or reading newspapers outside Roger's and Iris's doors. Other members of the night staff were drinking coffee, gossiping, laughing. As I passed by the glass-enclosed office, Mae looked up at me and smiled. "Having trouble sleeping, Barbara? Want some hot chocolate?"

"No, thanks, Mae but thank you for all the hot chocolates you've given me."

Mae. Did she know this was my last night; did this woman who had sent me to bed for five months know I was leaving? Did she know how terrified I was? Did she know I would miss her?

I walked past Jim's door, which was slightly ajar, and looked in to see him lost in sleep. Then finally, exhausted from my pacing, and from my own anxiety, I went back to my tiny room, pushed the suitcase to the side of the cot and lay down. I thought of Vivaldi and inaugurations and walks and coffee in the diner, and before I knew it I was asleep.

In the morning, my last morning on Six North, I took so much time putting on my make-up and my well clothes that the dining room was almost empty when I went for breakfast. Julie found me there. "All the therapy rooms are filled right now," she said. "Do you mind if we talk in your room?"

We went back there and sat on my cot.

"Well," she began.

"Well."

"Are you all packed?"

"Yes. This time."

"When's Edie coming?"

"Two o'clock, Julie, after lunch."

"Barbara, I have something I want to say. If you view this as regression, you'll be making a mistake. This is growth. And growth is always painful."

"But I'm still invisible to myself, Julie, and I hate that needful, selfish part of me."

"We all have that part in us, and you're not invisible, Barbara, not to me."

"But can't we meet for lunch, a drink? I'll bake you a quiche. If I write, won't you please answer? Oh, Julie, we live in the same city."

"Barbara, you know it's more than rules. It's what's best for you."

"But I never got a chance to find out who you are, are you in love, do you have sisters, why didn't you become a model, you are so beautiful? How can I tell you what you've meant to me? I can't imagine life without you. Really." I sat there trying to memorize her face so I could summon up her wisdom and tenderness in the days ahead.

"Will you go back to work?"

"Not yet. I have to be sure there's a Barbara without work."

"You've worked so hard here. Don't give up. Keep fighting. Don't give in to it."

"I'm so tired of fighting. And I'm not thrilled to be leaving."

"I'd be worried if you were."

Soon we both realized the time was almost up. "Do you know how much I wish for you?" Julie said. "Don't you know it's two-sided? Do you have any idea of the effect you've had on me, how much I will think of you, how painful it is for me to say goodbye?"

I hadn't thought of that. Selfish! "I wish happiness for you, too, Julie. Have a good life. Be a good therapist. Oh, but you are already. Be happy and love. Have a nice life."

"I'll miss you, Barbara."

"I'll miss you, too, and I don't care if our goodbye is symbolic and you represent the whole world and all that. I'll miss you, not because you're a great therapist, but because you're a person. You're a real person. You're whole."

"Take care of yourself, Barbara."

"If I don't, who will?"

Then we stood up. She reached out to hug me and we held each other for a long time. All the anger, the name-calling, the gigantic battles, were put aside. We were two women who loved each other intensely and now we had to say goodbye. I was trying to be a grownup and not cry, but remembering all her words, her counsel, her jokes, her laughter, I dissolved in tears.

When we drew apart, I straightened up proudly and said, "I'll be all you hoped I would be, Julie." She had given me back my life and that was the only present I could give her in return.

"Thank you, Barbara."

We walked out of my room to the hall. We stood there a moment together and then Julie turned away from me. I followed her with my eyes as she disappeared. This was really goodbye. Goodbye to Julie, goodbye to a part of myself.

Suddenly I saw Edie approaching from the other end of the hall. She hugged me. I looked at her clear blue eyes filled with tears, but even as I hugged her, Julie's face lingered in my mind.

Then I laughed, remembering the last time Edie had picked me up at a mental hospital. But that was a different Barbara, I knew, a Barbara that was light-years away from the person who was standing next to her now. "Edie, we're going to keep doing this until we get it right."

"Oh, no, we're not," she said gaily. "This is it, Barbara. I'm never taking you or picking you up from a mental hospital again, ever!"

Don joined us to help take my bags and paintings, the books and plants, to Edie's car. I looked around for Jim. He wasn't there. I asked Don where he was.

"I don't know, Barbara. I think he's having a session with Joyce."

"Say goodbye to him for me. And take care of him, Don. Please take care of him."

"I will."

Standing with me beside Edie's car, Don said, "There's one thing more I want to say to you, Barbara. You've called yourself selfish, selfish and needful, but I don't think you realize how much you gave to us on this hall, to Claudia, to Roger, to Jim, to me. You gave more than you know. You gave more than you took."

Edie took all this in quietly. She was beginning to understand the intensity of my new relationships. It wasn't only craziness that I was leaving behind. I kissed Don and quickly got into the car.

Once on the highway, Edie began to talk. "What a day! Blue sky, clear, new life, new you. Listen, baby, I'm going to keep you so busy—parties, yoga, swimming. It's time to start living again. Time to live."

I nodded. Yes, time to live. But listening to her, all I could think of was that I had never really said good-bye to Jim.

We drove into New York, the car filled with bags and paintings and Pablo Neruda, things Edie couldn't know about, part of my new self. Not a better self or a worse self, just part of whatever it was that I would become. I couldn't look back, and I was frightened to look ahead. Going home to loneliness, I was scared and happy. Relieved and filled with anticipation. I'm

Barbara. I am, I am, I am. And for the first time in months, I really began to believe it.

Edie was speeding down the West Side Highway. I looked out at the magnificent span of the George Washington Bridge. I saw the river, the Palisades on the far shore. It was all so familiar, yet so new, and I wanted to reexperience everything. I inhaled the fresh air, Edie's perfume, smells of health. Yes, I could forget the thick, musty hospital air.

Edie, sensing my mood, took her gloved hand off the wheel, grabbed my leg, squeezed it hard and said, "Smile, dammit. You're alive!"

14

Happy Business

In the months to come, I would draw on that reservoir of emotion: the pain of separation from Julie, Don and Jim, and the affection of a friend who had said, "Smile, dammit. You're alive!" And I would go to the well often to summon up the strength of the love I felt for them, for I was facing an emptiness that I knew would be terrible. I was determined that this return would be totally different from my return from Longview. But that determination wasn't enough to change the one thing that would remain the same, I would be alone.

Still, in many ways it *was* different. This time I had no illusions about Eric, no fantasies about remaking a life with him. I had no illusions about anything, not even about myself. Sitting alone in my apartment, I told myself, Barbara, you've got to rebuild your life. Sigmund Freud said health is the ability to love and to work. If you can work again, love again, you'll beat this bloody illness. I had produced a score of documentary films. And I was a good producer. Now I had to set about producing my own life. The trouble was that I also had to be the writer, the director, the researcher, the film editor, the cameraman. And despite all the supporting characters that were lurking about off camera, I was the entire cast.

How was I going to fight the screaming loneliness of an empty apartment, an empty life? And when I asked myself that question, I didn't mean life in the abstract. I meant eating, sleeping, bathing. Whom would I talk to, laugh with? Whom would I drink coffee with, make coffee for? Whom would I sleep with? Goddammit, other women lived alone, and I could do it, too. I had to be strong and inventive, as I was when I started to make a film. So I sat down with a pen and a long yellow pad and began a list of things to do. But I wasn't making notes on how much tape or whom to interview; this time I was trying to figure out how to fill the hours between waking and sleeping: make appointment with hairdresser, shop for food, pay bills, water plants, eat, walk. It was that primitive, that basic.

My friend Lisa had suggested that as a part of my attempt to put some structure in my life, I try charity work. I decided to read for the blind. And Edie had suggested I work on my sagging body, so I joined a gym. But my experiment with health worked out better than my charity work. Reading for the blind into a tape machine, telling myself I was helping some anonymous handicapped person, was a total failure. Although I felt it was urgent to matter, to matter to anyone—even a faceless person in Iowa who had requested a recording of *Das Kapital*—somehow sitting and reading in that glass booth made my sense of isolation worse. I had to stop. There wasn't enough of me to give yet, to be generous. So I gave up charity, despairing that I was so selfish, hating myself because I couldn't give.

At first I went to the gym just to exercise. But it soon became a sanctuary, a refuge. The bright, caring women who worked there, like Katie, who taught me exercises, and Janice, who tried to massage some life into my depersonalized self, became my friends. We talked about health and wheat germ and vitamins and finding peace. I told them my story and they were very kind to me. The past year had been rough on my body. So I began a vigorous campaign of daily exercise—a regimen that would continue for months as much for the battle against cellulite as for just a place to go.

I saw friends and even gave a dinner party. But it was all just marking time while I waited to go back to work. My former colleague Larry Gross had moved up at CBS, and he had been telling me that my old job would be ready soon—it was only a matter of days. Then he called me and we made a date for lunch. He had made it sound important, and as I sat there waiting for him, I was filled with excitement. This was going to be the day—my old job at last. I looked up, to see Larry handing his raincoat to the checkroom attendant and I rushed out of my seat to greet him. Together we had survived the slings and arrows of Nixon's attack on public television, and now we were two old friends, friends who had been colleagues.

Larry took a long sip of his Manhattan, asked how I was, and then launched into a brief summary of office gossip. "And of course, Steve is dying to make another film with you, and all the guys in the camera crew send love. You're missed, Barbara, you really are. We need you there."

I almost interrupted to say, "When, when?" But I repressed my eagerness and tried to sit there patiently.

"Let's order," Larry said. "You love the poached salmon, Barbara, and how about a nice Montrachet?"

I forced myself to look at the menu, put it down abruptly and said yes: Yes to the salmon, yes to the Montrachet—and I wanted to scream out yes to the job.

During lunch we talked about me, we reminisced about old times. This wasn't like Larry. Why the hell was it taking him so long to get to the point? Finally, over coffee, he said, "Barb, we need you back at CBS, but we've had a budget cut. The show I told you about has been canceled. Give me a few more weeks, a month on the outside, and you'll be back. You know these budget crunches. We'll work something out soon."

My heart sank. "The same old story," I said. "The public affairs department always gets it first." I marveled at how businesslike, how brisk, I sounded. Inside I was thinking, What will I do for a month? What the hell will I do? But then I reminded myself, Four weeks, that's not so bad. You've got to be Barbara without work, remember? It'll give you time to get your life in order.

Larry walked me a few blocks toward my apartment. We huddled together, sharing his umbrella, and after we said goodbye, I walked on alone in the light April rain, watching people with umbrellas dodging each other, hearing the horns honking, trying to look purposeful at two-thirty on a weekday afternoon with absolutely nothing to do, nowhere to go.

How to fill the endless hours of endless days? I browsed in department stores to kill time. The woman who couldn't go into stores in the past now wandered through them aimlessly, trying to get lost in the pretty clothes, find escape among the sweet scents, hoping the glamour, the freshness of the fashions, would lift my spirits. The hustle and bustle reminded me again that life was going on. But I was still so numb, so depersonalized, that deadness seemed to enshroud my head like fifty layers of Saran wrap.

Wherever I went, I discovered that at the drop of a "How are you?" or a "Have a good day," or a cab-driver's "Nice weather, isn't it?" my experience with mental illness came pouring out of me. I found myself telling my dark secret to perfect strangers. Maybe that was because it was all still unreal to me, and in telling strangers about my disorder I would connect, it would become authentic. I would engage someone in conversation and—zap!—I would exist for myself. Doormen, women at checkout counters—no one was immune from my spiel. But spilling my insides became repugnant to me after a few weeks. Soon I developed an early warning system and when I felt the impulse to blab, I'd check it instantly.

Eating became an almost religious experience. I had never eaten alone before. Never. And in the hospital I had eaten with twenty-four other people. Granted it was no banquet, but still they were company. Now I found myself unable to have anything more than a cup of coffee or an apple alone in the apartment. So I went to the local deli for dinner and sat there with sketch pad and newspapers for companions. The busboys and the waiters were my social connection with the world and I treated them like radii in the circle of my life.

Dr. Mildred Stanton was my connection to myself. I

saw her three times a week and I would sit in her luxurious penthouse apartment, talking while she drank her tea. She had an air-cleaning machine, and the purring of the machine was often the only response to my words. Unlike Julie, Dr. Stanton nodded a lot but spoke very litte. I later learned she was a dyed-in-the-wool Freudian, and as such didn't believe in the engaged, participatory style I was accustomed to with Julie. We talked about the same things: my childhood, my parents, but primarily Eric. And whenever she did speak, I often heard conflicting messages. She made me feel guilty when she asked me, "How could a woman like you let him do that? Why didn't you strike back at him sooner?" But then she would smile and say, "But you were never insane. You outwitted him. A psychotic person wouldn't have acted the way you did the night you got him to make that call." So I would walk out of there alternately disturbed by her sense of outrage that I hadn't fought back sooner, and proud—proud that I had outwitted my brilliant lover.

I began reading voraciously. Not with a pattern or in search of universal truths. Just reading—magazines, newspapers, novels, autobiographies—and in reading I often connected, became engaged in another reality. I read scores of articles and stories about women: their problems within the superstructure of corporations, the realigning of relationships with men, new opportunities, new lifestyles. And I sat there like a zombie, wondering about more elementary problems, such as eating, sleeping and peeing without disappearing from myself. It was a grim irony that all this was happening to me at a time when many American women were grappling with bigger questions. Or were they the same questions, only in my life magnified a thousand times over? I didn't know, but it seemed to me that my timing couldn't have been worse. In the past I had felt in step with the changing currents of American womanhood. Now I felt like a traitor.

My parents had wanted to visit me as soon as I was discharged from the hospital, but I told them, "No, I must do this alone. I must." I knew that living alone was what was in store for me and I didn't want it relieved by temporary company, or by the tenuous sense of connection that came to me from being with people I cared about. Because when they left, my alienation always seemed to return more intensely than before. However, I *was* eager to see my brother Eddie and his wife, Melinda. I had never known my sister-in-law well and I wanted to talk to my brother. So when they offered to fly up from Miami for a weekend, I jumped at the suggestion.

The first night we were together in a neighborhood Japanese restaurant, I forgot all my psychic aches and pains and delighted in the presence of this couple I hardly knew. Melinda had always impressed me. I had decided she was a strong, no-nonsense type the first time we met. Now she was a wife and the mother of three children. This was a formidable woman who was sitting across from me, her bright, dark eyes trying to hide the worry she felt. She was listening intently as Eddie and I caught up with each other's lives, about to take an excursion into our past.

"I play ball with the kids," he said, "take them on overnight hikes. Maybe it's compensation because Dad was too busy when I was young to do those things with me. But I love them and I want them to know me, to trust me. No matter how busy things are at the office, I make time."

And then we began to talk about our parents, about growing up in Miami. And I thought, I can't remember the last time Eddie and I spoke about a shared history, a mutual experience, about our connectedness.

Melinda was engrossed in our conversation. She sat quietly and took it all in, but she must have been reading my mind, for she interrupted us to say, "You mean you're talking about all this for the first time? How in the world did you avoid it?"

It was a good question. He was a boy, I was a girl. The difference in our ages. That was part of it. But in our family, there was always so much that was left unspoken.

We were talking about our father, when Eddie said, "Dad *is* tough, Barb, but he's a softie, too. He's sentimental, almost mushy sometimes, and I think he's afraid of that. He tries to protect himself and that's why it's hard for him to show love. I didn't know you felt it so deeply, too. I wish we had talked years ago. I feel guilty. Maybe if we had . . ."

"Stop that," I said. "Julie told me that guilt is the most wasteful emotion of them all. And we're talking now."

With the Japanese waiters plying us with brandy and tea, too polite to interrupt our intense conversation, we found ourselves at one in the morning the only people left in the restaurant. It was the beginning of four fine days together, talking, walking, eating, drinking, enjoying the city, enjoying each other. I got to know my brother and his wife. And it helped me to learn that I hadn't fabricated some of the more terrible memories from my childhood, to realize that some of them were not so terrible after all. We laughed over the warm, funny, wonderful memories, too. The good times—I was grateful he reminded me of them.

I missed Eddie and Melinda when they had to go back to Miami. I missed the brother I had just found. He was a man, a strong, tender, affectionate man; a father, a husband, a son—and my brother. How had he grown up like that? I asked myself. What had happened? And I remembered what Eddie had said. "They were different parents with me than they were with you, Barbara. We change as parents. I know I'm different with Jason than I was with David. And I'm different now with Michael. They learned on you." But then Melinda had said, giving my brother a loving kiss, "Don't worry, Barbara, he's not totally sane either. Sometimes I think he could use a week or two in that hospital. And you want to know something? With three kids on my heels all day, I was jealous of you sometimes, living up there in peace and quiet, walking the grounds, listening to music."

I had smiled and said, "Two things always look better in the movies, Melinda. Mental institutions and war."

One afternoon I was returning to my apartment

from an afternoon walk around the city in the suddenly warmish April afternoon. I was in the elevator when a man got in carrying a tennis racket. He looked at me and we began talking.

"Where do you play?" I asked.

"Wall Street courts, every day. Do you play, too?" he asked rather eagerly. He was about six feet tall, had a dark mustache and was built solidly. He could be attractive, but I wasn't sure.

We continued talking as the elevator stopped and started at the different floors. "Would you like to have a drink this evening?" he asked me when we reached his floor. "My name is Sigmund Myers. Would you?"

I was about to give an automatic no, my usual response to strange men, but then I thought better of it. We live in the same building, he plays tennis, he's attractive. "Sure," I said brightly, and we made a date for six o'clock that evening.

Back in my apartment, I had second thoughts. But he was on twelve, I was on sixteen, and if it was terrible I could always escape. Now, Barbara, don't be negative, I told myself. You haven't had a sane conversation that isn't about sickness with a member of the opposite sex in ages. Do it!

I did it.

I rang his bell, a little nervously, a few minutes after six. A date; I couldn't remember the last time I had had a date. Eric and I didn't date. We met in his office at first and talked about his clients, my show, and then it blossomed into talking about life, him, me. How do you talk to someone you haven't met at work or as part of the stream of your life?

He answered the door quickly and led me into an ultramodern chrome-and-glass room with the required plants, the paintings, the books. I smiled to myself. It was the apartment of an intelligent and civilized man. I asked for wine and we both sat for a few moments surveying each other. Then he began to talk about his career as a research biologist. I was fascinated by the new changes in neurobiology and he spoke knowledgeably about his field, then about the theater and politics.

I was impressed. More talk about his ex-wife, his children, and I listened to it all, thinking, I've never met anyone named Sigmund.

In the natural flow of our conversation, he told me he was in therapy and he wondered if I had ever been. Yes, I said, I had been in therapy.

"Good, excellent," he replied. "I think it's so important for people to know who they are."

I smiled.

"You know, Barbara," and now he seemed more animated than he had been a few minutes before, "I go up to Maine every weekend to a sort of psychological retreat. And I love it! I'm getting to know me. I'm getting in touch with my inner child. Are you aware that inside Barbara Gordon there is a little girl, your real self buried there?"

"Yes," I said softly. "I'm aware of a small child in me."

"It's crucial that you get in touch with that child, Barbara. Have you ever tried?"

I smiled again, trying to repress memories of my needful, demanding inner child. I wished desperately he would change the subject.

"My inner child is *angry,* Barbara," he said. "I feel so much anger." And then he began to pound his chest to indicate the site of his real self. "It's important to feel anger, Barbara. It really is. I have so much anger right now that it's impossible for me to love. It's even difficult to love my own inner child. But sometimes anger is better than love. When I'm with Ida—she's my therapist—we walk across the meadows and through the woods, and we talk about the need for human beings to experience their own anger, the need for me to feel the little boy within me, to feel my young self. It's wonderful, really!"

I was getting uncomfortable. I had so been looking forward to a conversation that didn't include love and anger, psychology, sickness. Is that all people talked about these days? I hadn't yet realized that this was the Me Decade. While I was in the hospital, the care and feeding of the self had become a popular preoccupation.

Just as I was thinking about all that, Sigmund leaped out of his chair, rushed over and put his arms around me, and tried to push my head back for a passionate kiss.

"What are you doing?" I cried shrilly. "What's the matter with you?"

"Come on, baby," he said, panting in my ear. "You know that's what you want. You know that's what you came here for. You want it as badly as I do."

I didn't want it. I was furious. I had wanted wine, a conversation, maybe even a friendship but not "it." I protested again and tried to push him away. But suddenly I found myself laughing out loud. The idea of a man jumping on top of me after telling me he has only anger and no ability to love struck me not as pathetic but as hilariously funny.

He tried to ignore my laughter, but I finally got away from him. "I don't want *it*," I said. "I don't want *you* and your inability to love. I'm getting out of here."

"Oh, Barbara, what a come-on you are. Why do you think I asked you here? You led me on, you bitch."

My laughter stopped. I couldn't think how I led him on by coming to *his* apartment. But the irony of his talking about anger and the need to regress to his inner child—to me of all people—I still found hilarious as I ran for the door. I rang for the elevator and was grateful that it came almost immediately.

Back in my own apartment, I fell on the bed laughing. Who would believe it? Who can I tell it to? I want to talk to someone about it, laugh about it with someone. Edie was home when I phoned, so I told her the story and she wept with laughter. "Welcome to the world of sanity, Barbara. I told you they're nuts out here too."

The weeks passed into a month, two months, and a thousand times I thought of calling Don or Julie. But I remembered the edict: Break it, learn to separate. It seemed so artificial not to hear from people you had lived with for five months, people who had touched your soul. But I did hear from Jim. He wrote long, funny letters and we talked by phone once a week. Sometimes I caught myself saying, "How's Don? How's Julie? Do you see them? Give them my love." He said he would.

He was going to be discharged soon, he told me, and we made plans to play tennis, to walk in the park, but first he would have to find an apartment, find a good therapist, find a job. He was overwhelmed by all the tasks that lay before him in the coming weeks, and I tried to assure him that they only sounded monumental. When we talked on the phone, I could hear Iris screaming in the background, hear the television and the phonograph blaring, and I tried to remember the me that had survived in that place night after night for five months. That person was beginning to become as alien to me as the person I was before I went to the hospital. How many Barbaras have there been? I wondered. And when am I going to become just me?

One day I read an article about megavitamins. They were described as a new, although controversial, method of treating mental illness, and a friend gave me the name of a psychiatrist who prescribed them. So I made an appointment with Dr. Lewis Fell, who seemed like the nine thousandth doctor I had seen on this odyssey of reintegration. When I walked into the enormous sterile office on Gramercy Park, his secretary asked me to fill out a questionnaire. It was a rapid diagnostic test for schizophrenia.

Dr. Fell, was straightforward, matter-of-fact, and I remembered thinking what a kind man he was. After I talked with him for a while, he looked up at me and said, "You are experiencing a schizophrenic reaction to drug withdrawal. Although it happened over a year ago, you are still in the grips of a drug reaction." I listened to him carefully.

He went on to explain that he had given up talk therapy. "But I think you should continue seeing Dr. Stanton. However, I'm going to give you some vitamins, huge doses of vitamins which I think can help reverse some of the terrible symptoms you have described."

I left his office feeling a lift. Maybe these were the magic pills I had always hoped for. They couldn't hurt. So I ran to a health food store and bought fifty dollars' worth of niacin, calcium, zinc, manganese, and things I had never heard of, like lecithin, choline, B_6. Dr. Fell said they were nutrients that would mend the neurons in my brain, nourish them and help them be at peace again, nutrients that would remedy the damage that going off the pills so quickly had done to me. He also said, "Give them time. Give them six months. It takes six months." I had plenty of time. And so I began patiently swallowing at least fifty pills at each meal.

Dr. Stanton did not approve of the vitamins. "They won't help you connect, Barbara," she said in that firm, dignified style I had grown accustomed to, "or end the depersonalization. Again you are looking for an external agent to solve your problems."

"I'm not going to get hooked on vitamins," I said, "but I must try them. I want to know. I've tried everything to help myself. I just can't go on living like a zombie. And I'm not convinced that they are as ineffective as you think."

That was that, and I would take vitamins for months.

Still more weeks passed of lonely dinners at the deli, sessions with Dr. Stanton, trips to the gym, broken by occasional evenings and weekends with my friends. I always had Edie's morning check-in calls, her visits to my apartment because "I just happened to be in the neighborhood." I was still waiting for Larry to tell me when there would be an opening at CBS. I really believed that once I went to work everything would be all right again. Love and work. At least I could handle half of that equation. But I was starting to think that there were people who thought I couldn't. Was there really a budget crunch at CBS?

Dr. Stanton remained the center of my life. Her apartment was dark, even on the sunniest days. The air-cleaning machine always purred in the background. It wasn't the real world, it wasn't my world, I was beginning to realize.

One day I was telling her about my loneliness. "It's not an emotion," I said. "It's a state of being, and I'm lousy at it."

"If you are lonely," she said, "why don't you take a lover?"

I was amazed. I think she was using the word in its old-fashioned sense: someone you saw occasionally, went to bed with. Someone who wasn't really a part of your life. I tried to explain that that's not what a lover meant to me. But it was hopeless.

"A lover will make you feel better," she said. "Think about it."

I walked all the way back to my apartment that afternoon thinking about Dr. Stanton. We weren't making any progress. She seemed more concerned with fitting me into her definition of things than helping me find my own. And after she advised me to take a lover, I don't think our therapeutic relationship was ever the same, that it ever had a chance. There was a chasm between us. She was like a relic from another time. She was a warm, smiling woman, but I knew that it was only a matter of time.

My mother didn't want to wait any longer to see me. She flew up for a short visit, and one night we were sitting in the same Spanish restaurant near my apartment that we had gone to the year before. I was filling her in on vitamins and Dr. Stanton and telling her a bit about what the hospital had been like.

"And I made such a friend, Mother. His name is Jim. He's younger than I am, but he helped me so much."

"Is he still there?" she asked.

"Yes, but he's getting out next week. I don't know what he'll do or where he'll live. I'm worried about him, but thank God he's getting away from the clutches of the therapist who's been treating him there. I was so lucky to get Julie. But that's all it was. Luck. It's an outrageous system."

Then I explained the psychic roulette of mental hospitals, the feeling of helplessness which is one of the most terrible emotions that all mental patients experience. But I couldn't tell her about the noise, the violence, the pain, the despair. She had had one brief glimpse of Six North and that was enough.

She shook her head sadly. "And the money, Barbara. What if your father and I couldn't give you the money? What would have happened?"

"I would have been put in a state hospital, Thorazined out of my mind and killed myself. That's part of the system, too. And you know, of course, I intend to pay back every penny."

She gave me one of those "thank God she doesn't have to" looks, and the two of us sat there in silence, drinking our wine, enjoying being together and having our first sane conversation since I became ill.

She was the first to speak again. "Barbara, there's something I want to say to you." She was leaning with both elbows on the table, her hands supporting her chin, and I knew that she had thought about what she was going to tell me, and that it would be difficult for her to say. "You know, darling, I'm not going to be around forever. And if there are things you need to know about your childhood, things that will help you in your therapy, things about when you were little, I remember everything. So ask me now, darling. I want to help any way I can." And I saw the tears filling her eyes, as she said again, "Please ask me anything. I won't always be here to help you. So please, darling, ask me."

I thought my heart would break in two. I remembered my rage, I remembered Julie saying, Let go of them, let go of cranberries, of scapegoating, of the old fears, of Chatahoochie, and I knew I loved my mother and my father more than anyone in the world. She was saying, Maybe we did something wrong when you were little, but you know we didn't mean to. We're not even sure we know what we did wrong. I don't understand what happened to you, I don't understand analysis or therapy, so all I can give you is my love. All I can give you are my memories of you as the little girl I used to hold in my arms. My memories are me, Barbara. All I can give you is me.

She was looking at me eagerly, waiting for my an-

swer. "There's nothing, Mother, nothing to ask. I remember everything." And in that moment I wanted to
erase all the angry words I had hurled at her when I
was in the hospital, and I didn't know how. I smiled
at her and took her hand. "There's nothing you need
to tell me, really. But I'll always appreciate what you
said. You've done everything you can, you and Dad.
I'll be all right. It just takes a long time for psyches to
mend. My back was easier. They fused my spine and
that was that. But honestly, psyches take longer. As a
matter of fact, I think I'll write an article, 'Psyches
Take Longer.'" I was trying to joke her out of her
sadness.

She returned my smile, seeing I was Barbara again.
And I thought, Is there any love like a mother's for her
child, anything in the world that special, that marvelous? I was flesh of her flesh and she would do anything
to help, even stirring up her old memories, her own
fears for me. And I didn't want her to do that. There
had been enough pain for everyone in this whole nasty
business.

Jim was released toward the end of April and we
met for lunch one weekend. He had begun working in
his father's business, had moved to a small apartment
of his own and was in therapy with a doctor recommended by a friend of his parents' who was a psychiatrist at Bellevue. We were sitting on the grass in Central
Park, watching people brave the cold April afternoon
to luxuriate in a few minutes of sun. We were talking as
friends, not lovers; our brief foray into romance was
over. It went unmentioned, but both of us knew it.

I was telling him about Dr. Stanton. "Jim, you're
right. I do miss Julie very much, but that has nothing
to do with the fact that I think Dr. Stanton isn't for
me. And I can't bear the idea of starting therapy all
over again. Do you know how many shrinks I've
seen?"

"I hate all of them," he said glumly, "all of them.
But if you don't like her, find someone else. You can't
do this alone."

Later that evening I sat in the apartment replaying

countless scenes with all the therapists I had encountered in the past year. Maybe Dr. Stanton wasn't so bad after all. But we weren't getting anywhere together and I knew Jim was right. I couldn't do this alone. I had to find someone else.

I picked up the phone and called Dr. Leon Roth, the therapist Edie had introduced me to the summer before. He was in his seventies and was considered one of New York's foremost psychoanalysts. He said how happy he was to hear from me; he had been wondering how I was doing since I got out of the hospital. I told him that the therapy with Dr. Stanton was not going well, that my symptoms of depersonalization were still plaguing me. And he said, "Miss Gordon, give me one week. You need to work with someone who is very sensitive, very special. Please give me one week and I'll call you."

The next day I walked into Dr. Stanton's office and told her I thought we should end our relationship.

She took a sip of tea, staring at me all the while, and then said, "You may die if you walk out of this office. I can help you."

"No," I said firmly. "It's been several months and we haven't made any progress. We talk about the same things every day and I don't want to stay, Dr. Stanton. I don't want to." I picked up my things and left her apartment feeling very independent, very proud—and very terrified. I hadn't been without a therapist for years.

Dr. Roth did call that week to say he knew of a therapist, Dr. David Aaron, who he thought could help me. There was just one thing that might be a problem. Dr. Aaron was younger than I was. But wouldn't I go and talk to him and see if I liked him?

Dr. Aaron's office was in the Village, on Charles Street. It was a third-floor walk-up, and as I trudged up the stairs I muttered to myself, what in God's name am I doing in Greenwich Village walking up two flights to see yet another therapist? When I entered the freshly painted white apartment, I saw plants and books everywhere. Obviously Dr. Aaron lived here as well. There was an enormous fireplace and a large cage in which six finches sat chirping accompaniment to the Mozart quintet playing on the radio. I was just about to sit down when a young man came out of another room and extended his hand. "Miss Gordon, I'm David Aaron. I looked up at a fair-skinned, dark-haired man whom I guessed to be in his late twenties. He's just a boy, I thought. What will he know about angst?

I followed him into the room that served as his office. It overlooked a beautiful garden, and from my chair I could see trees beginning to turn green. I gave Dr. Aaron the thirty-minutes extended version of my saga, from March 17—Valium Day—to the present. Then he suggested that we meet three times to see how we got along. He didn't suggest any pills; he didn't tell me I saddened or excited him. I liked him instantly. And he was very straightforward about the age thing. "If it's a problem for you," he said, "I can suggest some other people who I think can help you. It's up to you."

That afternoon I called Larry. I didn't want to beg. I didn't want him to hear how anxious I felt about going back to work, but I trembled as I waited for him to come to the phone. "We're having budget meetings this week, Barbara. It won't be long," he assured me brightly. "I'll be in touch."

It had been almost three months. I hadn't thought of looking for anything else to do, but I knew my life couldn't continue in this purposeless way. I was walking along Madison Avenue and saw a sign in the window of a chic boutique: SALES HELP NEEDED. I marshaled my sense of self and walked in. "I'm here to apply for the job," I said to a tall woman who wore an elegant black dress, her hair immaculately brushed back into a chignon.

She looked at me with professional detachment, but she was examining me closely. "What experience have you had as a salesperson?"

I couldn't lie. "None, but I promise you I know I can do it."

"I'm sorry; we only take people with experience."

"But I've worked before. I've worked for twenty years."

"I'm sorry," she said flatly, and turned to help a customer who had just entered the shop.

It was a ridiculous thing to have done, I thought as I walked out into the cool May afternoon. I should be calling friends at other networks, writing letters. I was not a salesperson, for God's sake. I was a documentary film producer. I will not consider this a rejection, I told myself. I will not.

The whole weekend was stretching before me, and I realized it was time to tie up another loose end in my life—the house at the beach. I called Frank, the man who took care of it for me. Yes, he told me, the water was on, everything was ready, the house was waiting for me. I packed some sweaters, picked up a bottle of wine, and found myself on the Long Island Rail Road. I would check out the old house to see if the winter had been hard on it. I'd read, make a fire, walk on the beach.

When I opened the door, I was greeted by my favorite paintings, the books. The shutters were off the glass windows facing the beach and the house was shining. I poured a glass of wine and walked out on the deck. I sat on the steps Eric had built that led down to the beach and looked out at the sea. The sun was setting behind me and I remembered that last weekend with Eric when we had made love right here facing the sea. Part of me expected to see him coming around the other side of the house carrying a hammer and some lumber. I had loved this house with him, I thought. And now I must love it for me before I can share it again.

I walked along the beach for a while, but when I returned to the house I discovered the wind had blown the door shut. I was locked out. I knocked, foolishly, half expecting Eric to open the door. Then I panicked. What could I do—force the lock, break a window? I began to collect my thoughts. I had seen people at one of the houses along the beach. I'd walk down and phone Frank.

He found me shivering on the deck. He let me in the house and we built a fire, drank some wine and laughed about being locked out. There was an extra key and we put it in a secret place outside the house. I'd never be locked out again. It was that simple. A key in a secret place—why hadn't I thought of that?

Was David Aaron the key that would let me back into my life? I was beginning to think so. There was something about the way we responded to each other that I liked. He was no cheerleader. At the end of our third session, he said to me, "I don't blame you for being suicidal. You've been given lousy advice. It's almost as if the mental health system and you conspired to make Barbara Gordon function less and less. And I don't blame you for being depressed. I'm surprised you're not more depressed. You've lost everything that matters in your life, not over a period of years, but in what was really an instant. You can't have your old life again. Too many things are different now. You're different. We can look back to see what happened and try to figure out why. But we've also got to look forward to see what can be done to make your life better. You're going to feel lousy for a while, maybe a long time, but I think you can beat this."

He made me think so, too, and I began therapy with Dr. David Aaron. His intelligence, wisdom really, tenderness and humor soon became very important in my life.

One day there was a message from Jim's parents from my answering service, asking me to call them right away; it was urgent. I had got to know them, and they knew I shared their concern for Jim. What was the matter? Had something happened to Jim? We had had dinner together just the week before and I thought he was fine. When I called his parents, they told me he was back in the hospital, in Mount Sinai in Manhattan. He wanted to talk to me.

I called the hospital immediately. "Barbara," he said, not sounding quite like Jim, "could you bring me some dried apricots and pistachio nuts and the Neruda book, please?" Reflexively and glibly I said yes. I ran out and bought the fruit and nuts and all the Neruda books I could find. And then I stopped so suddenly that people hurrying by stared at me. To give Jim these things, I suddenly realized, I would have to go to a mental hospital. And the old anxiety, the panic, started to seep through my numbness. No. I won't see him. I'll just leave the package with someone, I decided. I'll have to lie and tell Jim I had another appointment and couldn't stay.

I took a cab to the hospital, my thoughts churning: They'll keep me there; they'll lock me up and leave me alone. Then I remembered what David had said when I told him about Chatahoochie and my terror of mental illness. "For a child it is a heavy burden to grow up with the fear of mental illness. It's a heavy burden to feel he must constantly fight to stay free from punishment and incarceration. But let me emphasize, you are not psychotic. You had a psychotic reaction to drug withdrawal. You have a lot of unresolved conflicts, but you could have lived the rest of your life and not ended up in a mental hospital."

When I got to the hospital I heard myself asking, "What floor is psychiatric?" The eighth floor. I was about to leave my packages for Jim at the desk downstairs and run. But then I stopped short. If you run, Barbara, if you keep running from it, you'll go back to the old life, darting out of stores, terrified to walk the streets, living like a recluse. No one will lock you up. You are free. You *can* walk out of here. You lived in a place like this for five months. There is nothing to fear.

I rode the elevator to the eighth floor and heard a key rattling inside a locked door. The sound was all too familiar and I hated it. The attendant asked whom I was visiting and then let me in. I walked down a long, smoke-filled corridor, eyes fixed in front of me, not looking left, not looking right. But when I got to the day room, I realized it looked like an ordinary hospital: people playing cards, reading, talking in small groups. No one throwing a pool cue, no one walking in circles. But the smell was the same sick smell.

I saw Jim before he saw me. He was wearing the robe he had worn all those months in Greenwood, and he was sitting in a sort of daze, not talking to anyone, not watching the television in front of him. He recognized me at last, but when I sat down to talk we were strangely awkward with each other. For two people who had talked endlessly for five months, we had little to say. I began to realize after a few minutes of strained conversation how hard this was for him, seeing me as a visitor, not a patient.

"What happened, Jimmy? What happened? Why are you here?" I asked finally.

He picked listlessly at the pistachio nuts and said, "I don't know. I couldn't stand the job, I hated the loneliness of the apartment, and well, it just happened. Don't bug me, Barbara."

His speech was thick, his eyes lifeless. I couldn't see the merriment, the elfin spirit I had loved in him so very much. I told him I had been out to the beach house; I started to talk about Dr. Aaron, but I saw he wasn't interested.

"Barbara," he said softly, "would you mind leaving? I feel very tired."

I was saddened by the way he looked. He seemed more disturbed, more apathetic, than he had been in Greenwood. What could I do for him now?

I walked down that long corridor and waited for the attendant to open the door. For a moment I panicked again. He wasn't going to let me out. He was going to keep me there. But then it opened and I heard it being locked behind me as I waited for the elevator. I had done it! Goddammit, I had done it, and I was still alive. Only I knew how hard it had been for me to go there, and I had walked out. Standing on the street corner, breathing in the cold, penetrating air, I hailed a taxi. Central Park West, I practically sang out to the cabdriver. I'm going home.

Larry finally came through. "How about coming back next week, Barbara?" he said. "We've got the dough now. You can do a nice easy show. No tough investigative stuff. How about it? Are you ready?"

I was shocked. Suddenly I felt I couldn't handle it. The woman who had practically begged to go back to work had lost her courage. I had just started seeing David, and he was helping me look at things about myself I had never seen before. I wasn't ready to go back to work.

"Let's wait a month or two, for the fall season, Larry," I said. "I don't feel strong enough yet. After the summer, will you still want me?"

Larry didn't sound surprised. "Of course, Barbara, of course."

I was ashamed of myself for my cowardice, but I felt in two months I'll have had more time with David. "Was I wrong to turn Larry down?" I asked him the next time we met.

"I don't think so," he said. "You still feel rotten. But, Barbara, you've got to give up sickness as part of your personality. It's not entirely your fault. Many people who have endured long physical illnesses like your back trouble have psychological problems. Your anxiety was a replacement for your back pain because you were accustomed to being sick. And in sickness you at least felt connected to something. Without love, without work, you lost your identity, and a sick identity became preferable to none."

"But I don't want to be sick now. I want to be well and whole."

"Then you'll have to retain yourself. You have the options. Everyone will still love you when you're healthy, and those who don't have their own neurosis. But it's going to be tough. You are keeping all the symptoms of your illness because they serve a function, and as long as you keep them, you and everyone else will perceive you as sick Barbara and you'll be safe. Maybe it's time to start lying when people ask you how you're feeling. Lying is a sign of ego strength," he said with a smile.

"But I turned Larry down because of these bloody symptoms. I'm so ashamed, I'm so ashamed."

"You'll have another chance," he said.

Now it was important for me to understand, he went on, that neuroses functioned like ropes that tie a boat to its mooring. And like the ties to the boat, they keep the person landlocked, unable to live freely and unencumbered. Our therapy would be a careful untying of the ropes, one by one. Hopefully I would let go of each rope when I saw the malignant purpose it served.

"And then I'll be free, then I'll be healthy?" I asked.

"Yes, provided you can start the motor yourself and not just drift. . . . But along the way we have to look out for some dark clouds."

"Block that metaphor, David, tell it to me straight."

"I have to persist, just this once, with the metaphor, Barbara. Just as the boat becomes more unsteady as each rope is cast off, and can only proceed smoothly after all the ropes are discarded, so too you may find yourself growing more uncertain and frightened as you begin to shed the ropes. The boat is always more snug and safe tied to its moorings—but you can't go anywhere."

"Oh, David, I hope I don't have hundreds of ropes. And you're right, I'm not sure I won't feel shakier as we begin to let them go. But, O.K. It's a good metaphor, and I like it. I've never played it snug and safe, I'm for life and adventure."

He laughed.

The summer passed. I followed David's advice. I did lie a litle whenever I spoke to Larry, trying to convince him that I was ready this time, *really* ready. "I'll look into it, Barb," he always assured me. "We'll work something out soon." But nothing happened, and I was growing more concerned than ever that the people at CBS did not want me back. Were they worried that the old Barbara was gone, that I'd never be as good? Was Larry, as dear and wonderful as he was, worried about that, too?

I called Steve Isaacs, my old film editor, and made a date for lunch. I could ask him what was going on. We met at a Vietnamese restaurant on Eighth Avenue and he asked me about Eric, and how I was feeling. I said I didn't know anything about Eric, and didn't care, and I told him I was feeling fine. I didn't want to talk about me; I was trying to forget the sick Barbara. Then we began reminiscing about the films we had made together, especially the last one, about Jean Barris and her fight against cancer. "It was one of your best, Barbara," he said.

That gave me the opening I was waiting for, "Am I getting the run-around, Steve? If my films were so good, why don't they want me back?"

He took a puff on his big cigar. "As far as I know, there's nothing open right now. But I'm surprised at you, Barbara. Why are you waiting around to come back to CBS? You should be seeing people, writing letters. People know who you are. And you should get back to work."

That night I composed a résumé and started writing letters to everyone I had ever known in television. Two weeks later I received one answer, from ABC. They had heard of my work but wouldn't be hiring for a few weeks. They would call me.

The result: nothing.

"You've done films about stigma," David said, "films about mental illness."

Stigma? Me? Barbara, the three-time Emmy Award winner? I shook my head, no. Television is the most enlightened business in the world.

"Come on, Barbara. Only one reply to all those letters."

"They're busy, they're staffed, making documentaries is a small business."

"All of them busy? You mean you don't think everyone knows what happened to you? It *is* a small business. I agree with you. New York is a small town."

I didn't want to believe him. "No, I don't think everyone knows. And if they did, they'd hire me just to show there was no stigma."

"I'm not certain about what's going on, Barbara," David said, "but I've done some thinking and despite what you've told me, it's an unbelievable coincidence that no one will see you or even talk to you about a job. Even an appointment."

"Why don't you just say the words right out? She was in the nut house. Bonkers. Flipped out. Can't trust her with a hundred-thousand-dollar budget."

"Would you, Barbara? Would you as an executive?"

"Oh, don't do that, David. Let's not trust my liberal tendencies. If the person was as good before she was sick, as I was, yes. But I don't know what I'd do in general. I just don't know."

I wandered around the Village after the session. I wanted to think about what David had said. I found a quiet coffeehouse and went in for an espresso. Stigma? David must be wrong. Or was he right? Maybe it was stigma, maybe it was timing, but I couldn't find a job in the business I had worked in for twenty years.

I tried to imagine what it was like for mental patients who had never worked before, or who were stigmatized by people less sensitive, less intelligent, less knowing than the people I knew in television. I thought of Jim. How would he find work? What would Claudia do when she left the hospital school? All the mental health commissions and associations didn't mean a thing. All the books and movies—my documentary films—didn't matter a bit. Mental illness is a bloody black mark on your soul. Barbara Gordon can't find a job in a business where she had a solid-gold reputation. And that was, as you would say, Jimmy, my friend, a hell of a sock of reality.

I had blown apart, and the shrapnel of my experience with mental illness had scattered indiscriminately, hitting people I loved and cared for. But gradually, with David's help, I was beginning to put all the pieces back together. I did get another job, finally, and it wasn't a pleasant time. Stigma, in the form of an executive producer who systematically tried to whittle away my already shaky confidence in myself, moved from an abstraction to a reality. "I've heard about all your Emmies," he once said to me, "but I haven't seen any signs of talent from you yet." He had heard about my illness, too. Everyone on the show had, I discovered, and they were appalled by the way he treated me. I wasn't asking for pity or charity or outstretched hands. But I thought I deserved common, human decency. I was tempted to quit until David advised against it.

"This is what reality is all about, Barbara," he said.

"You just can't run and hide. I know you're not a coward. But you are a gambler. Why not take the risk and stick it out? If you quit, you'll be safe. But if you stay, you can grow. Love and work, Barbara. Bad as it is, you can have one of those now."

I stuck it out. I survived—and grew.

And I was beginning to learn about the different kinds of love.

My relationship with my parents was becoming more adult, more honest and, to use Julie's word, "cleaner" than it had ever been. I remembered what she told me in the hospital: "It's not a question of good friends, of bad friends. It's a question of cleaning up your relationships." Maybe my parents were still nervous with me, everybody tiptoeing around me because, "You know Barbara, she's not quite well yet." But I don't think I could make up the tenderness I felt for them now, and that they have continually shown me. Part of me says that it was always there, and the other part says maybe not, but still we are all imperfect persons. I have given up scapegoating. They did their best. They loved me, and I'm alive. So there are no more cringes on Sunday when the phone rings. As a matter of fact, it doesn't ring quite so regularly, but when it does I'm honestly happy to hear from them. And I am delighted by the new tenderness I have seen between them.

David calls what happened in my family, and what is common in many other families, a code of illusion. The unspoken, the things gone unsaid, build layer upon layer of unreality, and when that code is broken, the reality is sometimes obscenely clear. In a sense, my mother, my father and I were giving each other double messages. There may have been a silent conspiracy among the three of us that tended to exclude my father. And he learned to play his part by staying away. We all played our parts. We may not have been happy in these roles, yet once they had been set up, we felt helpless to change them. But as Jim once said in the hospital, "All neurosis is is lies . . . give up the lies and you're there." All the subconscious lies, the well-meaning lies, that protect us from the truth about loving and unloving, we sometimes think we need for survival. But they are the seeds of destruction of love and reality and truth.

I had made a new friend. Beth Morse was a tall, handsome woman, divorced and the mother of a small son, Oliver John. We had met shortly after I got out of the hospital and I had been attracted by her vitality, her openness, and I had fallen in love with O.J. instantly. He was four years old, going on seventy. He was the only child I had ever met who at that age was outside himself, so interested in the people around him. Beth and I had a lot in common. She worked for a television producer, her divorce had been grim and painful, and we were two women alone in New York.

One late spring weekend she and O.J. came to the beach house. Beth and I were sitting on the couch talking. O.J. was lying on his side on the floor, leaning on his elbow and watching the fire.

Beth put down her glass of wine. "What a year it's been, Barbara. We've both been through hell. But we've survived. And you—you're like a new person."

I smiled at her. "David says I'm getting well. I'm on my way."

"I *know* you are. Don't you remember how frightened and shaky you were when we first met?"

"I still am sometimes."

We went on to talk about jobs, life, love, men. We shared a fantasy—Mr. Marvelous, the man who would suddenly appear in our lives, strong, tender, loving, no pain, no problems, perfect. "We could advertise," I said. "Maybe he's listed in the phone book under M," Beth said, and we both began to laugh.

We were suddenly aware that O.J. was laughing, too. We had thought he was engrossed in the fire, that he wasn't listening to us. Then he said, "That's happy business, isn't it, Barbara? It's good to hear you talking happy business."

That night, after Beth and O.J. had gone to bed, I sat alone by the dying fire. Then on my way to bed, I looked into the guest room. O.J. was spread out on the bed, clutching his teddy bear in one hand. Beth was sleeping with her back to him, facing the wall. I marveled at the strength of women like Beth, who worked and brought up their children alone, playing out all the roles they have chosen for themselves, and some they haven't. There are so many kinds of love, I thought. Yes, O.J., it's happy business.

A week or so later, Jim was sleeping in that same bed. He had been released from Mount Sinai and he had a job as a construction worker. He happily accepted my invitation. The house on the beach, the dunes, the sky, the sea—it was something we had talked about endlessly when we were in the hospital together. But driving out in his parents' car, Jim was strangely silent, and that silence persisted for two days. The two people who had read poetry together, argued politics, laughed, fought, cried, loved, had very little to say to one another. At first I tried to make up for it with mindless prattling, trying to reestablish the connection between us. Then I accepted his silence, thinking that he felt tranquil being close to the sea. But I saw finally that he was a different Jim. And at last I realized I was a different Barbara. The intensity of our time together in the hospital was another incarnation.

We were having dinner on Saturday night in front of the fire, when he got up abruptly and said, "I'm going to bed now, Barbara."

"Sleep well, Jim," I said. There was nothing more I could say.

When I looked in his room later, I saw him still in his clothes, lying sound asleep on top of the spread. I wanted to sit by the side of the bed and stroke his head. I wanted to give him peace, a peace I hoped he would find someday. Part of me mourned the passing of our intimacy. It was gone. But it was an intimacy as profound as any I have ever known. And I will never forget that it was he who reminded me that I had a soul, that the real Barbara still existed under the numb, wooden woman he met in the hospital. And as I closed his door I prayed to a nameless deity that both of us would be able to make something of our lives. We're entitled, I thought. We really are.

It was a balmy May evening, and I sat out on the

deck for a while, listening to waves that were scarcely visible through the darkness. Two years, I thought. Two years out of my life. When had it all begun? I was making a film about a dying woman. . . . Jeanie always wanted to see this house, but time ran out. I was dying, too, Jean, but I didn't know it. Oh, there's been so much unhappy business. And in the darkness I thought of Eric. We had so much. We had it all. But it was us; it wasn't you, it wasn't me.

Now it was just me, and I remembered the Neruda poem I treasured, the poem I had hoped Jim and I would read together this weekend.

> But when I call upon my dashing being,
> out comes the same old lazy self,
> and so I never know just who I am,
> nor how many I am,
> nor who we will be being.
> I would like to be able to touch a bell
> and call up my real self, the truly me,
> because if I really need my proper self,
> I must not allow myself to disappear.

What bell can I touch to call up the truly me? Love and work, I answered. All kinds of work. All kinds of love, not just the Mr. Marvelous kind. Like the love I feel for my parents, for Eddie and Melinda, for Edie and Jonathan, Barry and Lisa, Beth and O.J., all my friends. Like the love I feel for Don and Julie, although I may never see them again. Like the love I feel for Jim. Like the love I feel for David, for the candor and clarity and humor we share. It will take many months to put Barbara Gordon back together, I thought, and the work will be a long and painful process, but with love I felt the courage to go through it, to do it all, to do it right.

I could hear the waves, but the night was dark and I couldn't see them. And I thought, That's what I feel like—like an ocean that can only be heard. I wanted to see it, to feel it. I wanted to experience everything, all of me to feel everything, nothing partial, no more halfways, no more almosts or might-have-beens. I wanted all of me.

I knew the ocean would be visible if I sat there long enough. And as I got up to lock the glass doors for the night and put out the fire, I told myself, Yes, I know that, just as I know I'll be wholly visible to myself soon. I will touch a bell. I will not allow myself to disappear.

15
Afterword

During the last several years, I have had to rely heavily on various members of the mental health establishment. I have encountered over twenty different therapists, been in two mental hospitals, had countless medications thrown at me, and amassed a staggering number of bills. I have been diagnosed schizophrenic, manic-depressive, cyclothymic personality, borderline psychotic, agitated depressive, hysterical, and just plain neurotic—to name a few of the labels this broad brush of scientific endeavor has pasted on me. I have been overmedicated, overanalyzed and underanalyzed. I have been given suicidal advice. But somehow along the way I have met a few wise and tender people. Too few.

All this is to say that psychiatry, because it probes the dark recesses of the human psyche, is a fragile science. And it is terrible to make the discovery, after a series of unfortunate circumstances, that you have also been a victim of the individual and collective ignorance of a profession that, because it is essentially unmonitored, attracts into its ranks a brand of charlatan that wouldn't dare practice in other branches of the medical establishment. A person with no more than everyday neurotic symptoms can handle the greed, the stupidity, the immaturity and the outright mistakes—including wrong diagnoses and prescriptions for inappropriate medications—of these inept practitioners. Although he shouldn't have to. But when you are ill, relying on them is like trying to read a book by the light of a firefly.

I managed to survive. But I'm not generous enough

of spirit to forgive or to forget the brutality of such a system. The road to recovery from mental illness is so interminable, so fraught with its own ups and downs, that fighting incompetence en route is intolerable excess baggage.

And that is at least one reason I have written this book. At first, I had no wish to tell anyone what had happened to me. I have always despaired of people who look for private salvation in the public marketplace. My book began as something to do when I got out of the hospital, something to help me process the overload of data that I had gathered about myself. But then I began to wonder: Was I alone? Was I the only average functioning neurotic who had almost OD'd on a tranquilizer? Could I have been that unique, that docile, that naïve? I couldn't be.

Still I scorned the idea of going public. It was too private, too painful, too embarrassing. People wouldn't hire me again, love me again, laugh with me again. I knew about the prejudice and suspicion that greet a mental patient wherever he goes. If I kept quiet, that wouldn't happen to me. But it did. And suddenly it was very important to write about what happened—to stop the whispers, the unreturned phone calls, the unanswered letters. I had to clean the air, my air. And if along the way I could unfog someone else's atmosphere, that would be my dividend, my reward.

I had another concern. It was my realization that almost everyone I met in the hospital had been a patient of a psychiatrist outside, and that they all had taken large amounts of mind-altering drugs, generally on the advice and with the consent of their doctors. The number of Americans being given large doses of tranquilizers by their internists, obstetricians, dentists —let alone psychiatrists—is staggering. But they aren't just medicines. They are drugs that can be anesthetics of the emotions. And their sudden withdrawal can precipitate psychosis or worse. Because of my strong feelings about medical mismanagement, because of the prevalence of drug abuse—and the soft-core prescription-pad variety is drug abuse all the same—I felt I had to tell my story.

And I began to think a lot about women and how we keep changing our skins, shedding our fur like animals in the spring, spiraling, growing, assuming new roles. At first I thought it was because of our estrogen cyle; but no, it's not menstrual or endocrinological, it's cultural. And our culture, like a giant supermarket, now offers a bewildering variety of choices for women. The choice I had to make was an extreme—the choice between life and death—but surrounding it were the concerns of identity that trouble so many women today: how to connect, to grow, to touch a bell, to emerge and be whole. I cannot wish that they take my life as an example. But I hope that in my experiences they may find the strength and courage to see themselves and their choices more clearly.

Friends. Had I never known before the richness, the importance of friends in my life? They have become like my nuclear family. They supported me like bookends for months. They made me laugh, they endured my tears, they reminded me that I was me. It was a bumpy ride, but they traveled with me every step of the way: Howard Aaron, Andree Abecassis, Joan Clayton, Stanley Cooney, Peter Dunn, Anthony and Lenore Hatch, Al and Sondra Markim, Marv Minoff, Phyllis Minoff, Sheila Nevins and Sidney Koch, Ann and George Popkin, Herb and Sara Ravis, Steve Seligman, Bob and Myrna Shevin, Mort and Rita Silverstein, Elizabeth Sykes. To all of you, my thanks.

And to my mother and father, for bearing the darts that came from this painful emergence of me, so long delayed. For loving me through it all, for being strong and brave enough to understand, I thank you with all my heart.

And to Eddie, whom I have just rediscovered after so many years, and to Melinda, my thanks for your love and understanding.

And to Edie and Jonathan, of course.

To Lucianne Goldberg and Morton Janklow, my thanks for their encouragement and help. To Buz Wyeth of Harper & Row, my gratitude for his faith in me. And to my editors, who in the process of helping me write this book became my friends: Elisabeth Jakab, who proved that it was possible to do what I wanted to do, and to Burton Beals, who made me do it right, my sincerest thanks.

And those tender people in the hospital, the friends I made there among the staff and patients, who touched my life so profoundly, I thank you, too.

And Jim, my dear Jim, I thank you for so very much—for your poems, for your love, for being you.

I have lived in the cellar of my soul, unable to feel warmth, unable to love, unable to cry, to taste, to smell. I have looked in the mirror and my own reflection shrugged back at me as if to say, "I don't know who you are either, Barbara." I think I know who I am now. But have I reached any decisions of cosmic importance? Not really.

Death is an indictment we all share. All human beings hold the tools of their own destruction. And I came perilously close to using mine. I decided against it, and now I am refashioning my life. Sometimes I still wobble and totter and lurch like a boat casting off its moorings and setting out to sea. But I am not sailing into the sunset. Not yet. Still when I look at the ocean from my house on the shore, the ever-changing colors of the sea, the motion of the waves, the view of the distant horizon, remind me once again that living is better than dying.

I think I know who I am now because of a new strength in myself, and the strength of the people who have been close to me. It is better to remember them than all the people who contributed to the illness along the way. No more scapegoats. And no happy ending either, no epiphany, no single moment of synthesis and complete understanding with flashing lights and the roar of drums. Long, laborious, painful, expensive, frustrating and time-consuming, living is. But living is preferable. As Woody Allen says, "I'm not afraid of death, I just don't like the hours."

BARBARA GORDON
ON
BARBARA GORDON

Ms. Gordon started writing I'M DANCING AS FAST AS I CAN, her first book, in early 1977, after her release from the hospital where she had undergone treatment. Her former job as an Emmy Award-winning documentary producer was no longer waiting for her.

As she tells it, "there I was, an ex-mental patient with no job. I didn't know what to do, so I sat down at the typewriter. I felt compelled to make myself understand who I was and where I had been."

Ms. Gordon began to write her book, as she states, "first as therapy but mostly to synthesize what happened. I thought this book was one woman's aberrant search for identity. I didn't know I'd be writing about universal truths."

She continues, "one month later I showed forty pages to an agent who didn't think it a good book, but might have movie potential." But then Ms. Gordon went home, wrote some more, showed it to a friend who took it to another agent. The result, as they say, is history.

Ms. Gordon hopes that the horror she experienced will lead to a change in patients' attitudes when they go shopping for psychiatric help. She says, "they must fight for their own health care. They should say they don't want to be treated like some submissive junkie." She stresses, "the profession needs a Ralph Nader. We give more thought to buying a car or winter coat than shopping for the right doctor."

"Because of my strong feelings about medical mismanagement," she adds, "because of the prevalence of drug abuse—and the soft-core prescription pad variety is drug abuse all the same—I felt I had to tell my story."

A year ago CBS offered Ms. Gordon her old job back, but she refused. She comments, "I love writing and have been afforded the luxury of changing careers at 43."

We Deliver!
And So Do These Bestsellers.

Special Offer
Buy a Bantam Book
for only 50¢.

Now you can have Bantam's catalog filled with hundreds of titles plus take advantage of our unique and exciting bonus book offer. A special offer which gives you the opportunity to purchase a Bantam book for only 50¢. Here's how!

By ordering any five books at the regular price per order, you can also choose any other single book listed (up to a $4.95 value) for just 50¢. Some restrictions do apply, but for further details why not send for Bantam's catalog of titles today!

Just send us your name and address and we will send you a catalog!